A VOYAGE TO NEW HOLLAND

By

WILLIAM DAMPIER

A VOYAGE TO NEW HOLLAND

By

WILLIAM DAMPIER

Edited, with Introduction, Notes
and Illustrative Documents, by
JAMES A. WILLIAMSON
D.Lit.

32 ILLUSTRATIONS

THE ARGONAUT PRESS

1939

Printed in Great Britain
by SIMSON SHAND LTD
London and Hertford

CONTENTS

	PAGE
Introduction	ix
Documents	lviii
Text	I
Notes	251
Index	255

MAPS AND ILLUSTRATIONS

*William Dampier. By T. Murray. From the painting in
the National Portrait Gallery* *Frontispiece*

General Map of Dampier's Voyage *Facing page* ix

The Canary Islands 6

The Cape Verde Islands 14

The Coast of Brazil 34

Plants found in Brazil 48

The Pintado Bird 66

The Coast of New Holland 82

Birds of New Holland 106

Plants of New Holland (I) 108

Plants of New Holland (II) 110

Dolphins 113

Fish of New Holland (I) 113

Fish of New Holland (II) 114

The Coast of Timor (I) 129

The Coast of Timor (II) 132

Plants of New Holland and Timor 166

Timor and adjacent Islands 178

The Coast of New Guinea (I) 180

Plants of New Guinea 182

Fish, Bat and Bird of New Guinea 185

The Coast of New Guinea (II) 186

The Coast of New Guinea (III) 192

The Coast of New Britain (I) 202

The Coast of New Britain (II) 206

Dampier's Course from Timor to New Britain 208

Fish of New Guinea (I) 214

Dampier's Passage   *Facing page* 216
Fish of New Guinea (II)   220
Islands on the Coast of New Guinea   222
Birds of New Guinea and Ceram   227
Gilolo and other Islands   228
Bouro and other Islands   230

NOTE

Owing to the fact that Dampier was at sea when the second part of his book was printed, and was dead when the second edition appeared in 1729, some of the illustrations are not as closely related to the text as he could have wished. All are here reproduced, with the exception of one which obviously belongs to another book.

INTRODUCTION

(i) DAMPIER'S LAST BOOK

THE account of the voyage to New Holland and adjacent regions is the last of Dampier's writings, if we except the brief *Vindication* of his conduct in the subsequent voyage of 1703, of which the full narrative was not from his pen. The present volume therefore completes the Argonaut Press edition of Dampier, of which the first volume, edited by Sir Albert Gray, was issued in 1927. To that work Mr. N. M. Penzer contributed an elucidation of the biographical complexities of Dampier's numerous editions[1]. The reader desirous of full information should refer to it, and here it need only be repeated that the *Voyage to New Holland* was originally published in two parts, the first in 1703 and the second in 1709, both parts being reprinted with continuous pagination by James Knapton in 1729. The text here given is reproduced from the 1729 edition, of which it forms the greater part of Vol. III. Since a fourth volume was added, the whole is sometimes described as "the four-volume Dampier"; but this is a misleading title, for the fourth volume contains nothing whatever by Dampier. He published no accounts of the two long expeditions in which he took part after returning from New Holland. One, the privateering venture of 1703–7, was described in rather inferior style by William Funnel and reprinted by Knapton in his fourth volume of 1729. The other, in which Dampier served as pilot under Woodes Rogers in 1708–11, was described by that officer[2] and also inde-

[1] Argonaut Press *Dampier*, I, pp. v–vii.

[2] Woodes Rogers, *A Cruising Voyage Round the World*, London, 1712.

pendently by Edward Cooke[1], and was not included in the so-called four-volume Dampier at all. Neither of these last two expeditions was a voyage of discovery. The voyage to New Holland was. It was made in the brief interval of peace between William III's war with France and the War of the Spanish Succession, and its purpose was purely geographical. To understand that purpose, and to estimate the success and failure of the voyage, a consideration of previous Australian exploration will be necessary.

(ii) AUSTRALIAN EXPLORATION BEFORE DAMPIER'S TIME

Long before the discovery of America, and indeed long before Europeans had pushed southwards into the tropics, it had been established by scientific reasoning that the earth was a sphere and that its climates were distributed in zones of decreasing warmth from the equator to the poles. The classical geographers of antiquity, who were aware of these facts, thought it probable that far away to the southward of the equator continental lands existed and might be peopled by an unknown race of men. The classical geography was never entirely forgotten, although during the decay of civilization after the fall of the Roman Empire there were few men who studied such things and there was no public interest in them. Of the few who did think of world-geography some applied passages from scripture to prove that the earth was flat, a conception which ruled out any idea of a southern continent; but this view never won general acceptance, and it is a mistake to

[1] Edward Cooke, *A Voyage to the South Sea and Round the World*, 2 vols, London, 1712.

INTRODUCTION

xi

suppose that mediæval Europe as a whole believed that the earth was flat. It would be truer to say that the majority of educated men gave no thought at all to the subject, and that there was always a minority who clung to the conception of the spherical earth. With the revival of interest in geographical matters from the twelfth century onwards the spherical earth was commonly accepted, and its geography was studied in paraphrases of the classical writings obtained from Saracen scholars. Later, in the fifteenth century, the true texts of the ancient authors were rediscovered, together with copies, long dormant in Byzantine libraries, of the maps drawn by Ptolemy of Alexandria in the second century of the Christian era. The men of the later Middle Ages were thus quite familiar with the concept of the spherical earth. They regarded it as floating motionless in space, with Europe, Asia and the known part of Africa occupying its upper surface; and since it was obvious that the minerals composing the soil were heavier than water, they held that there must be great continents south of the equator to balance the mass of northern continents and prevent the world from toppling over. The Terra Australis or southern land was thus demonstrated to exist, but the belief was long held that it must for ever remain Terra Australis Incognita. For it was a mediæval article of faith that the tropic zone was too intensely hot for human beings to survive in it, and therefore no northern man could ever penetrate to the temperate regions of the south. Here the Church stepped in with a further inhibition. Since all men were the sons of Adam and no man could pass the equator, it followed that there could be no men in the southern continent: it was heresy to assert the existence of the *antipodes*. Misconception of that statement has given wide currency to the

notion that the mediæval Church declared the earth
to be flat; but the *antipodes* which it denied were not
antipodean lands but antipodean peoples.

Portuguese discovery in the fifteenth century dis-
proved the error of supposing that the tropics were
impassable. By the middle of that century the explorers
were nearing the equator, and before its close they had
crossed it and rounded South Africa and sailed to India.
Under Vasco da Gama they reached Calicut in 1498,
but thirteen years then elapsed before they passed
through the Straits of Malacca and entered the waters
of the Pacific. They did this in 1511–12 under the
leadership of Antonio d'Abreu, the first Portuguese commander to reach the Spice Islands of the Eastern Archipelago. An Italian traveller, Ludovico di Varthema, had
forestalled them. He had made his way to the Far East
by land, and for some years he had been voyaging
among the islands in native shipping; and he had heard
that great countries lay to the southward. This may or
may not have been a vague indication of the existence
of Australia. When the Portuguese arrived, Varthema
joined them.

In 1513, less than two years after the Portuguese
entered the Pacific from Malacca, the Spaniards under
Balboa crossed the Isthmus of Panama and discovered
the other side of the great ocean. Thus began the period
of Spanish enterprise in the South Sea (so named by
Balboa) which was to accomplish important work for a
century to come. The first great Spanish expedition was
led by Ferdinand Magellan, a Portuguese who had
already been at Malacca. He discovered the Strait now
named after him, and sailed diagonally across the
Pacific from south-east to north-west. In the Philippine
Islands he was killed in battle with the natives, but the

survivors of his force threaded the archipelago and reached the Indian Ocean, returning by the Portuguese route round the Cape of Good Hope to Europe. This great voyage, the first circumnavigation of the globe, was accomplished in the years 1519–22. Spain immediately laid claim to the Moluccas or Spice Islands, and other voyages followed. But the Portuguese resisted, and in the end Charles V sold them his claim to the Moluccas, although not to the Philippines, by the Treaty of Saragossa in 1529. A deterrent to Spanish perseverance was the wind-system of the Pacific. In tropical latitudes it was possible to sail across from Spanish America to the archipelago with the North-East and South-East Trades, but impossible to sail back; and it was not until 1565, when Andres de Urdaneta cast northwards and found a belt of westerly winds, that any Spanish vessel succeeded in re-crossing the Pacific from Asia to America.

These early Portuguese and Spanish explorers discovered Java and the smaller islands to the eastward, Borneo and Celebes and the northern shore of the great land of New Guinea. Their ships were in the longitudes of Australia and only a few degrees of latitude north of it. Yet during the whole of the sixteenth century there is no positive record that Australia was seen by any European. In explanation of their apparent neglect to investigate southwards it may be said that both Portuguese and Spaniards were intent upon profit from the spice trade and that their man-power for exploiting the recorded discoveries was very scanty, leaving them little surplus energy for further probing of the unknown. Nevertheless there is some indirect and inconclusive evidence that Australia was discovered by the Portuguese in the first part of the sixteenth century. It consists of a series of world-maps drawn by French geographers in the period 1530–1550, and commonly known as the Dieppe maps. These maps are all of the library type, not charts intended to be used by navigators on board ship, but large and attractively drawn wall-pieces designed for the embellishment of rich men's studies. One apparent exception, drawn by Jean Rotz of Dieppe, is in the form of an Atlas sumptuously bound and presented to Henry VIII, but it also is in effect a great wall-map cut up into smaller sheets, which are copied in the leaves of the Atlas. Despite their magnificent appearance, these maps have not the authority as historical evidence that would reside in the humbler pilots' charts traced out on the spot by explorers of new coastlines. The pilots' charts must have been the more numerous type at the time, but few have survived, for they were worn out and destroyed in use, while the decorative specimens were preserved for their artistic value. There is, however, a relationship between the two types. The library maps are based upon information recorded in the pilots' charts, although it may be intermingled with theory derived from the works of academic geographers. Thus, in considering any strange part of the world, these Dieppe maps have to be criticized with three questions in mind: Is the information set down derived from the charts made by actual explorers? Is it evolved from the assertions contained in academic geographical treatises? Is it purely fictitious, the product of the cartographer's imagination?

The Dieppe maps all depict a continent to the southward of the Asiatic Archipelago. Its eastern, northern and western coasts bear rough resemblances to those of the true Australia, distorted indeed, but not so wildly as the contemporary representations of North and South America in the early period of their discovery. The latitudes and longitudes are incorrect, but so also and to much the same extent are those of the Americas in maps which we know to have been evolved from actual discovery. If the designers of the Dieppe maps had no real information, but were simply expressing the age-old theory of a southern continent, their guess-work was extraordinarily correct in placing that continent approximately where Australia actually exists, and nowhere else in the southern hemisphere; and their restraint was also remarkable in refraining from providing any fictitious southern coast to round off the conception after they had concocted the eastern, northern, and western coasts. The probabilities are really strong against the explanation that this early Australia was pure fiction or diluted classical lore.

On the other hand, if these French cartographers had access to some Portuguese explorer's chart they certainly took some liberties with it[1]. But after allowing for that, we must admit that in themselves the Dieppe maps do convey a powerful suggestion that they embody at second or third hand a record of veritable discovery. The difficulties in accepting it are circumstantial. When in the eighteenth century Bougainville drew near to the north-eastern coast of Australia and Cook actually traced its outline, the perils from shoals and reefs were so great that a combination of good luck, good ships and superb seamanship was required to surmount them. The Portuguese captains were good seamen, but their ships and equipment were very greatly inferior to those of Cook and his contemporaries. Thus, if they really coasted three sides of Australia, and if their "Dangerous Coast" (*Coste dangereuse* in the Dieppe maps) is actually that lined by the Great Barrier Reef, their achievement

[1] See the fuller discussion of this question in the present editor's *Observations of Sir Richard Hawkins*, Argonaut Press, 1933, pp. xvii–xx.

was so extraordinary that some have judged it incredible. The silence of all contemporary histories and of all written records so far discovered is at first sight an even greater argument against belief in the Portuguese discovery. But it is not by any means conclusive. It has been proved that Portuguese governments deliberately suppressed information about the West African coast for fear of aiding their rivals[1], and there was a good reason why they should do the same about Australia. For Spain was a potential rival for the wealth of the Moluccas, and it was conceivable that Spanish expeditions might cross the Pacific and establish a base of operations in Australia. It is true that in the outcome the suppression of African information was ineffective, but that was because the Portuguese were continually voyaging there and the details were known to too many persons for secrecy to be preserved. Australia, however, was of no immediate commercial value, and there was no incentive to maintain connexion with it. It is quite possible that after preliminary examination the discovery was purposely abandoned and the few navigators concerned enjoined to silence, and that, nevertheless, one of their charts came into French hands.

Later in the sixteenth century the Flemish geographers, Gerard Mercator and Abraham Ortelius, enlarged this Franco-Portuguese Australia to a great southern continent encircling the globe. Their inspiration was not, for the most part, geographical exploration, but the scientific reasoning that there *must be* land in the southern hemisphere of at least equal extent to that known in the northern hemisphere in order that the stability of the earth should be maintained. But they incorporated in their magnified Australian continent the

[1] See article by J. Cortesão, in *Lusitania*, January, 1924.

land-mass shown in the Dieppe maps, although it is evident that they knew of no narratives recording its discovery.

Finally, in 1597 Cornille Wytfliet appended to a map of the same general type the following remarks: "Terra Australis is the most southern of all lands. It is separated from New Guinea by a narrow strait. Its shores are hitherto but little known, since, after one voyage and another, that route has been deserted, and seldom is the country visited unless when sailors are driven there by storms." Again we have to choose between regarding this as pure fiction and seeing in it some tradition of a discovery once made but afterwards abandoned as unprofitable. The late Professor G. A. Wood explained away the passage as referring only to the Straits of Magellan and Tierra del Fuego[1]. But this obviously will not do, since Wytfliet was speaking of the southern land adjacent to New Guinea; and also there had been several voyages to the Straits of Magellan in the twenty years before 1597.

In the present account we are limiting ourselves to Australian discovery, and so need not pause over the voyage of 1567–8, in which Alvaro de Mendaña crossed the Pacific from Peru and found the Solomon Islands. Nearly thirty years later, in 1595, Mendaña sailed again with Fernandez de Quiros and discovered Santa Cruz, to the north of the New Hebrides. The ultimate objective of these expeditions was the Australian continent, thought to lie where it actually does lie; but Mendaña and Quiros exhausted their efforts before they drew near it.

The recorded discovery of Australia begins in 1606, by which time the Dutch were established in the East

[1] G. A. Wood, *Discovery of Australia*, London, 1922, pp. 112–13.

b

Indies. Early in that year Willem Janszoon, in command of a small vessel from the Dutch settlement at Bantam, passed along the south-western shore of New Guinea until he reached the western end of the strait that separates New Guinea from Australia. It was a dangerous region of shoals and islands, which Janszoon assumed to be an outlying barrier to solid land. He therefore failed to perceive the existence of the strait, and placed it on record that New Guinea and Australia were one continuous land, thus reversing Wytfliet's sixteenth-century tradition that there was a strait to the south of New Guinea. Janszoon penetrated some way into the Gulf of Carpentaria and examined the western coast of Queensland. He found both the land and its inhabitants utterly repellent, and returned to report that the discovery was valueless.

A few months afterwards, in the same year 1606, the strait that Janszoon had thought to be non-existent was actually traversed by a European ship. Mendaña had died in the voyage of 1595, but Quiros had survived. He was fired with the missionary spirit and eager to convert to Catholic Christianity the islanders of the South Sea, and thence to proceed to the discovery and conversion of the continent. In 1606 he was at length permitted to sail westwards from Peru. He reached the largest island of the New Hebrides, which he called Austrialia del Espiritu Santo. There his own crew, disaffected and anxious to return, allowed the ship to be blown away from the land by a strong wind, and then insisted on sailing back to America. Quiros thus drops out of the story; but there was another ship in which Diego de Prado and Luis Vaez de Torres held command. They decided to sail for the Philippines by the direct route along the northern coast of New Guinea. Adverse winds

prevented them from rounding the end of the great
island, and they had perforce to pass along its unknown
southern coast instead. They did so successfully, and
duly arrived at Manila. Torres and Prado had sailed
right through the passage between Australia and New
Guinea, the passage which now bears the name of
Torres Strait. But the discovery was not made public
either by them or by the Spanish Government. For a
century and a half it remained buried in secret archives,
and the erroneous theory of the Dutch, that there was
no strait, was generally accepted by geographers. The
story of Prado and Torres has its bearing upon the
question of prior Portuguese discovery. These officers
had sailed through a most perilous passage with an
indifferent crew and a ship very poorly equipped and
victualled; and their achievement was not placed on public
record, but came to light only in the mid-eighteenth
century by the accidental revelation of a manuscript
written by Torres. The corresponding account by Prado
has been found only in quite recent years[1]. These
circumstances go some way towards answering the case
against the Portuguese, which rests on the arguments of
impossibility and the non-existence of narratives.

Ten years after Janszoon's voyage the Dutch accidentally discovered Western Australia. The discovery re-
sulted from the adoption of a new route from the Cape
of Good Hope to Java. The old method of approach had
been through the tropic zone of the Indian Ocean,
where, at the correct season of the year, the south-west
monsoon could be utilized. But it was known that to the
south of the tropics there was a permanent belt of
westerly winds, and this, on being tested, was found to

[1] It is printed in *New Light on the Discovery of Australia*, ed. H. N.
Stevens, Hakluyt Society, 1930.

yield a much quicker passage to the East. The procedure was to run westwards until the longitude of Java was reached, and then to turn northward. But longitude was a matter of estimation, not of exact reckoning, and before long one Dutch ship after another overran the distance and sighted the western shores of the Australian continent. The first contact was made in 1616. In the course of the next decade the whole west coast came into view and was laid down with approximate correctness on the charts; and in 1627 a ship followed the south coast for about half its total extent before turning backwards to regain the track to Java. All these shores, as seen by navigators, were uniformly barren and dangerous, producing no merchantable goods, no foodstuffs, in most places not even fresh water; and their inhabitants, where any existed, were savages of the lowest type. The Dutch called the country New Holland, and showed little enthusiasm for it.

While the west coast was being revealed, something more was done in the north. In 1623 two vessels were sent out from Amboyna to examine further into the Gulf of Carpentaria. They passed south of the point reached in 1606, but found the conditions similar: the country contained "nothing fit for the use of man". One ship returned to Amboyna by the same route. The other crossed the Gulf westwards and discovered Arnhem Land on the other side. Neither had penetrated to the end of the Gulf, and its true nature therefore remained unknown; it might not, after all, be a gulf, but a channel cutting New Holland in two. Other voyages made it seem probable that Arnhem Land was continuous with the western discoveries, but even this was not certainly known.

The Dutch period of Australian exploration culmin-

ated with the voyages of Abel Tasman, who owed his
successes to his sound qualities as a commander, and also
to the co-operation of two other men, Frans Visscher, his
chief pilot, who had the knowledge and vision requisite
for planning great discoveries, and Anthony van
Diemen, Governor-General of the Dutch East Indies,
who provided the equipment for work on a great scale.

The Dutch were still at war with Spain, as they had
been almost continually since they had declared their
independence from her rule in the sixteenth century.
The Spanish colonies of Chile and Peru and Central
America were rich and worth attacking. The only
known means of access to them from the Dutch East
Indies was by the wide northern sweep through the
temperate zone of the North Pacific to a landfall in
California, and thence by coasting painfully southwards
in a region of calms and adverse winds. Van Diemen
wished to learn whether Chile and Peru could be more
easily approached through the southern zone of westerly
winds, south of the tropics, which was already being
utilized in the section between the Cape of Good Hope
and Western Australia. It was primarily for this purpose
that he sent out Tasman in 1642. To achieve it, Tasman
would need to pass south of Australia, since all its
northern coasts, and those of New Guinea, were in the
tropical belt. Tasman had to discover, not only whether
it was possible to pass completely clear of Australia by
the south, but also whether the unknown continental
land, generally assumed to lie between Australia and
America, formed an obstacle in the latitudes of the
westerly winds; for if such land projected into the tropics
as Australia did, it would thrust the navigator northwards into the trade-wind belt, and so bar his progress
towards America.

Tasman therefore sailed to seek an ocean passage rather than to reveal more details of the Australian coast, although it is true that the latter object was included in the very comprehensive instructions issued to him. He went from Batavia west and south to Mauritius, and thence struck southwards into higher latitudes than those traversed by the regular Dutch Indiamen. The strong west winds carried him past southern Australia in 43° of latitude, far out of sight of land until, in November 1642, he discovered a hitherto unknown country lying athwart his track. It is now called Tasmania, but he named it Van Diemen's Land. He had the choice of coasting it northward or southward. If the former, he would discover whether it was part and parcel of the known Australian continent; if the latter, whether it stretched away indefinitely to the Antarctic and blocked progress on the desired eastern passage. He chose to turn southward and was rewarded by finding that he could round his new discovery, which must either be a separate island or the southern extremity of New Holland. He left that question unsettled, and after making a semi-circle round Van Diemen's Land he turned away eastwards into the open ocean in 42°. This course brought him to another unknown land, which the Dutch named New Zealand. He assumed that it must be a part of the great unknown continent which all the geographers believed to border the southern ocean, and he therefore coasted it northwards until he reached its northernmost extremity at Cape Maria van Diemen (named after the Governor-General's wife). The latitude, between 34° and 35°, convinced him that the west-wind track to South America was possible, and he turned for the tropics without pursuing that track further. He wished to rediscover Mendaña's Solomon Islands, but passed well to the east and north of them, and completed his return to Batavia along the fairly well-known northern coast of New Guinea.

In this voyage Tasman had completed the circle round Australia and proved that it must be a great island. But he had not seen any of its southern coast unless Van Diemen's Land could be accounted part of it, and he had passed hundreds of miles clear of its eastern coast, to whose nature not a single clue was known to the science of the time. The existence of Torres Strait was buried knowledge, and even the Dieppe maps lay unregarded in the libraries of Europe, not to be rediscovered and studied by practical geographers until the eighteenth century.

The early Dutch voyagers into the Gulf of Carpentaria, as we have seen, had failed to find Torres Strait and had concluded that New Guinea and Australia were continuous. But they had reached that conclusion only from the shallowness of the water and the prevalence of banks and islands, and not because they had actually seen a connecting link of mainland. The prospect of sailing by a short route to South America reopened the question; for if there was after all a strait between New Guinea and Australia, its use would still further shorten the voyage between Batavia and Chile. Alternatively there was another possibility. No one had yet been to the bottom of the Gulf of Carpentaria. It might yet turn out to be a strait and not a gulf, a strait cutting Australia in two and coming out somewhere on the unknown southern or eastern coasts. To solve these problems Van Diemen sent out Tasman once more in 1644.

In the same manner as his predecessors, Tasman wen by south-western New Guinea into the Gulf of Carpentaria, and failed to perceive Torres Strait while doing so. He concluded that there was no strait and that the lands were all one. He examined the Gulf more fully and confirmed that it was a gulf, with no southern outlet. He returned by its western shore and coasted Arnhem Land and made reasonably certain that it was all continuous with the western New Holland which the Indiamen sighted, and on which they were sometimes wrecked. Next year Van Diemen died, and the East India Company's policy changed. It was decided that there should be no further attempts to exploit New Holland and the southern route to Chile, and that the Dutch should concentrate their efforts on developing their own East Indies.

It was to be yet half a century before Dampier should come upon the Australian scene, but the geographical position as he found it was substantially as Tasman left it; for only a few details were added to the west coast chart in the interval. We may therefore at this point summarize what was known of Australia at the close of the seventeenth century. The general trend of about half of the outline of the continent was fairly accurately plotted on the charts—from the mid-point of the south coast in the Great Australian Bight, round clockwise to the west coast, and thence round the north coast into the Gulf of Carpentaria. In addition there was the southern part of Tasmania as an isolated discovery, with its connexions undetermined. All the rest was either misinterpreted or completely unknown. The greatest error was the belief that south-eastern New Guinea was continuous with north-eastern Australia. The unknown comprised the eastern half of the south coast and the entire extent of the east coast, regions which the belated explorations of the eighteenth century were to reveal as the most attractive parts of the great country. Meanwhile, the known was decidedly unattractive, although legitimate imagination might conceive that the whole could not be so utterly disappointing as the forbidding outward part.

(iii) DAMPIER'S VOYAGE

The chief interest of Dampier's book is not in the narrative of events, but in the descriptions of lands, seas and weather, of birds and beasts, fishes and plants, the whole range of natural phenomena which the author found so much more to his taste than the characters and actions of his fellow men. The narrative is of quite secondary importance, and rightly so, for in respect of geographical discovery the voyage was substantially a failure, and as an exhibition of leadership it was second-rate. The preponderance of description over narrative renders the sequence of events sometimes a little difficult to follow, and in addition Dampier omits certain matters and alludes very slightly to others. A brief account of the course of the expedition is therefore given here, while the natural history is left to speak for itself from the pages of the text.

In 1697 an end was made to "King William's War", the first of the series of Anglo-French contests which were destined to continue, with intervals of peace, until 1815. The struggle was for world-trade and oceanic power quite as much as for European objects, and in the record of empire-building, and especially of geographical exploration, the peaceful periods were on the whole more fruitful than the warlike. The first peace-interlude, from 1697 to 1702, witnessed Dampier's expedition to Australia. Many circumstances combined to produce public and government interest in the far South. The Scottish people, under the inspiration of

William Paterson, had formed a national company to compete with the English in oceanic trade, in any part of the world in which profit seemed possible; and the English East India merchants were greatly, and, as it turned out, unnecessarily, perturbed. The Spanish colonial empire, regarded commercially as a great and undeveloped estate with important frontages on the Pacific, was about to come into the market with the extinction of the Spanish royal family, whose last male representative, Carlos II, was dying fast. The French were preparing to assert their claims, and it was desirable for England to know more about the possibilities of the South Sea. Then again there was a purely scientific interest. It was partly a manifestation of the general impetus to research which had set in towards the close of the seventeenth century, and partly had been excited by Dampier himself with his widely read *New Voyage Round the World*, whose publication in 1697 had come at a fortunate moment.

The *New Voyage* brought Dampier to the notice of the authorities as a man with useful knowledge of the South Sea and the Indian Ocean. Shortly after its publication he was summoned before the Council of Trade and Plantations, together with Lionel Wafer, another ex-buccaneer, to give information about the Isthmus of Darien and the Scottish design to colonize it. On July 2, 1697, Dampier and Wafer attended and were orally examined, being afterwards directed to draw up their report in writing. Further entries in the Journal of the Council of Trade show Dampier being consulted during the ensuing twelve months on Darien, piracy, and the navigation of the Indian Ocean[1].

[1] *Calendar of State Papers Colonial, America and West Indies, 1696–7,* No. 1120; *1697–8,* Nos. 661, 830, 850, 851.

Meanwhile the Admiralty was also preparing to employ him. It was anxious for an accurate discovery to be made of all that lay in the vast area to the south and south-east of the Dutch Indies, the region of Southern New Guinea and Eastern Australia, of which absolutely nothing was yet known. The discoveries of Torres, it must be repeated, were buried in oblivion, and the accepted doctrine was that New Guinea and north-eastern Australia were all one land, with a coast that must face eastwards; but no one had yet seen this coast, so far as knowledge went in 1698. Tasman had proved that Australia must be a great continental island, for he had sailed round it, although far out of sight of its eastern shores. But even Tasman's work was not clearly understood in England, by Dampier or by anyone else, for we have allusions to the possibility that southern Australia stretched right away into the Antarctic. Dampier, as will be shown, believed that such might be the truth, and planned his voyage on that assumption. Historical research was not then accorded its place as an activity with any practical importance in the work of discovery. It was an omission that the eighteenth century was to remedy, for Cook was to sail seventy years later with a very complete knowledge of all the records of his predecessors.

The English interest of 1698 was an unconscious revival of an old project. The Elizabethans had speculated on the possibilities of the very region that Dampier was to approach; and Drake, as is now known, had sailed in 1577 with orders to investigate the southern continent from Tierra del Fuego to Australia. Drake had preferred the more lucrative occupation of raiding the treasures of Peru, and his original programme had been lost to sight. Then had followed the Elizabethan war with Spain, and after it a century of American colonization and East Indian trade. Now the old plan had come to life again, but there is not the slightest evidence that Dampier's employers knew it to be an old plan. In their minds it was entirely novel, the outcome of the existing situation in world affairs. The neglect of historical research in its bearing on contemplated action was characteristic of seventeenth-century England, where it never occurred to practical organizers that they could have anything to learn from scholars. It had been far different in Tudor England, where John Dee and Michael Lok and Richard Hakluyt had eagerly ransacked the records of the past in search of material for present projects; and these men had not merely been consulted, but had taken a leading part in directing the discoveries of their time.

The Admiralty allowed Dampier to frame his own plan for the voyage. His most important objectives were the unknown eastern coasts of New Guinea and Australia and the partly known islands between northwestern Australia and the Dutch Indies. Any visit to the known northern or western coast of Australia would be mainly incidental, for the purpose of watering and refreshment. He had been on that coast with the buccaneers ten years before, and knew that it offered no attraction to empire-builders. At first, on the assumption that he would be able to sail by September, he proposed to go by Cape Horn, and then westwards across the Pacific so as to arrive at the unknown coast in latitudes 35°–40° S. This was substantially what Cook afterwards did in 1769; and the experiences of Cook and other eighteenth-century navigators make it seem improbable that Dampier, poorly equipped as he was, would have achieved success by this route. Improbable, it must be said, but not impossible; for Torres, also poorly equipped, had surmounted difficulties such as Dampier would have met with. Dampier, however, through no fault of his own, was unable to sail in time to attempt Cape Horn, and on November 21, 1698, he wrote to the Admiralty saying that the season was gone and that he must proceed by the Cape of Good Hope. In another letter he outlined this route. From the Cape he would go by Madagascar to northern Australia, and thence to the north coast of New Guinea, examining the islands by the way for prospects of spices. From New Guinea he might double back to investigate Gilolo, one of the northernmost of the Moluccas, but in any case he would go on to round New Guinea eastwards and then southwards down that eastern shore of Australia which no one had yet seen. Here he expected to make the most fruitful discoveries, and thence would sail homewards round the world by Cape Horn. There was, of course, another way of reaching the unknown east coast, by going round the south of Australia. But to attempt this would entail missing the hypothetical spice islands, and Dampier himself thought that it might lead him to an impassable barrier; for in one of his letters, ignoring Tasman, he remarks that Australia may extend unbroken to the South Pole[1]. In accordance with the above suggestions the Admiralty framed their formal instructions to the explorer, and despatched them on November 30[2].

[1] Dampier's letters to the Admiralty are preserved in the Public Record Office, Ad. 1/1692 (Captains' Letters). This is a large volume containing letters from various officers. It is impossible to give a more precise reference, since the folios are not numbered. Moreover, only the letter of Nov. 21 is dated, so that the development of Dampier's ideas is not made perfectly clear.

[2] The instructions are given in Mr. John Masefield's *Dampier's Voyages* (London, 1908), II, p. 331. His reference is R. O., Adm. Sec. Out-Letters, 25.

Preparations had been in hand since the early part of the year. Dampier desired to have two vessels, as was prudent for the purpose of distant and dangerous exploration, but he was allowed only one. On March 25, 1698, he was appointed to the *Jolly Prize*. He found her hopelessly unfit for the voyage, and on June 30 he reported to that effect. The *Roebuck* was then selected for his purpose. If she was an improvement upon the *Jolly Prize*, the latter must have been indeed a wreck, for the *Roebuck* was far advanced in rottenness. With careful nursing she endured two years of ocean sailing, and then opened up and "foundered through perfect age", as her commander himself phrased it. She was a ship of 290 tons and carried a crew of fifty, with provisions for twenty months.

The fitting-out at Deptford was a slow process, and it was not until October 22 that the *Roebuck* was clear of the Thames and anchored in the Downs. It was then more than another month before Dampier received his instructions, and nearly seven weeks after that before he finally set sail from the Downs. Neither he nor his employers seem to have been in any hurry.

Dampier's qualification to lead a difficult expedition lay solely in the literary talent which had enabled him to describe the distant parts of the earth in a book that has become a classic. He had no record of command, or even of service as an officer. He had occupied twelve years in drifting round the world, for the most part in ruffianly company, and always in subordinate positions in which he had displayed no promise of leadership. Other drifters had done the like, and there were doubtless many scally-wags who had seen as much as he had. But his book set him in a class of his own. It proved him to be a man of intellect, if not of character. The Admiralty took the character for granted, and sent the poor man out in command of a cheap expedition, with a rotten ship and an inferior crew, and without a single officer of any moral quality to supply his captain's deficiencies. The result was another classic and a quantity of dirty linen for public laundering.

His first lieutenant was George Fisher, an officer of the regular Navy, who took an instant dislike to his captain, and made no effort to conceal it from the date of joining the ship at Deptford, in July, 1698. Fisher had begun his career as a soldier in the Irish campaigns of 1688–9, and had been a volunteer, that is, a prospective though not yet commissioned officer, at the relief of Londonderry. He was then transferred, with a recommendation, to the Navy. With the rank of gunner, he was present at the Battle of Beachy Head in 1690, and was soon afterwards promoted lieutenant. Thenceforward he served in several large ships under well-known captains, including Sir George Rooke, until, as he put it, he had the misfortune to be appointed to the *Roebuck*. He was able to produce testimonials from his various captains, and had evidently been a passable junior officer[1]. Now, from being fourth lieutenant of a big ship under regular discipline he became chief officer of a small one with all its discipline to make; and he was not equal to the position. Fisher may have been technically a gentleman, if Dampier was not. But both of them behaved equally as boors without a spark of dignity or self-respect, and while they sailed in company they were alternately drinking together, backbiting one another to their confidants, and breaking into personal abuse and even fisticuffs in presence of the crew. The other officers,

[1] His own account of himself, with copies of his testimonials, is in Ad. 1/5262 (Courts Martial).

including the master, two mates, gunner and surgeon, were a colourless lot, and the crew were the usual raw material swept up by impressment, most of them not sailors, who could be made efficient only by good leadership.

The *Roebuck* sailed from the Downs on January 14, 1699, and passed down Channel with a fair wind. A fortnight later the Canary Islands came in sight, and Dampier steered for Teneriffe, anchoring at Santa Cruz on the 30th. He gives a full description of the islands, and mentions that the Governor of the group was Don Pedro de Ponto, a native of Teneriffe. It would be interesting to know if this man was a descendant of Pedro de Ponte, the Teneriffe merchant who had been the confederate of John Hawkins in his attempt to force a trade with Philip II's American colonies in 1562-8.

Dampier's story ignores the difficulties which had already arisen with George Fisher. Dissension had begun at Deptford, when Dampier brought into the crew a friend of his, a Spaniard named Andres Garcia, and announced that he intended to make him an officer. Fisher prevented this by appealing to a regulation against foreigners exercising authority in the King's ships. Next, while lying in the Downs there was a good deal of skirmishing between the captain and his first lieutenant. Fisher said that some of the men were insubordinate, and tried to make Dampier get rid of them. Dampier retained them and was alleged to have incited them to be disrespectful to Fisher. The latter's contention was that he alone was trying to have the ship's work properly conducted, and that Dampier was ignorant of the Navy's methods and customs and altogether a poor seaman and navigator—"a very mean artist". On the passage to Teneriffe the situation became worse, and at that island Fisher alleged that he was in danger of his life. Dampier, he said, arranged with the Spaniard Garcia to get Fisher engaged in a brawl and murdered while on shore, but the plot miscarried. It is hard to believe this of Dampier, although no doubt he would have been pleased if Fisher had been arrested for some offence against Spanish law, which would have been a good excuse for leaving him behind.

The victuals being insufficient for the probable duration of the voyage, it was necessary to obtain a quantity of salt for the preservation of future supplies, and for this purpose a course was set to the Cape Verde Islands. The *Roebuck* reached the Isle of Maio on February 11, and took in seven or eight tons of salt, and thence proceeded to St. Iago to water. Here Fisher claimed that Dampier ran the ship into a position of great danger and then lost his nerve and was unable to extricate her. Fisher, seeing the ship about to be cast away, asked his captain what he meant to do, to which "he answered (as if crying) he did not know what the master designed". Fisher retorted that no one else did, since the master was at the moment dead drunk. Dampier then left the quarterdeck, and Fisher gave the necessary orders which saved the ship. How much, if any, truth there was in the story, no one can tell. Dampier in his book merely says that he had some difficulty in entering the roadstead of St. Iago and was at length towed in with assistance from two Portuguese boats.

The next destination was Brazil, where it would be possible to obtain final supplies for the direct run to Australia. Dampier says also that his crew were so raw and unaccustomed to hardship that it was necessary to refresh them before undertaking the long ocean passage. From the Cape Verdes to Brazil was a month's sailing,

during which time the feud reached its climax. Fisher
got it into his head that Dampier meant to turn pirate,
and that he and his friends were always hinting at it and
sounding the crew about it. At a drinking party the talk
turned upon pirates, whom Dampier defended, while
Fisher righteously maintained that they ought to be
hanged. It was, of course, a transparent dig at the ex-
buccaneer. A few days later the two engaged in a scuffle
up and down the deck. After a reprimand to which
Fisher answered in the style of a little vulgar boy,
Dampier collared him and caned him to his cabin,
where the delinquent was locked up, emitting loud
shouts of "old rogue, old dog, old villain". Fisher
finished his passage in irons, strictly confined in his stuffy
little box, and not liberated even for the most necessary
purposes. The crew, much edified, took sides, and a
mutiny appeared to Dampier to be imminent. He dared
not sleep in his cabin, but lay on the quarterdeck, with
arms at hand, and surrounded by those whom he could
trust. All this, and a great deal more, was deposed at the
court-martial two years later.

The state of indiscipline compelled Dampier to change
his Brazilian port of call from Pernambuco to Bahia.
At the first-named he would have been obliged to
anchor a long way from the town, and it would have
been possible for the crew to make off with the ship while
he was ashore. At Bahia, on the other hand, he could lie
under the guns of the forts, and he counted on the
Portuguese authorities to assist him. He arrived there on
March 25[1] and was well received by the Governor,
whom he describes as a very good man of ancient English

[1] The date given in the *Voyage* (p. 33); Fisher at the court-martial
said that he was sent to Bahia jail on March 8. Dampier's must be
the correct date.

ancestry. The Governor was certainly complaisant to Dampier in putting the jail at his disposal without asking too many questions, for Fisher was immediately bundled ashore and locked up on his captain's mere word, without any legal proceedings and without any formal charge being made against him. There he remained for four months enduring tropical imprisonment with the status of a common malefactor. In July he was shipped to Lisbon and there liberated, returning to England in December of the same year, 1699. It was quite indefensible treatment for any man, and especially for a commissioned officer. But Dampier, with his buccaneering ethics, seems to have thought that he had acted generously in putting his enemy in the way of reaching home instead of marooning him at some desolate spot. He wrote to the Admiralty an account of Fisher's insubordination, but took no pains to collect the evidence and place it on formal record; and he evidently considered that no more would be heard of the matter. His carelessness supports the assertion that he was ignorant of naval procedure.

As before, the book contains no mention of the Fisher affair. All it says is that its author found at Bahia an opportunity "to allay in some measure the ferment that had been raised among my men", without specifying its nature. In spite of the improvement the crew were still very disinclined for the voyage into unknown seas, and both hoped and believed that they would soon be turning homewards.

Dampier, however, was determined to go on, and, once rid of Fisher, exercised more effective authority. He sailed from Bahia on April 23, meaning to pass the Cape without touching. His description of the voyage through southern latitudes, and of all the natural phenomena which he delighted to observe, forms one of the best passages in the book. He was more than a lover of nature, and was concerned to make accurate scientific records. He gives a table of observed variations of the compass at a large number of positions, spread over a period of two years. This was a work of first-rate import-ance, for the old idea that lines of similar variation were identical with meridians was only then in process of being discredited. The notion had been held for nearly two centuries and had been propounded as a method of finding longitude at sea. Dampier pays tribute to the work of Halley on variation, modestly disclaims any scientific competence on his own part, and offers his data as raw material for others to work upon. "For my part I profess myself unqualified for offering at anything of a general scheme; but since matter of fact, and whatever increases the history of the variation, may be of use towards the settling or confirming the theory of it, I shall here once for all insert a table of all the variations I observed beyond the equator in this voyage." This is Dampier at his best; and his best might have been much more fruitful if he had been sent out solely as a scientific observer, with the cares of command allotted to someone better qualified to fulfil them.

On June 3 the *Roebuck* spoke an East Indiaman, and shortly afterwards sighted the South African coast, which she passed without stopping. Then she ran on with mainly westerly winds until various indications showed that she was nearing the western shore of Aus-tralia. Dampier worked cautiously towards it, for there were known to be outlying shoals, and sighted land on August 1st, 1699, in $27\frac{1}{2}°$ S. From this point he turned northwards to Shark's Bay in $25°$. He had a copy of Tasman's chart, which he was able to amend in certain particulars during the ensuing exploration; but it must be confessed that he added little or nothing to the general knowledge of the country which had been obtained by the Dutch.

Fresh water was running short, and the chief occupation of the landing parties was to search for supplies. At Shark's Bay none could be obtained, and after a week's stay in different anchorages Dampier went on to follow the coast northwards and eastwards. On August 21, after standing off to sea, he closed the land again and sighted a line of small islands, now called the Dampier Archipelago, in $20\frac{1}{2}°$. Tasman had shown this region as a broken coastline, but not as islands, which inclined Dampier "to think that he came not so near the shore as his line shows". Dampier ventured in among the islands, at considerable risk to the ship, but again found no fresh water and was obliged to pass on. The strong tides made him suspect that the archipelago masked a channel leading deep into the continent, but he was unable to investigate what was in fact an erroneous supposition.

He was now on the north coast of Australia and working in a general easterly direction, but the shoal water compelled him to keep well away from the land. On some days it was not in sight. On August 31 he went ashore in the neighbourhood now named Roebuck Bay, with a party equipped to dig for water, and also, fortunately, armed with muskets and cutlasses. An encounter took place with a group of natives. It need not be detailed here, since it is vividly described in Dampier's text. But one passage in his account of this locality needs comment: "When we came to the top of the hill where they [the savages] first stood, we saw a plain savannah, about half a mile from us, farther in from the sea. There were several things like hay-cocks, standing in the savannah; which at a distance we thought were houses, looking just like the Hottentots' houses at the Cape of Good Hope: but we found them to be so many rocks." Later writers have suggested that they were more probably anthills. But the fact is interesting because one at least of the Dieppe maps of the sixteenth century depicts these Hottentot huts as characteristic of the landscape of the country which may or may not be intended for Australia. The aborigines of the true Australia do not build dwellings of this sort. But what if some old Portuguese navigator, who had been at the Cape, had, like Dampier, beheld these misleading anthills and not come near enough to discern their real nature?

On September 1st the digging party struck water for the first time. It was so brackish as to be unfit for drinking, but Dampier filled a few casks, as he thought that it might do for making porridge, and to that extent spare the drinking water. He now decided to leave the coast, which he had visited principally for water and had never expected to be the scene of important discoveries. They, as he thought, lay still ahead, on the unknown eastern face of Terra Australis. And so on September 5 he set sail, meaning indeed to touch once again for water at the point he had visited in 1688, but soon changing his purpose and shaping his course directly for Timor. Here it may be noted that Dampier uniformly refers to Western and Northern Australia, known to the Dutch, as New Holland, and names the unknown part beyond New Guinea as Terra Australis. In the interval between his letters to the Admiralty in 1698 and the writing of the second part of his book some years later he had presumably given further study to Tasman's discoveries. For in the opening pages of the *Continuation*, in discussing his reasons for rounding Australia by the north instead of by the south, he no longer alludes to the possibility of a barrier, but attributes his decision to the undesirability of going into high latitudes in winter weather, and says that he thought of returning by the southern route if it could be done in the summer season. He still thought that there was probably a strait leading eastwards through New Holland from the coast which he had been investigating. It had been too risky to probe deeply for this strait, but he hoped that he might discover its farther end on the eastern coast which he was seeking to reach.

On his previous voyage Dampier had sighted Timor but had not landed. He had heard of the existence of Dutch and Portuguese settlements, but did not know their positions; and he had no accurate chart of the coast. He was therefore approaching what was in a sense a field of new discovery.

On September 14 he sighted the middle of the south side of Timor, and decided to stand eastwards. But four days later, having found neither a port nor water, he turned back westwards, and on the 21st entered the strait between Timor and the island of Anamabao. Here he met with a sloop under Dutch colours, and learned that he was only five leagues from Concordia, the only Dutch post in Timor. The Dutch were at first very suspicious, having had a bad experience with French pirates two years before. Dampier anchored within four miles of the fort and sent his clerk to interview the Governor, who refused to allow landing or watering. On September 23 and 24 Dampier twice sent "an officer" (name not given), who reported the Governor to be very hostile. It appeared later that this was a deliberately false statement, and that the officer had sought to foment distrust with a view to compelling

Dampier to turn back. But for the time the deception was not exposed, and Dampier passed clear of Concordia and began his voyage along the north side of Timor. He says that this same officer attempted to incite a mutiny, and it is quite possible that some lurid passages have here been suppressed. But since they led to no subsequent court-martial, we hear nothing further about the affair.

The north coast at length provided the much-desired water. On September 30 it was found in quantity at a good anchorage, where the ship remained for a week taking in supplies. Then Dampier stood on to the eastwards, and on October 12 came to the Portuguese settlement at Liphao, where he was well received. He heard of another Portuguese post at Sesial, twenty leagues farther on, and of a third at Porto Novo, at the eastern end of the island. On the 23rd he reached Sesial, which he found to be a bad harbour, exposed to the north. The ship now needed at least a month's work in refitting, and the northerly monsoon was due, with accompanying gales. Dampier therefore determined not to proceed farther along the north coast, but to return to the sheltered anchorage of Babao, in Copang Bay, at the Dutch or western end of Timor.

From October 28 to December 12, the *Roebuck* lay at Babao undergoing an extensive refit. On the anniversary of the gunpowder treason, which was also that of the landing of King William on English soil, there was a jollification with much firing of guns. It was heard by the Dutch, who came to investigate the cause. By this means Dampier got into touch again with the Governor of Concordia, cleared up the misunderstanding, and established good relations. The monsoon did not come, and when the ship again sailed eastwards she encoun-

INTRODUCTION xli

tered head winds and took a week to make good the
forty leagues to Liphao. Dampier therefore did not
examine the extreme east of Timor, but passed north
between the small islands of Omba and Fetter, and
thence stood away north-east for the nearer end of New
Guinea. The foregoing represents a summarized
itinerary extracted from a great amount of descriptive
matter on Timor, which Dampier evidently viewed as
an island of importance to the purposes for which he
had been sent out.

In going from Timor to western New Guinea, and
purposing thence to sail along its northern side, Dampier
missed a chance of discovering Torres Strait. No doubt
he accepted the Dutch belief that there was no such
strait. But he should not be accused of too easily taking
an unenterprising view, for his policy was to attain as
soon as possible the unknown eastern side of New Guinea
and Terra Australis, and from there work back by any
new passage he could discover. This, with the winds generally prevailing, was a defensible plan, although it was
not in the outcome followed far enough to yield any
really important discovery.

On New Year's Day, 1700, Dampier sighted New
Guinea at a point some two hundred miles from its
western end. He followed the trend of the coast and
examined the adjacent islands until by February 4 he
was off Cape Mabo, the north-westerly point of the
great country. Thence he worked eastwards along its
north coast, not keeping close to it, but visiting various
islands, some of them marked on the Dutch charts, and
others not. One such island, north of Cape Mabo, he
named King William's Island. In taking this course, he
was adding details to the existing chart but not discovering anything radically new; for northern New

Guinea had been visited in turn by Portuguese, Spaniards and Dutch since the early sixteenth century.

At the beginning of March, having latterly kept far out of sight of the mainland, Dampier turned south-east in order to close it. He passed the islands named Garret Dennis, Anthony Cave, and St. John's, all well inhabited by untrustworthy natives, and on March 8 and 9 found the main coast trending south-west. At this point the Dutch charting ceased, and Dampier believed, rightly, that he was in the unknown waters clear of the eastern end of New Guinea. Here at length he was in the most important of the regions towards which his voyage was directed. To the southwards lay an unlimited area never yet described by any recorded navigator, and full of speculative possibilities—the hidden eastern face of Terra Australis. We know now that there were many hundreds of miles of coast worth discovering, and we know also that it would have needed a better seaman than Dampier and a better ship than the *Roebuck* to perform the task. It needed, in fact, James Cook and his *Endeavour*.

What Dampier did was as follows. He sailed along his new mainland until he came to a cape, pointing south, which he called Cape St. George[1]. West of it was a deep opening, St. George's Bay, and the enclosing cape at the other side he called Cape Orford. Thence he followed the coast south-west to another indentation, Port Montague. He reached it on March 14 and stayed until the 22nd; and he gives a long and interesting description of the land and its people. Going on from that point he found on March 24 that the shore trended north-west, with only a faint loom of further land far to the westward. It was another deep gulf. He steered into it and found it to be a strait which brought him out on the northern side

---

[1] All the localities are marked on his own map.

of New Guinea once more. It thus appeared that the land which he had been coasting was not part of New Guinea, but a separate large island. He named it Nova Britannia—it is still called New Britain[1]—and the strait Dampier's Passage. This was the principal, indeed the sole, important discovery of the voyage. And it was important only relatively to the rest. Compared with the great unfulfilled possibilities it was insignificant.

Having traversed his Passage and arrived on the northern side of New Guinea, Dampier examined and charted the adjacent islands, and then steered westwards and homewards. He had reached the promised land and was turning back. He gives only one reason, which he says was the main one, namely, that his pinnace required repairs and that he had only one skilled carpenter on board. If one tries to enter into the realities of his position, that may well be accepted as adequate. To take a large sailing-ship close in to uncharted shores was a great risk, to mitigate which an able auxiliary vessel was essential. So far as can be discerned, it was not Dampier's fault that his expedition was wretchedly equipped and manned; and if he had resolutely pushed on southward the odds are heavy that nothing would ever have been heard of him again. The answer to any charge of faintheartedness lies in the record of Cook's Australian passage. Whether, with Cook's crew and equipment, Dampier would have done anything effective, is an unanswerable question. Indeed, since he lacked Cook's leadership, he could probably never have had Cook's crew.

[1] It was left to a later explorer, Captain Philip Carteret, to reveal the smaller strait that subdivides New Britain and New Ireland on the modern map. Dampier's St. George's Bay was actually the mouth of this strait.

On March 31, then, Dampier was steering west. He kept closer to the coast and saw some parts of northern New Guinea which he had missed on the outward passage. A northerly set in the tides caused him to conjecture the existence of another strait cutting New Guinea in two; but this, as we know, was wrong. On April 17 he was back at King William's Island, and next day was abreast of Cape Mabo.

From this point Dampier worked back to Timor by a more westerly track than that taken on the outward journey. He sighted Gilolo, Ceram and many smaller islands, and made a record useful to any commander who might follow him. This was all pertinent to the service on which he was engaged, but it was in no sense new discovery. At Timor he stayed to take in water at his old anchorage of Babao. He then departed southwestwards, with some hope of locating the Tryal Rocks, where an English ship had long ago been wrecked, and whose position had never been rediscovered. This unknown danger still lurked in the track of vessels approaching the Dutch Indies from the Cape; but Dampier, who was ill and unable to remain on deck, failed to clear up the mystery. He turned away northwards for Java and anchored at Batavia on July 3.

Dampier stayed two and a half months at Batavia. One of his tasks was to repair the ship. He obtained such stores as were necessary for the carpenter, but drily remarks that the *Roebuck* "proved more leaky after he had caulked her than she was before"; so that it was necessary to undertake the heavy job of careening, which entailed removing the whole of the contents of the ship, guns included, to smaller vessels lying alongside.

On October 17 he was ready to sail. The passage across the Indian Ocean was prosperous, and he arrived at the Cape of Good Hope on December 30. He gives not a single detail of his stay there, merely recording that he left on January 11, 1701. In the same manner he omits any account of St. Helena, which he reached on February 2 and quitted on the 13th. The *Roebuck* had now run her course. She sprang a serious leak on February 22, providentially when in sight of the island of Ascension. While Dampier steered in towards the land his carpenter and boatswain were working on repairs. But the rotten timber broke away like dirt as they touched it, and their efforts only served to increase the flow of water. With the pumps going ceaselessly the ship crept in close to the shore, and there, full to the hatches, she took the ground in three and a half fathoms. All hands were saved, but Dampier lost many of his books and papers. He gives in the text a detailed story of the efforts to stop the leak. At the official enquiry into the loss he put in a shorter account, which is printed at the end of this Introduction. It has been said that his published work was touched up by skilled editors after it left his hand, and this short paper, not meant for publication, may serve for comparison.

The castaways lived on Ascension without hardship until April 3, when they were taken off by three of the King's ships and an East Indiaman which touched at the island. On May 8 the men-of-war bore away for Barbados, while the East Indiaman sailed directly for England. Dampier and his officers took passage in her, leaving the majority of the crew to come later in the others. There is no record of the date on which Dampier reached England, but a letter from him to the Admiralty, written on August 21, 1701, mentions that the men who had been carried to Barbados have now returned. He therefore asks for a speedy court-martial on the loss of the *Roebuck*[1].

(iv) THE COURTS-MARTIAL

As a result of the events of his voyage, Dampier had to face three trials by court-martial: the first, on his responsibility for losing the ship; the second, on his treatment of Lieutenant Fisher; and the third, on an allegation by the widow of John Norwood, his boatswain, that the man's death at Barbados was in great measure due to harsh usage by his captain while on board the *Roebuck*. The third need not detain us: the court found that the charge was unsubstantiated; and it certainly appears as though it was a speculative attempt by the widow to profit from the odium then being raised against Dampier by Fisher.

The enquiry into the loss of the ship was held before the close of 1701, probably in October. Dampier's version of the facts was supported by Jacob Hughes, the master, and other witnesses. Together they made it evident that everything possible had been done, and the court, with entire justice, exonerated the captain. Whether the officials responsible for sending the *Roebuck* to sea could have been equally exonerated, if brought to trial, may be doubted; for the decay which caused the final and fatal leak seems to have been too extensive to have arisen in the course of the voyage.

The Fisher trial was delayed until the following year. Fisher, on reaching home at the close of 1699, had immediately begun to work up his case against Dampier, who on his side had written a brief statement to the Admiralty from Bahia. Pending Dampier's return,

[1] Ad. 1/1692 (Captain's Letters).

Fisher had been suspended from the King's service and told that he might seek employment in merchantmen. This he had done, and he was away on a long voyage when Dampier arrived. Fisher was again in England in 1702, and in May was asking for a speedy trial, as his witnesses might soon be going to sea.

The court-martial, which was a trial of both men on their mutual accusations, was held on board H.M.S. *Royal Sovereign* on June 8, 1702. The president was Sir George Rooke, and the court included Sir Cloudesley Shovell and thirty-four captains. They form an impressive list, from whose character and position impartial justice might be expected. Yet there was conceivably an element of prejudice, for they were to judge between a regular officer and an ex-buccaneer, and some of them, including the president, had been former commanding officers of Fisher's and had already given him testimonials of good conduct. Whether this really influenced them, we cannot tell; it would be pleasant to think that the future heroes of Gibraltar were not ungenerous men.

The court listened patiently to the whole degraded story of pettiness and ill-temper, which revealed no trace of any proper sense of discipline on either side. Fisher produced eleven witnesses to his being caned and manhandled by Dampier, and others reeled off all the ill-guarded remarks and tittle-tattle of six unpleasant months. The substance of it was that Dampier accused Fisher of repeated contempt and bad language, altering course contrary to orders, and inciting to mutiny; while Fisher accused Dampier of professional incompetence, inciting to piracy, personal violence, and illegal imprisonment. The hearing must have represented a long day's work. The result was that the court refused to act on the story of the recriminations and their causes, and

decided only on the established facts of the imprisonment
of Fisher on board ship and in Brazil. They concluded
that Dampier had been guilty of very hard and cruel
usage of his lieutenant, without any grounds for it, and
that the charges brought by Dampier against Fisher had
not been made good. The court acquitted Fisher and
fined Dampier the whole of his pay[1], and further declared that "the said Captain Dampier is not a fit person
to be employed as commander of any of her Majesty's
ships".

There exists[2] the following memorandum presumably
made by a member of the court:

"Upon full examination of all the Articles sett forth by
Captn Dampier & Lieu[nt] Fisher against each other,
the Court was of opinion that many of them were in
their own nature frivolous, and others not sufficiently
prov'd. So the chief matter before them seem'd to bee
the severity of Capt. Dampier's confinement of Lt
Fisher & other ill usage of him; and the grounds hee
had for so doing. The matter of fact of his beating his
said Lieut[nt] on Board, his confining him for many
months[3] on Board & then sending him ashore in Irons
to bee imprisoned there were notorious and past a
dispute. The reasons hee gave for so doing were his
Informations hee had of some mutinous practices
fomented by the sd Lt in the ship & the Jealousy hee
had of him, but the Captain failing in his proof of them,
amounting only to suppositions and surmise, induc'd the

---

[1] The forfeited money was to go to "the Chest at Chatham",
that is, the fund for disabled seamen founded long before by Drake
and Hawkins—except for £50 adjudged to the Queen for advances
already made to Fisher for his expenses in getting home from Brazil.

[2] This, with all the other court-martial papers, is in Ad. 1/5262.

[3] An exaggeration.

Court Martiall in their sentence to declare in favour of the Lieuten^t."

So unsatisfactorily ended the trial. For it really does appear that Fisher was not guiltless and that the court acquitted him in the face of convincing evidence; and that Dampier, although undoubtedly to blame and perhaps justly declared unfit to command, himself suffered "hard and cruel usage" in losing nearly three years' pay, which none can deny that he had earned. He never did thereafter command any of Her Majesty's ships, but it looks as though higher authority considered that the court-martial had been too severe. For, on April 16, 1703, not a year afterwards, when about to sail in charge of a privateering expedition, he was introduced to the Queen's presence by the Lord High Admiral, and had the honour to kiss the royal hand. It can only be interpreted as a censure upon Sir George Rooke and his captains.

The late Sir J. K. Laughton says of the *Roebuck* voyage that Dampier "showed himself an incompetent commander, whose sobriety, honesty, and courage even were impugned, and whose highest idea of discipline was calling his subordinate officers rogues, rascals, or sons of bitches"[1]. This, while in part true, implies acceptance of charges which the court dismissed. Dampier's other biographers, on the other hand, have gone too far in exonerating him, and have yielded too readily to the charm of his literary style and to sympathy with the hard lot of a man of sensibility who spent most of his life in uncongenial society. The truth may well be that Dampier

[1] Dictionary of National Biography, art. Dampier. For a very unfavourable picture, based on newly discovered evidence, of Dampier's conduct in the voyage of 1703, see B. M. H. Rogers, *Dampier's Voyage of 1703*, in *Mariner's Mirror*, 1924, October, pp. 366–81.

d

was one of those men of intellect who adapt themselves without difficulty to low company. The buccaneers
of his time were in effect pirates, whatever their predecessors may have been, and their way of life was
criminal. Dampier joined them willingly and continued
long in their association. His sea manners and ethics
were theirs, and were a good deal too crude for a
generation of the Royal Navy that was by no means
fastidious. But Dampier with a pen in his hand was a
different man, pleasant, tolerant and urbane. He says
not a word of the broils with Fisher, and rather mini-
mizes than emphasizes the general disaffection. In the
whole of his book he never mentions one of his sub-
ordinates by name. They are "the gunner" or "the
master", and when they do anything regrettable, not
even that, but merely "an officer". We can well imagine
a man with a meaner literary instinct seizing the opportunity to score off old enemies and vindicate himself,
unrestrained, as was then the case, by any effective law
of libel. He did not do it, although many a literary man
of action has yielded to the temptation even in our own
enlightened times. In sum, Dampier deserves sympathy,
not as a good man maligned, but as a questionable character with saving graces, a man of unequal parts, who
must sometimes have been as bitterly at war with himself
as with his fellows.

(v) THE EFFECTS OF DAMPIER'S WORK

As in his character, so in his influence upon events, the
literary inspiration was most estimable, the practical
achievement of small account. Dampier's permanent
service to his countrymen was to arouse their interest in
the exploration of the Pacific. He did it so effectively that

in the eighteenth century they took the lead in revealing the tropical islands and the coasts of Australia and New Zealand; and two dominions of the British Commonwealth are, among other things, the outcome of that enterprise. Dampier's agency in the process is demonstrable.

In the sixteenth century the versatile Elizabethans, taking the whole world as their field, had speculated on the South Sea and its supposed great unknown continent. They had sent out Drake to explore Terra Australia Incognita, but he had preferred to raid Peru. His success led others to imitate him, and then followed the war with Spain, during which projects of discovery were suspended. After the war came the century of empire-building in which the American and West Indian colonies were founded and the East India Company firmly established. The Atlantic and Indian oceans absorbed the national energies, and the efforts of explorers were devoted almost exclusively to seeking a better route to India than that round the Cape of Good Hope. The explorers failed to open the North-West Passage, and the Cape route became the only frequented path to the East.

During that seventeenth century the English people became imbued with the importance of the long-distance trades as producers of wealth and sea-power. The West Indies with their sugar plantations, and the East Indies with their spices and rare fabrics, became as lucrative as the Spanish silver mines; and it was recognized that the process of acquiring this wealth produced, in large ships and numerous seamen, the means of defending it and strengthening the whole nation against its rivals. In the middle of the seventeenth century the Dutch seemed the most formidable rivals, but by its close the French had

taken their place. The Dutch had begun by excluding
the English from any effective share in the trade of the
East Indian archipelago, and had forced them to restrict
themselves to continental India. But the English returned, and gradually pushed their way back into the
islands' trade, and even beyond to the tea-market of
China. In Dampier's writings we find frequent mention
of English merchantmen at Batavia, treated as a matter
of course. Thus the English by his time were on the
western fringe of the Pacific.

On its eastern or American side they had done almost
nothing since Drake's time. Their only representatives—
if we except an isolated voyage by Sir John Narborough
under Charles II—had been the buccaneers with whom
Dampier himself had served. But the buccaneers were
cosmopolitan, disreputable, and destructive. They ac-
knowledged no allegiance to the English government, sold
no wares for English merchants, made no discoveries of
value to anyone. They had no roots in the English state
or nation. For practical purposes the Pacific was a closed
and unknown ocean to Stuart England. Yet it covered
half the earth's surface, and the possibilities of the other
half were known and measured. For France under
Louis XIV the position was similar, and France and
England were sworn enemies after 1689. The rivalry, it
seemed, must extend into the new field. The Pacific was
"ripe for development".

The appositeness of Dampier's first book, the *New
Voyage Round the World* (1697), to this situation has
already been noticed, and the fact that it was a best-
seller shows how ready the public was to be interested in
its topics. His second book, *Voyages and Discoveries* (1699),
published while he was lying in the Downs waiting to
sail in the *Roebuck*, was to the same general purpose,

interest in distant seas and lands. His third and last
book, the *Voyage to New Holland* (1703 and 1709), con-
centrated attention more particularly on the western and
southern Pacific. It might have been more aptly described as a voyage to New Britain and a project for
Eastern Australia, for there essentially lay the focus of its
interest. The repulsiveness of New Holland had a
merely scientific appeal, but the fertility and populous-
ness of Nova Britannia and the adjacent islands attracted
the attention of empire-builders. Not only did this region
offer a value of its own, but its position marked it as a
base from which enterprise might radiate—to the north
the Asiatic seas, to the south the still unknown Australia,
to the east New Zealand, seen once by Tasman and
thenceforward unvisited, but thought to be a part of the
mighty continent bordering the South Sea.

These incentives were talked of, but did not at once
produce action. Meanwhile Dampier's later career had
its significance. The War of the Spanish Succession
called forth immediate French and British enterprise on
the Spanish coasts of the Pacific. The majority of the
Spanish people rejected the Austrian candidate for their
throne, who was backed by the British and their allies,
and accepted the French candidate, who was substantially King of Spain from the beginning of the struggle.
The French were therefore able to appear on the west
coast of America as friends and helpers, while the
British organized privateering expeditions in quest of
plunder. Dampier sailed in 1703 in command of a
privateer enterprise. It was an utter failure, mainly by
reason of his own irresolution and incapacity to work
with others. Not even he could write a book that would
put a good face upon it, and he passed it over in silence,
save for a brief and unconvincing pamphlet of 3,000

words in which he sought to answer the criticisms of
William Funnell, who had published an account of the
voyage. He was now thoroughly discredited as a commander, but his knowledge of meteorology and geography rendered him still a useful man to advise in, if
not to direct, the strategy of a distant voyage. In that
capacity he sailed again in 1708 as an officer under
Captain Woodes Rogers with the *Duke* and *Dutchess*, two
privateers for the South Sea. Owing to the excellence of
Rogers in all the qualities that Dampier lacked, the
voyage was a brilliant success, and its commander's well-
written narrative confirmed the public belief that the
South Sea was the coming field of enterprise. Dampier
himself wrote nothing upon it, but his own books had
laid the foundation upon which the new national
consciousness was being built.

In the sphere of national policy, as contrasted with
privateering enterprise, the first fruit of the movement
was the foundation in 1711 of the South Sea Company,
chartered by the British government to organize and
monopolize the prospective national interest. Like so
many of our first steps, it failed. The ministers who
founded the Company hoped to secure concessions for
trade with the South Sea at the peace negotiations which
they were then initiating. But the Treaty of Utrecht, two
years later, gave them only the right of limited general
trading and supplying slaves to the Atlantic ports of
Spanish America. Indirectly there was some dealing at
Porto Bello in the produce of the remoter coast; but the
South Sea Company never sent a ship of its own into the
South Sea, and the hopes with which it was founded
were unrealized.

Privateering in the Pacific had a fresh lease of life with
another short Spanish War in 1718-19, but afterwards

there was a cessation of British enterprise during the twenty years of the Walpole Peace. Discovery was like-wise dropped. The War of the Spanish Succession had left Great Britain supreme in the Atlantic, and the energies of the peace were devoted to extensive coloniza-tion and expansion of commerce in that area. Explora-tion had now reached the phase in which scientific information, but no immediate financial profit, could be expected from an expedition on the lines of the Voyage to New Holland. It was therefore regarded as a matter for the State and not for private initiative. English capitalists were making fortunes in the Atlantic sugar trade and slave trade, but the tradition had not yet arisen that the successful business man should devote some of his winnings to public objects. Meanwhile the State under Walpole was unadventurous; he was all for economy, consolidation, and the defence of existing assets.

But the intellectual interest continued keen, in France no less than in Great Britain; and since French books were even more widely read in this country than they are now, and the more important of them translated, the British mind continued to be well nourished with fact and speculation on the Western and Eastern Pacific. The French Jesuits in China published many volumes of their *Lettres édifiantes et curieuses*, from which the cream of the *curieux*—omitting the conversions as merely *édifiant*—was brought out in three successive English translations. Du Halde's massive *History of China*, 1735, was translated into English in the following year, and again, inde-pendently, in 1738. Under Queen Anne, John Churchill had brought out four volumes of *Voyages and Travels*, to which he added two more in 1732. John Harris had also published two volumes of *Voyages* in 1705, and in 1744

John Campbell revised and extended the collection into a four-volume work. Knapton, as we have seen, had answered a public demand by re-publishing all Dampier's works in 1729, with much additional matter; and the fact that the general collection was incorrectly known as "the four-volume Dampier", is significant of the spell which his name still exercised. Fiction also was entering into the new field. Swift located all of Gulliver's fantastic discoveries in the Pacific, north or south; while Defoe's numerous novels, although not containing much on the unknown South Sea—for their author preferred to write of things on which he could obtain real information—powerfully excited the public sense of the romance of distant countries.

Through all this mental activity the leaven of Dampier was a working and indeed a vitalizing agent. For he alone of the English navigators had come to the fringe of the unknown; the privateer captains had traversed only the regular Pacific tracks of the Spaniards. He also was pre-eminent in satisfying the mind that studied for delight, the imagination that fed itself on strange birds and beasts and peoples and glowing tropic scenes, the calculation that dwelt more on rare commodities than on blood and battle-smoke. In his life he was an antithesis, a shady adventurer, an untrustworthy colleague, a morose, unstable captain, who inspired neither affection nor respect; and at the same time the wielder of a pen of gold, which imparted to the materialism of empire-building a gleam of humane and scientific enlightenment. Gradually the memory of Dampier the adventurer faded, while the genius of Dampier the writer continued to live. And, when, after half a century, the great age of the South Sea set in, and Byron and Wallis, Carteret, Bougainville and Cook revealed in fifteen years all the hidden mysteries, they did so in the best manner of the eighteenth century and not in its worst, approaching their task as civilized captains without envy or avarice, following the tradition of Dampier, the seeker of knowledge, untainted by that of the buccaneer.

J. A. WILLIAMSON

DAMPIER'S UNPUBLISHED ACCOUNT OF THE LOSS OF THE "ROEBUCK."

(Public Record Office, Admiralty 1/5262.)

An account of the Loss of His Majesty's Ship Roebuck Febry 21st 1700/1. At three aclock in the afternoon being in Sight of the Island Ascension, and not haveing day Light enough to carry us into the Bay where design'd to anchor, we brought to under a pair of Courses and stood to the Eastward, At half an hour after 8 in the night we sprung a Leake on the Larboard bow about four Strakes from the Keele, which oblig'd us to keep our Chain pump constantly going, at twelve at night having a moderate gale, we bore away for the Island and be day light were close in with it, at nine aclock in the morning anchored in the N.W.bay in ten fathom and half water, sandy ground about half a mile from the shoare, the S. point of the bay bore S.S.W. dist. one mile and half and the Northermost point, N.E. ½N. dist. two mile, Being come to anchor I ordered the Gunner to cleare his Powder roome, that we might there search for the Leake, and endeavour to stop it within board if possible, for we could not heele the Ship so low, neither was there any convenient place to haule her ashoare, I ordered the Boatswain and several men to assist the Gunner, which they did, and at ten aclock (the Powder roome being cleare) I ordered the Carpenter's Mate (who was the only Carpenter I had aboard) with the Boatswain and some others to goe downe and search for the Leake, the Carpenter's Mate and Boatswain told me that they could not come at it unless they cut the Cieling, which I bidd them doe, which done they found the Leake against one of the foothook timbers, it was very large, and the water gushed in with great violence, then I went down to view it, and the Carpenter's Mate and Boatswain told me it could not be stopt, unless the timber were cutt, I made answer that I never was in any ship whose timbers were cutt to find Leakes, but am no shipwright, therefore advise you that understand it to be very cautious not to weaken or endanger the Ship more, And if it cannot be otherwise stopt but by cutting the timber, I bidd them first get all things in readiness to stop the Leake before they cutt too farr, for I knew the water would rush in with such force that it would be hardly possible for any to stand there, unless great circumspection and Diligence were us'd to stop it soon, To this the Carpenter's

Mate and Boatswain replied, that they did not doubt but that they should stop it before four a clock, But after they had cutt the timber, notwithstanding all that could be done the Leake so increased that with pumping and bealing we could not stay in the place where the Leake was, The water gained so much upon us, I ordered a bulkhead to be cutt open to give passage to the water, and withall ordered to cleare away abaft the bulkhead, that we might beale, and at this time we had both Pumps going and as many bealing as could, by which meanes the water began to decrease, and the Carpenter's Mate said be ten aclock at night he would engage to stop the Leake. But about 11 aclock at night the Boatswain came to me, told me that the Leake still encreas'd, and that the Plank was quite rotten, and that now it was impossible to save the Ship, because they could not come at the Leake, for the water in the Powder roome was gott above it, The rest of the night we spent in pumping and bealing, but the water still encreas'd, we thought on nothing now but saving our Lives, I therefore hoysted out the boate, and next morning, being the 23rd, we weigh'd anchor and warped in nearer the shoare, but to little purpose till in the afternoon we had a Sea breeze by which we gott in within a Cable's length of the Shoare, then made a Raft to carry men's chests and bedding ashoare, and before Eight at night most of them were gott ashoare, She struck not before nine aclock at night, and so continued, I ordered some sailes to be cutt from the yards to make us some tents, etc, and the next morning being the 24th myself and Officers went ashoare on the forenamed desolate Island Ascension.

WM DAMPIER

29° die Septem: 1701

A PLAN FOR AUSTRALIAN EXPLORATION, 1715

The document printed below is contained in a volume of unpublished Naval Miscellanea in the Library of the National Maritime Museum. It was written by John Welbe and enclosed with a covering letter to an unknown "Your Lordship", with date May 27, 1715. In the letter Welbe says that he has proposed the scheme to His Majesty and that it is now before the Council. The writer adds that he has not two shillings in the world, but knows His Lordship to be "a bright patron of ingenuity." Nothing came of the proposal, but it is interesting as illustrating the state of knowledge and speculation after Dampier's work. Welbe had sailed with Dampier in the privateering voyage of 1703, but not in the voyage to New Holland. The editor's thanks are due to the librarian of the National Maritime Museum for his kindness in tracing this document and affording facilities for copying it.

A SCHEME OF A VOYAGE ROUND THE GLOBE FOR THE DISCOVERY OF TERRA AUSTRALIS INCOGNITA

There ought to be a good fourth Rate Ship carrying 180 men having her upper tire of guns mounted, the lower tire of guns being left a Shore for the conveniency of stowage and the ease of the Ship; The Copper hung like a Still so that when water is wanted we can distill the Salt water and make it fresh.

A good Brigantine of about 100 Tuns, carrying 20 men 6 guns and 6 patereros. This Brigantine will be usefull to send a head upon occasion, when it will not be convenient to goe so nigh with a great ship before we have sounded.

I propose to sail directly for the Island of St. Iago, one of the Cape de Verd Islands, in the Lat 14^d : 56^m North Long^{td} west 24^d : 47^m, to get fresh water, frome thence to the Island of Legrand on the Coast of Brazil, South Lat^d 23^d : 20^m to get wood and water, From thence make the Island Siboldewards[1] Lat^d 51^d : 35^m So, Long^{td} west 51^d : 37^m then take a fresh departur and endeavour to get my passage about Cape Horn Lat^d 57^d : 30^m So, then hale in with the Coast of Chilly, and make the Island Lamocha, Lat^d 38^d : 40^m So, then take a fresh departur, and stear away for the Island of Juan de fardinandos, Lat^d 33^d : 40^m South to get wood and water, from thence sail downe to the Coast of Peru. Thence take my departur and stear west till I come to the Solomons Islands, which are reported by the Spaniards to abound in Gold; They were discovered above 100 years agoe, but the Court of Spain did not thinck fit to settle them, by reason they had not intirely setled the main land of Peru.

These Islands lying out of the way of all foreign Trade, and the Accapulca Ships which trade betweene the Phillippine Islands in the East Indies and Accapulca on the Coast of Mexico in the South Seas, keepe always in the North East Trade wind, when they sail from Accapulca to the Philippines, and when they come from the Indies to Accapulca, they Sail to 40 or 45 degrees North to meete with a westerly wind to run them to the Eastward, for which reason those parts are not yet fully discovered, nor any part of them setled, by any Nation except the Indians, who are very populous, as soon as I come to theese Islands, I propose to goe a Shore with about 150 men to search and discover what the Country abounds in, and then trapan some of the Inhabitants on board, and bring them for England, who when they have learnd our language, will be proper interpreters.

From the Solomon Islands I propose to sail west, to the Coast of Nova Guinea, which is the East Side of

[1] The Falkland Islands.

Nova Hollandia, in the East Indies, and make a true discovery of that Coast, and search what the Country abounds in: it lying North and South as Peru does, and in the same Lat^d I believe it abounds in Gold and Silver mines, which if discoverd and setled may be of vast advantage to Great Britain. This Coast is full of Harbours, according to the Account I have had out of Spanish Journals of the discovery of the Solomon Islands. After I have made a discovery of this Coast of Nova Guinea, and taken away some of the Inhabitants, I propose to make a farther discovery of Nova Britannia and the adjacent Islands, and search what they abound in, and take off some of the Inhabitants likewise. For tho Capt Dampire discoverd Nova Britannia yet he never was at Shore at any place, except Port Montegue, and only as far as the watering place, he having only 50 men in his Ship, was not strong enough to search the Country, and consequently it is unknowne what those parts abound in.

From Nova Britannia I propose to Sail to the westward, and sail between the west end of Nova Guinea and the Island of Gillolo, and stand away to the South ward of the Island of Java, and Stear directly towards the Cape de bon Espirance, to get fresh provision, from thence sail for England.

A

VOYAGE
TO
NEW-HOLLAND, &c.
In the YEAR 1699.

Wherein are defcribed,
The *Canary*-Iflands, the Ifles of *Mayo* and St. *Jago*.
The Bay of *All-Saints*, with the Forts and Town
of *Bahia* in *Brazil*. Cape *Salvadore*. The Winds
on the *Braſilian* Coaſt. *Abrohlo* Shoals. A Table
of all the *Variations* obferv'd in this Voyage. Occurrences near the Cape of *Good-Hope*. The
Courfe to *New-Holland*. *Shark's* Bay. The Ifles
and Coaſt, *&c.* of *New--Holland*.

Their Inhabitants, Manners, Cuſtoms, Trade, *&c.*
Their Harbours, Soil, Beaſts, Birds, Fiſh, *&c.*
Trees, Plants, Fruits, *&c.*

Illuftrated with feveral MAPS and DRAUGHTS: Alfo divers
Birds, Fiſhes and Plants not found in this Part of the
World, Curiouſly Ingraven on Copper-Plates.

VOL. III.

By Captain WILLIAM DAMPIER.

The THIRD EDITION.

LONDON,
Printed for JAMES *and* JOHN KNAPTON, at the
Crown in St. *Paul's* Church-Yard. MDCCXXIX.

To the Right Honourable

THOMAS, EARL OF PEMBROKE

Lord President of Her Majesty's Most Honourable

Privy-Council, &c.

MY LORD,

*T*HE *Honour I had of being employ'd in the Service of his late Majesty of Illustrious Memory, at the time when Your Lordship presided at the Admiralty, gives me the Boldness to ask Your Protection of the following Papers. They consist of some Remarks made upon very distant Climates, which I should have the Vanity to think altogether new, could I persuade my self they had escap'd Your Lordship's Knowledge. However I have been so cautious of publishing any thing in my whole Book that is generally known, that I have deny'd my self the Pleasure of paying the due Honours to Your Lordship's Name in the Dedication. I am asham'd, my Lord, to offer You so imperfect a Present, having not time to set down all the Memoirs of my last Voyage: But as the particular Service I have now undertaken, hinders me from finishing this Volume, so I hope it will give me an Opportunity of paying my Respects to Your Lordship in a new one.*

The World is apt to judge of every thing by the Success; and whoever has ill Fortune will hardly be allow'd a good Name. This, my Lord, was my Unhappiness in my late Expedition in the Roe-Buck, *which founder'd thro' perfect Age near the Island of* Ascension. *I suffer'd extreamly in my Reputation by that Misfortune; tho' I comfort my self with the Thoughts, that my Enemies cou'd not charge any Neglect upon me. And since I have the Honour to be acquitted by your Lordship's Judgment, I*

e

*should be very humble not to value my self upon so compleat a
Vindication. This, and a World of other Favours, which I have
been so happy as to receive from Your Lordship's Goodness, do
engage me to be with an everlasting Respect,*

My Lord,

Your Lordship's

Most Faithful and

Obedient Servant,

WILL DAMPIER

THE PREFACE

THE favourable Reception my two former Volumes of *Voyages and Descriptions* have already met with in the World, gives me Reason to hope, That notwithstanding the Objections which have been raised against me by prejudiced Persons, this *Third Volume* likewise may in some measure be acceptable to Candid and Impartial Readers, who are curious to know the Nature of the Inhabitants, Animals, Plants, Soil, &c. in those distant Countries, which have either seldom or not at all been visited by any *Europeans*.

It has almost always been the Fate of those who have made new Discoveries, to be disesteemed and slightly spoken of, by such as either have had no true Relish and Value for the *Things themselves* that are discovered, or have had some Prejudice against *the Persons* by whom the Discoveries were made. It would be vain therefore and unreasonable in me to expect to escape the Censure of all, or to hope for better Treatment than far Worthier Persons have met with before me. But this Satisfaction I am sure of having, that the *Things themselves* in the Discovery of which I have been imployed, are most worthy of our diligentest Search and Inquiry; being the various and wonderful Works of God in different Parts of the World: And however *unfit a Person* I may be in other respects to have undertaken this Task, yet at least I have given a faithful Account, and have found *some* Things undiscovered by any before, and which may at least be *some* Assistance and Direction to better qualified Persons who shall come after me.

It has been objected against me by some, that my Accounts and Descriptions of Things are dry and jejunc, not filled with variety of pleasant Matter, to divert and gratify the Curious Reader. How far this is true, I must leave to the World to judge. But if I have been exactly and strictly careful to give only *True* Relations and Descriptions of Things (as I am sure I have;) and if my Descriptions be such as may be of use not only to my self (which I have already in good measure experienced) but also to others in future Voyages; and likewise to such Readers at home as are more desirous of a Plain and Just Account of the true Nature and State of the Things described, than of a Polite and Rhetorical Narrative: I hope all the Defects in my Stile, will meet with an easy and ready Pardon.

Others have taxed me with borrowing from other Men's Journals; and with Insufficiency, as if I was not my self the Author of what I write, but published Things digested and drawn up by others. As to the first Part of this Objection, I assure the Reader, I have taken nothing from any Man without mentioning his Name, except some very few Relations and particular Observations received from credible Persons who desired not to be named; and these I have always expressly distinguished in my Books, from what I relate as of my own observing. And as to the latter; I think it so far from being a Diminution to one of my Education and Employment, to have what I write, Revised and Corrected by Friends; that on the contrary, the best and most eminent Authors are not ashamed to own the same Thing, and look upon it as an Advantage.

Lastly, I know there are some who are apt to slight my Accounts and Descriptions of Things, as if it was an easie Matter and of little or no Difficulty to do all that I have done, to visit little more than the Coasts of unknown Countries, and make short and imperfect Observations

of Things only near the Shore. But whoever is experienced in these Matters, or considers Things impartially,
will be of a very different Opinion. And any one who is
sensible, how backward and refractory the Seamen are
apt to be in long Voyages when they know not whither
they are going, how ignorant they are of the Nature of
the Winds and the shifting Seasons of the Monsoons,
and how little even the Officers themselves generally are
skilled in the Variation of the Needle and the Use of the
Azimuth Compass; besides the Hazard of all outward
Accidents in strange and unknown Seas: Any one, I say,
who is sensible of these Difficulties, will be much more
pleased at the Discoveries and Observations I have been
able to make, than displeased with me, that I did not
make more.

Thus much I thought necessary to premise in my own
Vindication, against the Objections that have been
made to my former Performances. But not to trouble
the Reader any further with Matters of this Nature;
what I have more to offer, shall be only in relation to
the following Voyage.

For the better apprehending the Course of this Voyage,
and the Situation of the Places mentioned in it, I have
here, as in the former Volumes, caused a Map to be
Ingraven, with a prick'd Line, representing to the Eye
the whole Thread of the Voyage at one View; besides
Draughts and Figures of particular Places, to make the
Descriptions I have given of them more intelligible and
useful.

Moreover, which I had not the opportunity of doing
in my former Voyages; having now had in the Ship with
me a Person skill'd in Drawing, I have by this means
been enabled, for the greater Satisfaction of the Curious
Reader, to present him with exact Cuts and Figures of

several of the principal and most remarkable of those
Birds, Beasts, Fishes and Plants, which are described in
the following Narrative; and also of several, which not
being able to give any better or so good an Account of,
as by causing them to be exactly Ingraven, the Reader
will not find any further Description of them, but only
that they were found in such or such particular Countries. The Plants themselves are in the Hands of the
Ingenious Dr. *Woodward.* I could have caused many
others to be drawn in like manner, but that I resolved
to confine my self to such only, as had some very remarkable difference in the Shape of their principal Parts
from any that are found in *Europe.* I have besides several
Birds and Fishes ready drawn, which I could not put
into the present Volume, because they were found in
Countries, to the Description whereof the following
Narrative does not reach. For, being obliged to prepare
for another Voyage, sooner than I at first expected;
I have not been able to continue the ensuing Narrative
any further than to my Departure from the Coast of
New Holland. But, if it please God that I return again
safe, the Reader may expect a Continuation of this
Voyage from my departure from *New Holland*, till the
foundring of my Ship near the Island of *Ascension.*

In the mean time, to make the Narrative in some
measure compleat, I shall here add a Summary Abstract
of that latter part of the Voyage, whereof I have not had
time to draw out of my Journals a full and particular
Account at large. Departing therefore from the Coast of
New Holland in the beginning of *September*, 1699. (for
the Reasons mentioned *Page* 107.) we arrived at *Timor*,
Sept. 15. and anchored off that Island. On the 24th we
obtain'd a small Supply of fresh Water from the Governor
of a *Dutch* Fort and Factory there; we found also there a

Portuguese Settlement, and were kindly treated by them. On the 3d of *December* we arrived on the Coast of *New Guinea;* where we found good fresh Water, and had Commerce with the Inhabitants of a certain Island call'd *Pulo-Sabuti.* After which, passing to the Northward, we ranged along the Coast to the Eastermost Part of *New Guinea*; which I found does not join to the main Land of *New Guinea*, but is an Island, as I have described it in my Map, and call'd it *New-Britain.*

It is probable this Island may afford many rich Commodities, and the Natives may be easily brought to Commerce. But the many Difficulties I at this time met with, the want of Convenience to clean my Ship, the fewness of my Men, their Desire to hasten home, and the Danger of continuing in these Circumstances in Seas where the Shoals and Coasts were utterly unknown, and must be searched out with much Caution and length of Time; hindred me from prosecuting any further at present my intended Search. What I have been able to do in this Matter for the Publick Service, will, I hope, be candidly receiv'd; and no Difficulties shall discourage me from endeavouring to promote the same End, whenever I have an Opportunity put into my Hands.

May 18. in our Return, we arrived at *Timor. June* 21, we past by part of the Island *Java. July* 4, we anchored in *Batavia*-Road; and I went ashore, visited the *Dutch* General, and desired the Privilege of buying Provisions that I wanted, which was granted me. In this Road we lay till the 17th of *October* following; when, having fitted the Ship, recruited my self with Provisions, filled all my Water, and the Season of the Year for returning towards *Europe* being come; I set Sail from *Batavia*, and on the 19th of *December* made the Cape of *Good Hope;* whence departing *Jan.* 11, we made the Island of *Santa Hellena* on the 31st; and *February* the 21st, the Island of *Ascension*; near to which my Ship, having sprung a Leak which could not be stopped, foundred at Sea; with much difficulty we got ashore, where we liv'd on Goats and Turtle; and on the 26th of *February* found, to our great Comfort, on the S. E. Side of a high Mountain, about half a Mile from its Top, a Spring of fresh Water. I returned to *England* in the *Canterbury East-India*-Ship. For which wonderful Deliverance from so many and great Dangers, I think my self bound to return continual Thanks to Almighty God; whose Divine Providence if it shall please to bring me safe again to my Native Country from my present intended Voyage; I hope to publish a particular Account of all the material Things I observed in the several Places which I have now but barely mentioned.

PART I

THE CONTENTS

CHAP. I

THE A.'s departure from the Downs. A Caution to those who sail in the Channel. His Arrival at the Canary-Islands. Santa Cruz in Teneriffe; the Road and Town, and Spanish Wreck. Laguna T. Lake and Country; and Oratavia T. and Road. Of the Wines and other Commodities of Teneriffe, &c. and the Governors at Laguna and Santa Cruz. Of the Winds in these Seas. The A's Arrival at Mayo. Of the C. Verd Islands; its Salt-pond, compar'd with that of Salt Tortuga; its Trade for Salt, and Frape-boats. Its Vegetables, Silk-Cotton, &c. Its Soil, and Towns; its Guinea-Hen's, and other Fowls, Beasts, and Fish. Of the Sea-Turtles, &c. laying in the Wet Season, Of the Natives, their Trade and Livelihood. The A.'s Arrival at J. St. Jago; Proga, and St. Jago Town. Of the Inhabitants, and their Commodities. Of the Custard-Apple, St. Jago Road. J. Fogo.

CHAP. II

The A.'s Deliberation on the Sequel of his Voyage, and Departure from St. Jago. His Course, and the Winds, &c. in crossing the Line. He stands away for the Bay of All-Saints in Brazil; and why. His Arrival on that Coast and in the Bay. Of the several Forts, the Road, Situation, Town, and Buildings of Bahia. Of its Governour, Ships and Merchants; and Commodities to and from Europe. Claying of Sugar. The Season for the European Ships, and Coire Cables: Of their Guinea-

trade, and of the Coasting-trade, and Whale-killing. Of the Inhabitants of Bahia; *their carrying in Hammocks: Their Artificers, Crane for Goods, and Negro-Slaves. Of the Country about* Bahia, *its Soil and Product. Its Timber-trees; the Sapiera, Vermiatico, Comesserie, Guitteba, Serrie, and Mangroves. The Bastard-Coco, its Nuts and Cables; and the Silk-Cotton-trees. The* Brasilian *Fruits, Oranges, &c. Of the Sour-sops, Cashew's, and* Jennipah's. *Of their peculiar Fruits,* Arisah's, Mericasah's, Petango's, Petumbo's, Mungaroo's, Muckishaw's, Ingwa's, Otees, *and* Musteran de Ova's. *Of the Palm-berries, Physick-nuts,* Mendibee's, *&c. and their Roots and Herbs, &c. Of their Wild-Fowl,* Maccaw's, Parrots, *&c. The* Yemma, *Carrion-Crow and Chattering-crow, Bill-bird, Curreso, Turtle-dove and Wild-pigeons; the* Jenetee, *Clocking-hen, Crab-catcher, Galden, and black Heron: The Ducks, Widgeon and Teal; and Ostriges to the Southward, and of the Dunghil-fowls. Of their Cattle, Horses, &c. Leopards and Tiger's. Of their Serpents; the Rattle-Snake, small Green-Snake,* Amphisbæna, *small Black and small Grey-Snake; the great Land, and the great Water-Snake; and of the Water-dog. Of their Sea-fish and Turtle; and of St.* Paul's *Town.*

CHAP. III

The A.'s Stay and Business at Bahia: *Of the Winds, and Seasons of the Year there. His departure for* N. Holland. C. Salvadore. *The Winds on the* Brasilian *Coast; and* Abrohlo *Shoal; Fish, and Birds: The Shear-water Bird, and Cooking of Sharks. Excessive number of Birds about a dead Whale; Of the Pintado Bird, and the Petrel, &c. Of a Bird that shews the* C. of G. Hope *to be near: Of the Sea-reckonings, and Variations: And a Table of all the Variations observ'd in this Voyage. Occurrences near the* Cape; *and the A.'s passing by it. Of the Westerly Winds beyond it: A Storm, and its Presages. The A.'s Course to* N. Holland; *and Signs of approaching it. Another* Abrohlo Shole *and Storm, and the A.'s Arrival on part of* N. Holland. *That part describ'd; and* Shark's Bay, *where he first anchors. Of the Land there, Vegetables, Birds, &c. A particular sort of* Guano: *Fish, and beautiful Shells; Turtle, large Shark, and Water-Serpents. The A.'s removing to another part of* N. Holland: *Dolphins, Whales, and more Sea-Serpents: And of a Passage or* Streight *suspected here: Of the Vegetables, Birds, and Fish. He anchors on a third Part of* N. Holland, *and digs Wells, but brackish. Of the Inhabitants there, and great Tides, the Vegetables and Animals, &c.*

A *Voyage to* Terra Australis

CHAP. I

The A.'s Departure from the Downs. *A Caution to those who sail in the*
Channel. *His Arrival at the* Canary-Islands. Santa Cruz *in* Teneriffe;
the Road and Town, and Spanish *Wreck.* Laguna *T. Lake and
Country; and* Oratavia *T. and Road. Of the Wines and other Com-
modities of* Teneriffe, *&c. and the Governours at* Laguna *and* Santa
Cruz. *Of the Winds in these Seas. The A.'s Arrival at* Mayo, *one of the*
C. Verd *Islands; its Salt-pond, compar'd with that of* Salt-Tortuga;
its Trade for Salt, and Frape-boats. *Its Vegetables, Silk-Cotton, &c. Its
Soil, and Towns, its* Guinea-Hen's, *and other Fowls, Beasts, and Fish.
Of the Sea-Turtle's (&c.) laying in the wet Season. Of the Natives, their
Trade and Livelihood. The A.'s Arrival at* J. St. Jago, *and* St. Jago
Town. *Of the Inhabitants, and their Commodities. Of the* Custard-Apple,
and the Papah. *St.* Jago *Road,* J. Fogo.

I Sail'd from the *Downs* early on *Saturday, Jan.* 14.
169$\frac{8}{9}$. with a fair Wind, in his Majesty's Ship the
Roe-buck; carrying but 12 Guns in this Voyage, and 50
Men and Boys, with 20 Month's Provision. We had
several of the King's Ships in Company, bound for *Spithead* and *Plimouth;* and by Noon we were off *Dungeness.*
We parted from them that Night, and stood down the
Channel, but found our selves next Morning nearer the
French Coast than we expected; C. *de Hague* bearing S. E.
and by E. 6 L. There were many other Ships, some
nearer, some farther off the *French* Coast, who all
seem'd to have gone nearer to it than they thought they
should. My Master, who was somewhat troubled at it at
first, was not displeas'd however to find that he had
Company in his Mistake: Which, as I have heard, is a
very common one, and fatal to many Ships. The Occasion of it is the not allowing for the Change of the Variation since the making of the Charts; which Captain

B

Hally has observ'd to be very considerable. I shall refer the Reader to his own Account of it which he caus'd to be publish'd in a single Sheet of Paper, purposely for a Caution to such as pass to and fro the *English* Channel. And my own Experience thus confirming to me the Usefulness of such a Caution, I was willing to take this Occasion of helping towards the making it the more publick.

Not to trouble the Reader with every Day's Run, nor with the Winds or Weather (but only in the remoter Parts, where it may be more particularly useful) standing away from C. *la Hague*, we made the *Start* about 5 that Afternoon; which being the last Land we saw of *England*, we reckon'd our Departure from thence: Tho' we had rather have taken it from the *Lizard*, if the hazy Weather would have suffer'd us to have seen it.

The first Land we saw after we were out of the Channel was C. *Finisterre*, which we made on the 19th; and on the 28th made *Lancerota*, one of the *Canary* Islands; of which, and of *Allegrance*, another of them, I have here given the *Sights*, as they both appeard to us at two several Bearings and Distances. [Table I. N°. 1, 2.]

We were now standing away for the Island *Teneriffe*, where I intended to take in some Wine and Brandy for my Voyage. On *Sunday*, half an hour past 3 in the Afternoon, we made the Island, and crouded in with all our Sails till 5; when the N. E. Point of the Isle bore W. S. W. dist. 7 Leagues: But being then so far off that I could not expect to get in before Night, I lay by till next Morning, deliberating whether I should put in at *Santa Cruz*, or at *Oratavia*, the one on the E. the other on the W. side of the Island; which lies mostly North and South; and these are the principal Ports on each Side. I chose *Santa Cruz* as the better Harbour (especially at this Time of the Year) and as best furnish'd with that Sort of Wine which I had occasion to take in for my Voyage: So there I come to an Anchor *Jan.* 30th, in 33 Fathom-water, black slimy Ground; about half a Mile from the Shore; from which Distance I took the Sight of the Town [Table I. N°. 3.]

In the Road, Ships must ride in 30, 40, or 50 Fathom-water, not above half a Mile from the Shore at farthest: And if there are many Ships, they must ride close one by another. The Shore is generally high Land, and in most Places steep too. This Road lies so open to the East, that Winds from that Side make a great Swell, and very bad going ashore in Boats: The Ships that ride here are then often forced to put to Sea, and sometimes to cut or slip their Anchors, not being able to weigh them. The best and smoothest Landing is in a small sandy Cove, about a Mile to the N. E. of the Road, where there is good Water, with which Ships that lade here are sup-ply'd; and many Times Ships that lade at *Oratavia*, which is the chief Port for Trade, send their Boats hither for Water. That is a worse Port for Westerly than this is for Easterly Winds; and then all Ships that are there put to Sea. Between this Watering-place and *Santa Cruz* are two little Forts; which with some Batteries scatter'd along the Coast command the Road. *Santa Cruz* its self is a small unwalled Town fronting the Sea, guarded with two other Forts to secure the Road. There are about 200 Houses in the Town, all two Stories high, strongly built with Stone, and covered with Pantile. It hath two Con-vents and one Church, which are the best Buildings in the Town. The Forts here could not secure the *Spanish* Galleons from Admiral *Blake*, tho' they hall'd in close under the main Fort. Many of the Inhabitants that are now living remember that Action; in which the *English*

batter'd the Town, and did it much Damage; and the
Marks of the Shot still remain in the Fort-Walls. The
Wrecks of the Galleons that were burnt here, lie in 15
Fathom-water: And 'tis said that most of the Plate lies
there, tho' some of it was hastily carried ashore at
Blake's coming in Sight.

Soon after I had anchor'd I went ashore here to the
Governour of the Town, who receiv'd me very kindly,
and invited me to dine with him the next Day. I return'd
on Board in the Evening, and went ashore again with
two of my Officers the next Morning; hoping to get up
the Hill Time enough to see *Laguna*, the principal Town,
and to be back again to dine with the Governour of
Santa Cruz; for I was told that *Laguna* was but 3 Miles off.
The Road is all the way up a pretty steep Hill; yet not so
steep but that Carts go up and down laden. There are
Publick Houses scattering by the Way-side, where we
got some Wine. The Land on each Side seemed to be
but rocky and dry; yet in many Places we saw Spots of
green flourishing Corn. At farther Distances there were
small Vineyards by the Sides of the Mountains, intermixt
with Abundance of waste rocky Land, unfit for Cultivation, which afforded only Dildo-bushes. It was about
7 or 8 in the Morning when we set out from *Santa Cruz*;
and it being fair clear Weather, the Sun shone very bright
and warmed us sufficiently before we got to the City
Laguna; which we reached about 10 a Clock, all sweaty
and tired, and were glad to refresh our selves with a
little Wine in a sorry Tipling-house: But we soon found
out one of the *English* Merchants that resided here; who
entertained us handsomely at Dinner, and in the Afternoon shew'd us the Town.

Laguna is a pretty large well-compacted Town, and
makes a very agreeable Prospect. It stands part of it

against a Hill, and part in a Level. The Houses have mostly strong Walls built with Stone and covered with Pantile. They are not uniform, yet they appear pleasant enough. There are many fair Buildings; among which are 2 Parish-Churches, 2 Nunneries, an Hospital, 4 Convents, and some Chapels; besides many Gentlemens Houses. The Convents are those of St. *Austin*, St. *Dominick*, St. *Francis*, and St. *Diego*. The two Churches have pretty high square Steeples, which top the rest of the Buildings. The Streets are not regular, yet they are mostly spacious and pretty handsome; and near the middle of the Town is a large Parade, which has good Buildings about it. There is a strong Prison on one Side of it; near which is a large Conduit of good Water, that supplies all the Town. They have many Gardens which are set round with Oranges, Limes, and other Fruits: In the middle of which are Pot-herbs, Sallading, Flowers, *&c*. And indeed, if the Inhabitants were curious this way, they might have very pleasant Gardens: For as the Town stands high from the Sea, on the Brow of a Plain that is all open to the East, and hath consequently the Benefit of the true Trade-wind, which blows here, and is most commonly fair; so there are seldom wanting at this Town, brisk, cooling, and refreshing Breezes all the Day.

On the Back of the Town there is a large Plain of 3 or 4 Leagues in length and 2 Miles wide, producing a thick kindly Sort of Grass, which lookt green and very pleasant when I was there, like our Meadows in *England* in the Spring. On the East-side of this Plain, very near the Back of the Town, there is a natural Lake or Pond of fresh Water. It is about half a Mile in Circumference; but being stagnant, 'tis only us'd for Cattle to drink of. In the Winter-time several Sorts of wild Fowl resort hither affording Plenty of Game to the Inhabitants of *Laguna*. This City is called *Laguna* from hence; for that Word in *Spanish* signifies a Lake or Pond. The Plain is bounded on the W. the N. W. and the S.W. with high steep Hills; as high above this Plain as this is above the Sea; and 'tis from the Foot of one of these Mountains that the Water of the Conduit which supplies the Town, is conveyed over the Plain, in Troughs of Stone rais'd upon Pillars. And, indeed, considering the Situation of the Town, its large Prospect to the East (for from hence you see the *Grand Canary*) its Gardens, cool Arbors, pleasant Plain, green Fields, the Pond and Aqueduct, and its refreshing Breezes; it is a very delightful Dwelling, especially for such as have not Business that calls them far and often from Home: For the Island being generally mountainous, steep and craggy, full of Risings and Fallings, 'tis very troublesome Travelling up and down in it, unless in the Cool of the Mornings and Evenings: And Mules and Asses are most us'd by them, both for Riding and Carriage, as fittest for the stony, uneven Roads.

Beyond the Mountains, on the S. W. side, still further up, you may see from the Town and Plain a small peeked Hill, overlooking the rest. This is that which is called the *Pike of Teneriffe*, so much noted for its Heighth: But we saw it here at so great a Disadvantage, by Reason of the Nearness of the adjacent Mountains to us, that it looked inconsiderable in Respect to its Fame.

The true *Malmesy* Wine grows in this Island; and this here is said to be the best of its Kind in the World. Here is also *Canary-Wine*, and *Verdona*, or Green-wine. The *Canary* grows chiefly on the West-side of the Island; and therefore is commonly sent to *Oratavia*; which being the chief Sea-port for Trade in the Island, the principal *English* Merchants reside there, with their Consul; because

Table I.   Canary Islands

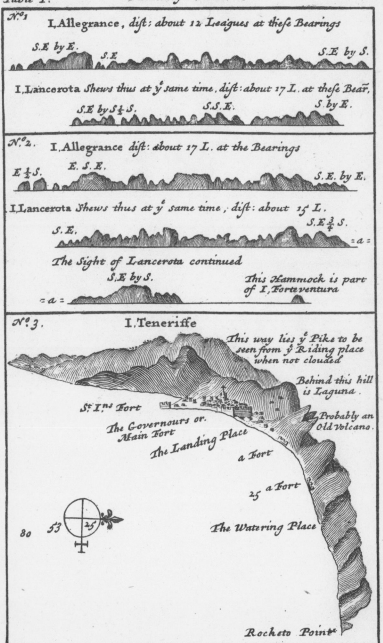

Nᵒ 1.

I, Allegrance, *dist: about 12 Leagues at these Bearings*

S.E by E.   S.E   S.E by S.

I, Lancerota *Shews thus at y̆ same time, dist: about 17 L. at these Bear,*

S.E by S¼ S.   S.S.E.   S by E.

Nᵒ 2.

I, Allegrance *dist: about 17 L. at the Bearings*

E ½ S.   E.S.E.   S.E by E.

I, Lancerota *Shews thus at y̆ same time, dist: about 15 L.*

S.E.   S.E ¾ S.

= a =

The Sight of Lancerota continued

S.E by S.

This Hammock is part
of I, Forteventura

= a =

Nᵒ 3.   I, Teneriffe

This way lies y̆ Pike to be
seen from y̆ Riding place
when not clouded

Behind this hill
is Laguna.

Sᵗ Iⁿˢ Fort

Probably an
Old Volcano.

The Governours or.
Main Fort

The Landing Place

a Fort

25 a Fort

The Watering Place

80   53   25

Rocketo Pointᵉ

we have a great Trade for this Wine. I was told, that that
Town is bigger than *Laguna;* that it has but one Church,
but many Convents: That the Port is but ordinary at
best, and is very bad when the N. W. Winds blow. These
Norwesters give notice of their Coming, by a great Sea
that tumbles in on the Shore for some Time before they
come, and by a black Sky in the N. W. Upon these
Signs Ships either get up their Anchors, or slip their
Cables and put to Sea, and ply off and on till the
Weather is over. Sometimes they are forced to do so 2 or
3 Times before they can take in their Lading; which 'tis
hard to do here in the fairest Weather: And for fresh
Water, they send, as I have said, to *Santa Cruz. Verdona* is
green, strong-bodied Wine, harsher and sharper than
Canary. 'Tis not so much esteemed in *Europe,* but is exported to the *West-Indies,* and will keep best in hot
Countries; for which Reason I touch'd here to take in
some of it for my Voyage. This Sort of Wine is made chiefly
on the East-side of the Island, and shipt off at *Santa Cruz.*

Besides these Wines, which are yearly vended in great
Plenty from the *Canary* Islands (chiefly from *Grand
Canary, Teneriffe,* and *Palma*) here is Store of Grain, as
Wheat, Barly and Maiz, which they often transport to
other Places. They have also some Beans and Peas, and
Coches, a Sort of Grain much like Maiz, sow'd mostly
to fatten Land. They have Papah's, which I shall speak
more of hereafter; Apples, Pears, Plumbs, Cherries, and
excellent Peaches, Apricocks, Guava's, Pomegranates,
Citrons, Oranges, Lemons, Limes, Pumpkins, Onions the
best in the World, Cabbages, Turnips, Potato's, &c.
They are also well stocked with Horses, Cows, Asses,
Mules, Sheep, Goats, Hogs, Conies, and Plenty of Deer.
The *Lancerot* Horses are said to be the most mettlesome,
fleet, and loyal Horses that are. Lastly, here are many

Fowls, as Cocks and Hens, Ducks, Pidgeons, Partridges, &c. with Plenty of Fish, as Mackril, &c. All the *Canary* Islands have of these Commodities and Provisions more or less: But as *Lancerota* is most fam'd for Horses, and *Grand Canary*, *Teneriffe*, and *Palma* for Wines, *Teneriffe* especially for the best Malmesy, (for which Reason these 3 Islands have the chief Trade) so is *Forteventura* for Dunghil-Fowls, and *Gomera* for Deer. Fowls and other Eatables are dear on the Trading Islands; but very plentiful and cheap on the other; and therefore 'tis best for such Ships that are going out on long Voyages, and who design to take in but little Wine, to touch rather at these last; where also they may be supply'd with Wine enough, good and cheap: And for my own Part, if I had known before I came hither, I should have gone rather to one of those Islands than to *Teneriffe:* But enough of this.

'Tis reported they can raise 12000 armed Men on this Island. The Governor or *General* (as he is call'd) of all the *Canary* Islands lives at *Laguna:* His Name is *Don Pedro de Ponto.* He is a Native of this Island, and was not long since President of *Panama* in the *South Seas:* who bringing some very rich Pearls from thence, which he presented to the Queen of *Spain,* was therefore, as 'tis said, made General of the *Canary* Islands. The *Grand Canary* is an Island much superiour to *Teneriffe* both in Bulk and Value; but this Gentleman chuses rather to reside in this his native Island. He has the Character of a very worthy Person; and governs with Moderation and Justice, being very well beloved.

One of his Deputies was the Governor of *Santa Cruz,* with whom I was to have din'd; but staying so long at *Laguna,* I came but Time enough to sup with him. He is a civil, discreet Man. He resides in the main Fort close by the Sea. There is a Centinel stands at his Door; and he has a few Servants to wait on him. I was treated in a large dark lower Room, which has but one small Window. There were about 200 Muskets hung up against the Walls, and some Pikes; no Wainscot, Hangings, nor much Furniture. There was only a small old Table, a few old Chairs, and 2 or 3 pretty long Forms to sit on. Having supp'd with him, I invited him on Board, and went off in my Boat. The next Morning he came aboard with another Gentleman in his Company, attended by 2 Servants: But he was presently Sea-sick, and so much out of order, that he could scarce eat or drink any Thing, but went quickly ashore again.

Having refresh'd my Men ashore, and taken in what we had occasion for, I sail'd away from *Santa Cruz* on *Feb.* 4. in the Afternoon; hastening out all I could, because the N. E. Winds growing stormy made so great Sea, that the Ship was scarce safe in the Road; and I was glad to get out, tho' we left behind several Goods we had bought and paid for: For a Boat could not go ashore; and the Stress was so great in weighing Anchor, that the Cable broke. I design'd next for the I. of *Mayo*, one of the C. *Verd* Islands; and ran away with a strong N. E. Wind, right afore it, all that Night and the next Day, at the Rate of 10 or 11 Miles an Hour; when it slackened to a more moderate Gale. The *Canary* Islands are, for their Latitude, within the usual Verge of the true or general Trade-Wind; which I have observ'd to be, on this Side the Equator, N. Easterly: But then lying not far from the *African* Shore, they are most subject to a N. Wind, which is the *Coasting and constant Trade*, sweeping that Coast down as low as to C. *Verd*; which spreading in Breadth, takes in mostly the *Canary* Islands; tho' it be there interrupted frequently with the true Trade-Wind, N. West-Winds, or other Shifts of Wind that Islands are subject to; especially where they lie many together. The *Pike of Teneriffe*, which had generally been clouded while we lay at *Santa Cruz*, appear'd now all white with Snow, hovering over the other Hills; but their Height made it seem the less considerable; for it looks most remarkable to Ships that are to the Westward of it. We had brisk N. N. E. and N. E. Winds from *Teneriffe;* and saw Flying-fish, and a great deal of Sea-thistle-Weed floating. By the 9th of *Feb.* at Noon we were in the Lat. of 15 d. 4 m. so we steered away W. N. W. for the I. of *Mayo*, being by Judgment, not far to the E. of it, and at 8 a Clock in the Evening lay by till Day. The Wind was then at W. by South, and so it continued all Night, fair Weather, and a small easy Gale. All these were great Signs, that we were near some Land, after having had such constant brisk Winds before. In the Morning after Sun-rise, we saw the Island at about 4 Leagues distance. But it was so hazy over it, that we could see but a small Part of it; yet even by that Part I knew it to be the Isle of *Mayo*. See how it appear'd to us at several *Views*, as we were compassing the E. the S. E. and the S. of it, to get to the Road, on the S. W. of it, [Table II. N°. 1, 2, 3.] and the Road it self [N°. 4.]

I got not in till the next Day, *Feb.* 11. when I come to an Anchor in the Road, which is the Lee-ward Part of the Island; for 'tis a general Rule, never to anchor to Wind-ward of an Island between the Tropicks. We anchored at 11 a Clock in 14 Fathom clean Sand, and very smooth Water, about three quarters of a Mile from the Shore, in the same Place where I anchor'd in my *Voyage round the World;* and found riding here the *Newport of London*, a Merchant Man, Captain *Barefoot* Commander, who welcomed me with 3 Guns, and I returned one for Thanks. He came from *Fayal* one of the *Western*

Islands; and had Store of Wine and Brandy aboard. He was taking in Salt to carry to *New-found-land*, and was very glad to see one of the King's Ships, being before our coming afraid of Pyrates; which, of late Years, had much infested this and the rest of the Cape *Verd Islands*.

I have given some Account of the Island of *Mayo*, and of other of these Islands, in my *Voyage round the World*, [Vol. I. p. 60] [1] but I shall now add some further Observations that occurr'd to me in this Voyage. The I. of *Mayo* is about 7 Leagues in Circumference, of a roundish Form, with many small rocky Points shooting out into the Sea a Mile, or more. Its Lat. is 15 d. N. and as you sail about the Isle, when you come pretty nigh the Shore, you will see the Water breaking off from those Points; which you must give a Birth to, and avoid them. I sail'd at this Time two Parts in three round the Island, but saw nothing dangerous besides these Points; and they all shew'd themselves by the Breaking of the Water: Yet 'tis reported, that on the N. and N. N. W. Side there are dangerous Sholes, that lye farther off at Sea; but I was not on that side. There are 2 Hills on this Island of a considerable Heighth; one pretty bluff, the other peeked at top. The rest of the Island is pretty level, and of a good Heighth from the Sea. The Shore clear round hath sandy Bays, between the rocky Points I spake of; and the whole Island is a very dry Sort of Soil.

On the West-side of the Isle where the Road for Ships is, there is a large sandy Bay, and a Sandbank, of about 40 Paces wide within it, which runs along the Shore 2 or 3 Miles; within which there is a large *Salina* or Salt-pond, contained between the Sand-bank and the Hills beyond it. The whole *Salina* is about 2 Miles in length, and half a Mile wide; but above one half of it is com-

[1] All cross-references are to the Argonaut Press edition.

monly dry. The North End only of the Pond never wants
Water, producing Salt from *November* till *May*, which is
here the dry Season of the Year. The Water which
yields this Salt, works in from out of the Sea through a
Hole in the Sand-bank before-mentioned, like a Sluce,
and that only in Spring-tides; when it fills the Pond
more or less, according to the Height of the Tides. If
there is any Salt in the Ponds when the Flush of Water
comes in, it presently dissolves: But then in 2 or 3 Days
after it begins to kern; and so continues kerning till either
all, or the greatest part of the Salt-water is congeal'd or
kern'd; or till a fresh Supply of it comes in again from
the Sea. This Water is known to come in only at that
one Passage on the N. part of the Pond; where also it is
deepest. It was at a Spring of the *New* Moon when I was
there; and I was told that it comes in at no other Time
but at the New Moon Spring-tides: But why that should
be I can't guess. They who come hither to lade Salt rake
it up as it kerns, and lay it in Heaps on the dry Land,
before the Water breaks in a-new: And this is observable
of this Salt-pond, that the Salt kerns only in the dry
Season, contrary to the Salt-ponds in the *West-Indies*,
particularly those of the Island *Salt-Tortuga*, which I
have formerly mentioned [Vol. I. p. 47.] for they never
kern there till the Rains come in about *April;* and continue to do so in *May, June, July,* &c. while the wet
Season lasts; and not without some good Shower of
Rain first: But the Reason also of this Difference between
the Salt-ponds of *Mayo*, and those of the *West-Indies*, why
these should kern in the wet Season, and the former in
the dry Season, I shall leave to Philosophers.

Our Nation drives here a great Trade for Salt, and
have commonly a Man of War here for the Guard of
our Ships and Barks that come to take it in; of which I

have been inform'd that in some Years there have not
been less than 100 in a Year. It costs nothing but Men's
Labour to rake it together, and wheel it out of the Pond,
except the Carriage: And that also is very cheap; the
Inhabitants having Plenty of Asses, for which they have
little to do besides carrying the Salt from the Ponds to
the Sea-side at the Season when Ships are here. The
Inhabitants lade and drive their Asses themselves, being
very glad to be imploy'd; for they have scarce any other
Trade but this to get a Penny by. The Pond is not above
half a Mile from the Landing-place, so that the Asses
make a great many Trips in a Day. They have a set
Number of Turns to and fro both Forenoon and Afternoon, which their Owners will not exceed. At the
Landing-place there lies a *Frape*-boat, as our Seamen
call it, to take in the *Salt*. 'Tis made purposely for this
Use, with a Deck reaching from the Stern a third Part of
the Boat; where there is a kind of Bulk-head that rises,
not from the Boat's Bottom, but from the Edge of the
Deck, to about 2 Foot in Heighth; all calk'd very tight.
The Use of it is to keep the Waves from dashing into the
Boat, when it lies with its Head to the Shore, to take in
Salt: For here commonly runs a great Sea; and when the
Boat lies so with its Head to the Shore, the Sea breaks
in over the Stern, and would soon fill it, was it not for
this Bulk-head, which stops the Waves that come flowing
upon the Deck, and makes them run off into the Sea
on each Side. To keep the Boat thus with the Head to
the Shore, and the Stern to the Sea, there are two
strong Stantions set up in the Boat; the one at the Head,
the other in the Middle of it, against the Bulk-head, and
a Foot higher than the Bulk-head. There is a large
Notch cut in the Top of each of these Stantions big
enough for a small Hazer or Rope to lie in; one End of

which is fasten'd to a Post ashore, and the other to a
Grapling or Anchor lying a pretty way off at Sea: This
Rope serveth to hale the Boat in and out, and the
Stantions serve to keep her fast, so that she cannot swing
to either Side when the Rope is hal'd tight: For the
Sea would else fill her, or toss her ashore and stave her.
The better to prevent her staving and to keep her the
tighter together, there are two Sets of Ropes more: The
first going athwart from Gunnal to Gunnal, which,
when the Rowers Benches are laid, bind the Boats Sides
so hard against the Ends of the Benches that they cannot
easily fall asunder, while the Benches and Ropes mutu-
ally help each other; the Ropes keeping the Boat's Sides
from flying off, and the Benches from being crush'd
together inwards. Of these Ropes there are usually but
two, dividing the Boat's length, as they go across the
Sides, into there equal Parts. The other Set of Ropes are
more in Number, and are so plac'd as to keep the Ribs
and Planks of the Boat from starting off. For this Purpose
there are Holes made at certain Distances through the
Edge of the Keel that runs along on the Inside of the
Boat; through which these Ropes passing are laid along
the Ribs, so as to line them, or be themselves as Ribs
upon them, being made fast to them by Rattan's brought
thither, or small Cords twisted close about both Ropes
and Ribs, up to the Gunnal: By which Means tho'
several of the Nails or Pegs of the Boat should by any
Shock fall out, yet the Ropes of these two Sets might hold
her together: Especially with the Help of a Rope going
quite round about the Gunnal on the out-side, as our
Long-boats have. And such is the Care taken to streng-
then the Boats; from which girding them with Ropes,
which our Seamen call *Fraping*, they have the Name of
Frape-boats. Two Men suffice to hale her in and out,

Table II.

Cape Verd Iſlands

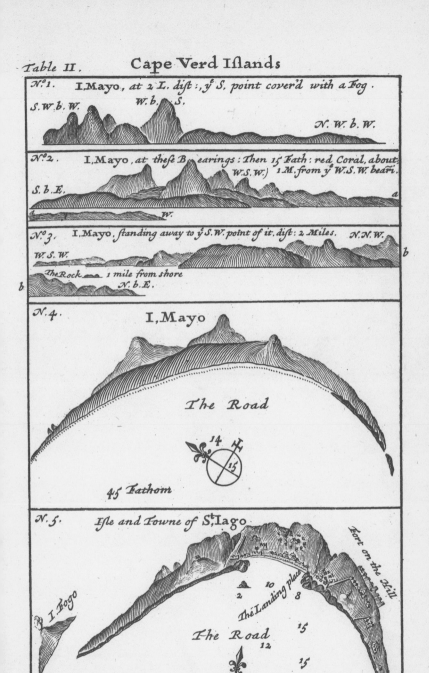

Nº 1. I. Mayo, at 2 L. diſt:, yͤ S. point cover'd with a Fog.

S. W. b. W. W. b. S.

N. W. b. W.

Nº 2. I. Mayo, at theſe Bͤ earings: Then 15 Fath: red Coral, about

W. S. W.) 1 M. from yͤ W. S. W. beaͬī.

S. b. E.

a

4 W.

Nº 3. I. Mayo, ſtanding away to yͤ S. W. point of it. diſt: 2 Miles. N. N. W.

W. S. W.

b

The Rock 1 mile from shore

N. b. E.

b

N. 4.

I, Mayo

The Road

14

15

45 Fathom

N. 5. Iſle and Towne of Sͭ Iago

Fort on the Hill

I. Fogo

10

2

The Landing place

8

The Road

12

15

15

and take in the Salt from Shore (which is brought in Bags) and put it out again. As soon as the Boat is brought nigh enough to the Shore, he who stands by the Bulk-head takes instantly a turn with the Hazer about the Bulk-head-Stantion; and that stops her fast before the Sea can turn her aside: And when the two Men have got in their Lading, they hale off to Sea, till they come a little without the Swell; where they remove the Salt into another Boat that carries it on board the Ship. Without such a *Frape*-boat here is but bad Landing at any Time: For tho' 'tis commonly very smooth in the Road, yet there falls a great Sea on the Shore, so that every Ship that comes here should have such a *Boat*, and bring, or make, or borrow one of other Ships that happen to be here; for the Inhabitants have none. I have been thus particular in the Description of these *Frape*-boats, because of the Use they may be of in any Places where a great Sea falls in upon the Shore: as it doth especially in many open Roads in the *East* and *West-Indies;* where they might therefore be very serviceable; but I never saw any of them there.

The Island *Mayo* is generally barren, being dry, as I said; and the best of it is but a very indifferent Soil. The sandy Bank that pens in the Salt-pond hath a Sort of Silk Cotton growing upon it, and a Plant that runs along upon the Ground, branching out like a Vine, but with thick broad Leaves. The Silk-Cotton grows on tender Shrubs, 3 or 4 Foot high, in Cods as big as an Apple, but of a long Shape; which when ripe open at one End, parting leisurely into 4 Quarters; and at the first opening the Cotton breaks forth. It may be of use for stuffing of Pillows, or the like; but else is of no Value, any more than that of the great Cotton-tree. I took of these Cods before they were quite ripe, and laid them in my Chest; and in 2 or 3 Days they would open and throw out the Cotton. Others I have bound fast with Strings, so that the Cod could not open; and in a few Days after, as soon as I slackned the String never so little, the Cod would burst, and the Cotton fly out forceably, at a very little Hole, just as the Pulp out of a roasting Apple, till all has been out of the Cod. I met with this Sort of Cotton afterwards at *Timor* (where it was ripe in *November*) and no where else in all my Travels; but I found two other Sorts of Silk-cotton at *Brazil*, which I shall there describe. The right Cotton-shrub grows here also, but not on the Sand-bank. I saw some Bushes of it near the Shore; but the most of it is planted in the Middle of the Isle, where the Inhabitants live, Cotton-cloth being their chief Manufacture; but neither is there any great Store of this Cotton. There also are some Trees within the Island, but none to be seen near the Sea-side; nothing but a few Bushes scattering up and down against the Sides of the adjacent Hills; for, as I said before, the Land is pretty high from the Sea. The Soil is for the most part either a Sort of Sand, or loose crumbling Stone, without any fresh Water Ponds or Streams, to moisten it; but only Showers in the Wet-season, which run off as fast as they fall; except a small Spring in the Middle of the Isle, from which proceeds a little Stream of Water that runs through a Valley between the Hills. There the Inhabitants live in three small Towns, having a Church and Padre in each Town: And these Towns, as I was inform'd, are 6 or 7 Miles from the Road. *Pinose* is said to be the chief Town, and to have 2 Churches: St. *John's* the next; and the third *Lagoa*. The Houses are very mean; small, low Things. They build with Fig-tree; here being, as I was told, no other Trees fit to build with. The Rafters are a

Sort of wild Cane. The Fruits of this Isle are chiefly Figs, and Water-Melons. They have also *Callavances* (a Sort of Pulse like *French* Beans) and Pumpkins, for ordinary Food. The Fowls are Flamingo's, Great Curlews, and *Guinea*-Hens; which the Natives of those Islands call *Gallena Pintata*, or the Painted Hen; but in *Jamaica*, where I have seen also those Birds in the dry Savannah's and Woods, (for they love to run about in such Places) they are call'd *Guinea*-Hens. They seem to be much of the Nature of Partridges. They are bigger than our Hens, have long Legs, and will run apace. They can fly too, but not far, having large heavy Bodies, and but short Wings and short Tails: As I have generally observed that Birds have seldom long Tails unless such as fly much; in which their Tails are usually serviceable to their turning about, as a Rudder to a Ship or Boat. These Birds have thick and strong, yet sharp Bills, pretty long Claws, and short Tails. They feed on the Ground, either on Worms, which they find by tearing open the Earth; or on Grashoppers, which are plentiful here. The Feathers of these Birds are speckled with dark and light Grey; the Spots so regular and uniform, that they look more beautiful than many Birds that are deck'd with gayer Feathers. Their Necks are small and long; their Heads also but little. The Cocks have a small Rising on their Crowns, like a Sort of a Comb. 'Tis of the Colour of a dry Wallnut-shell, and very hard. They have a small red Gill on each side of their Heads, like Ears, strutting out downwards; but the Hens have none. They are so strong that one cannot hold them; and very hardy. They are very good Meat, tender, and sweet; and in some the Flesh is extraordinary white; tho' some others have black Flesh: But both Sorts are very good. The Natives take them with Dogs, running them down whenever they

c

please; for here are Abundance of them. You shall see
2 or 300 in a Company. I had several brought aboard
alive, where they throve very well; some of them 16 or 18
Months; when they began to pine. When they are taken
young they will become tame like our Hens. The
Flamingo's I have already describ'd at large, [Vol. I.
p. 56.] They have also many other Sort of Fowls, *viz.*
Pidgeons and Turtle-doves; *Miniota's*, a Sort of Land-
fowls as big as Crows, of a grey Colour, and good Food;
Crufia's, another Sort of grey-colour'd Fowl almost as
big as a Crow, which are only seen in the Night (probably a Sort of Owls) and are said to be good for con-
sumptive People, but eaten by none else. *Rabek's*, a Sort
of large grey eatable Fowls with long Necks and Legs,
not unlike Herons; and many Kinds of small Birds.

Of Land-Animals, here are Goats, as I said formerly,
and Asses good Store. When I was here before they were
said to have had a great many Bulls and Cows: But the
Pirates, who have since miserably infested all these
Islands, have much lessen'd the Number of those; not
having spar'd the Inhabitants themselves: for at my
being there this Time the Governor of *Mayo* was but
newly return'd from being a Prisoner among them, they
having taken him away, and carried him about with
them for a Year or two.

The Sea is plentifully stock'd with Fish of divers Sorts,
viz. Dolphins, Boneta's, Mullets, Snappers, Silver-fish,
Gar-fish, *&c.* and here is a good Bay to hale a Sain or
Net in. I hal'd mine several Times, and to good Purpose;
dragging ashore at one Time 6 Dozen of great Fish,
most of them large Mullets of a Foot and a half or two
Foot long. Here are also Porposes, and a small Sort of
Whales, that commonly visit this Road every Day. I have
already said, [Vol. I. p. 60.] That the Months of *May*,

June, July and *August,* (that is, the wet Season) are the Time when the green Turtle come hither, and go ashore to lay their Eggs. I look upon it as a Thing worth taking Notice of, that the Turtle should always, both in North and South Latitude, lay their Eggs in the wet Months. It might be thought, considering what great Rains there are then in some Places where these Creatures lay, that their Eggs should be spoiled by them. But the Rain, tho' violent, is soon soaked up by the Sand, wherein the Eggs are buried; and perhaps sinks not so deep into it as the Eggs are laid: And keeping down the Heat may make the Sand hotter below than it was before, like a Hot-bed. Whatever the Reason may be why Providence determines these Creatures to this Season of laying their Eggs, rather than the dry, in Fact it is so, as I have constantly observ'd; and that not only with the Sea-Turtle, but with all other Sorts of amphibious Animals that lay Eggs; as Crocodils, Alligators, Guano's, &c. The Inhabitants of this Island, even their Governour and *Padre's*, are all Negro's, Wool-pated like their *African*-Neighbours; from whom 'tis like they are descended; tho' being Subjects to the *Portugeuze*, they have their Religion and Language. They are stout, lusty, well-limb'd People, both Men and Women, fat and fleshy; and they and their Children as round and plump as little Porposes; tho' the Island appears so barren to a Stranger as scarce to have Food for its Inhabitants. I inquired how many People there might be on the Isle; and was told by one of the *Padre's* that here were 230 Souls in all. The Negro-Governour has his Patent from the *Portugueze* Governour of St. *Jago*. He is a very civil and sensible poor Man; and they are generally a good Sort of People. He expects a small Present from every Commander that lades Salt here; and is glad to be invited aboard their Ships. He spends most of his Time with the *English* in the Salting Season, which is his Harvest; and indeed, all the Islanders are then fully employed in getting somewhat; for they have no Vessels of their own to trade with, nor do any *Portugueze*-Vessels come hither: scarce any but *English*, on whom they depend for Trade: and tho' Subjects of *Portugal*, have a particular Value for us. We don't pay them for their Salt, but for the Labour of themselves and their Beasts in lading it: for which we give them Victuals, some Money, and old Cloaths, *viz.* Hats, Shirts, and other Cloaths: By which Means many of them are indifferently well rigg'd; but some of them go almost naked. When the Turtle-season comes in they watch the Sandy-bays in the Night to turn them; and having small Huts at particular Places on the Bays to keep them from the Rain, and to sleep in: And this is another Harvest they have for Food; for by Report there come a great many Turtle to this and the rest of the *Cape Verd Islands*. When the Turtle Season is over they have little to do, but to hunt for *Guinea*-Hens, and manage their small Plantations. But by these Means they have all the Year some Employment or other; whereby they get a Subsistence, tho' but little else. When any of them are desirous to go over to St. *Jago* they get a Licence from the Governour, and desire Passage in any *English* Ship that is going thither: And indeed all Ships that lade Salt here will be obliged to touch at St. *Jago* for Water, for here at the Bay is none, not so much as for drinking. 'Tis true there is a small Well of brackish Water not half a Mile from the Landing-place, which the Asses that carry Salt drink at; but 'tis very bad Water. Asses themselves are a Commodity in some of these Islands, several of our Ships coming hither purposely to freight

with them, and carry them to *Barbadoes* and our other
Plantations. I stay'd at *Mayo* 6 Days, and got 7 or 8 Ton
of Salt aboard for my Voyage: In which Time there
came also into this Road several Sail of Merchants Ships
for Salt; all bound with it for *Newfoundland*.

The 19th Day of *February*, at about One a Clock in the
Morning I weighed from *Mayo*-Road, in order to water
at St. *Jago*, which was about 5 or 6 Leagues to the Westward. We coasted along the Island *St. Jago*, and past by
the Port on the East of it, I mention'd formerly [Vol. I.
p. 60.] which they call *Praya;* where some *English* out-
ward-bound *East-India* Men still touch, but not so many
of them as heretofore. We saw the Fort upon the Hill,
the Houses and Coco-nut Trees: But I would not go in
to anchor here, because I expected better Water on the
S. W. of the Island, at St. *Jago* Town. By 8 a Clock in
the Morning we saw the Ships in that Road, being
within 3 Leagues of it: But were forc'd to keep Turning
many Hours to get in, the Flaws of Wind coming so
uncertain; as they do especially to the *Leeward* of Islands
that are high Land. At length two *Portugueze* Boats came
off to help tow us in; and about 3 a Clock in the Afternoon we came to an Anchor; and took the Prospect of
the Town, [Table II. N°. 5.] We found here, besides two
Portugueze Ships bound for *Brazil*, whose Boats had tow'd
us in, an *English* Pink that had taken in Asses at one of
the *Cape Verd* Islands, and was bound to *Barbadoes* with
them. Next Morning I went ashore with my Officers to
the Governour, who treated us with Sweet-meats: I told
him, the Occasion of my coming was chiefly for Water;
and that I desired also to take in some Refreshments of
Fowls, &c. He said I was welcome, and that he would
order the Townsmen to bring their Commodities to a
certain House, where I might purchase what I had occa-

sion for: I told him I had not Money, but would exchange some of the Salt which I brought from *Mayo* for
their Commodities. He reply'd, that Salt was indeed an
acceptable Commodity with the poor People, but that if
I designed to buy any Cattle, I must give Money for
them. I contented my self with taking in Dunghill Fowls:
The Governour ordering a Cryer to go about the Town
and give Notice to the People, that they might repair to
such a Place with Fowls and Maiz for feeding them,
where they might get Salt in Exchange for them: So I
sent on Board for Salt, and order'd some of my Men to
truck the same for the Fowls and Maiz, while the rest of
them were busy in filling of Water. This is the Effect of
their keeping no Boats of their own on the several Islands,
that they are glad to buy even their own Salt of Foreigners,
for want of being able to transport it themselves from
Island to Island.

St. Jago Town lies on the S. W. part of the Island, in
Lat. about 15 Deg. N. and is the Seat of the General
Governour, and of the Bishop of all the *Cape Verd* Islands.
This Town stands scattering against the Sides of two
Mountains, between which there is a deep Valley, which
is about 200 Yards wide against the Sea; but within a
quarter of a Mile it closes up so as not to be 40 Yards
wide. In the Valley, by the Sea, there is a straggling
Street, Houses on each Side, and a Run of Water in the
Bottom, which empties it self into a fine small Cove or
sandy Bay, where the Sea is commonly very smooth; so
that here is good Watering and good Landing at any
Time; tho' the Road be rocky and bad for Ships. Just by
the Landing-place there is a small Fort, almost level
with the Sea, where is always a Court of Guard kept.
On the Top of the Hill, above the Town, there is
another Fort; which, by the Wall that is to be seen from

the Road, seems to be a large Place. They have Cannon mounted there, but how many know I not: Neither what use that Fort can be of, except it be for Salutes. The Town may consist of 2 or 300 Houses, all built of rough Stone; having also one Convent, and one Church.

The People in general are black, or at least of a mixt Colour, except only some few of the better Sort, *viz.* the Governour, the Bishop, some Gentlemen, and some of the Padres; for some of these also are black. The People about *Praya* are Thievish; but these of *St. Jago* Town, living under their Governour's Eye, are more orderly, tho' generally poor, having little Trade: Yet besides chance Ships of other Nations, there come hither a *Portugueze* Ship or two every Year, in their way to *Brazil.* These vend among them a few *European* Commodities, and take of their principal Manufactures, *viz.* striped Cotton-cloth, which they carry with them to Brazil. Here is also another Ship comes hither from *Portugal* for Sugar, their other Manufacture, and returns with it directly thither: For 'tis reported that there are several small Sugar-works on this Island, from which they send home near 100 Ton every year; and they have Plenty of Cotton growing up in the Country, wherewith they cloath themselves, and send also a great deal to *Brazil.* They have Vines, of which they make some Wine; but the *Eoropean* Ships furnish them with better; tho' they drink but little of any. Their chief Fruits are, (besides Plantains in Abundance) Oranges, Lemons, Citrons, Melons, (both Musk and Water-melons) Limes, Guava's, Pomegranates, Quinces, Custard-Apples, and Papah's, &c.

The Custard-Apple (as we call it) is a Fruit as big as a *Pomegranate,* and much of the same Colour. The out-side Husk, Shell or Rind, is for Substance and Thickness

between the Shell of a Pomegranate, and the Peel of a
Sevil-Orange; softer than this, yet more brittle than that.
The Coat or Covering is also remarkable in that it is
beset round with small regular Knobs or Risings; and
the Inside of the Fruit is full of a white soft Pulp, sweet
and very pleasant, and most resembling a Custard of
any Thing, both in Colour and Taste; from whence
probably it is called a Custard-Apple by our *English*. It
has in the Middle a few small black Stones or Kernels;
but no Core, for 'tis all Pulp. The Tree that bears this
Fruit is about the Bigness of a Quince-tree, with long,
small, and thick-set Branches spread much abroad: At
the Extremity of here and there one of which the Fruit
grows upon a Stalk of its own about 9 or 10 inches long,
slender and tough, and hanging down with its own
Weight. A large Tree of this Sort does not bear usually
above 20 or 30 Apples; seldom more. This Fruit grows in
most Countries within the *Tropicks*. I have seen of them
(tho' I omitted the Description of them before) all over
the *West-Indies*, both Continent and Islands; as also in
Brazil, and in the *East-Indies*.

The *Papah* too is found in all these Countries, though
I have not hitherto describ'd it. It is a Fruit about the
Bigness of a Musk-Melon, hollow as that is, and much
resembling it in Shape and Colour, both Outside and
Inside: Only in the Middle, instead of flat Kernels,
which the Melons have, these have a handful of small
blackish Seeds, about the Bigness of Pepper-corns; whose
Taste is also hot on the Tongue somewhat like Pepper.
The Fruit it self is sweet, soft and luscious, when ripe;
but while green 'tis hard and unsavory: tho' even then
being boiled and eaten with Salt-pork or Beef, it serves
instead of Turnips, and is as much esteemed. The Papah-
Tree is about 10 or 12 Foot high. The Body near the

Ground may be a Foot and an half or 2 Foot Diameter; and it grows up tapering to the Top. It has no Branches at all, but only large Leaves growing immediately upon Stalks from the Body. The Leaves are of a roundish Form and jagg'd about the Edges, having their Stalks or Stumps longer or shorter as they grow near to or further from the Top. They begin to spring from out of the Body of the Tree at about 6 or 7 Foot heighth from the Ground, the Trunk being bare below: But above that the Leaves grow thicker and larger still towards its Top, where they are close and broad. The Fruit grows only among the Leaves; and thickest among the thickest of them; insomuch that towards the Top of the Tree the *Papahs* spring forth from its Body as thick as they can stick one by another. But then lower down, where the Leaves are thinner, the Fruit is larger, and of the Size I have describ'd: And at the Top, where they are thick, they are but small, and no bigger than ordinary Turnips; yet tasted like the rest.

Their chief Land-Animals are their Bullocks, which are said to be many; tho' they ask us 20 Dollars apiece for them; They have also Horses, Asses, and Mules, Deer, Goats, Hogs, and black-fac'd long-tail'd Monkeys. Of Fowls they have Cocks and Hens, Ducks, *Guinea-*Hens, both tame and wild, Parrakites, Parrots, Pidgeons, Turtle-Doves, Herons, Hawks, Crab-catchers, Galdens (a larger Sort of Crab-catchers), Curlews, &c. Their Fish is the same as at *Mayo* and the rest of these Islands, and for the most part these Islands have the same Beasts and Birds also; But some of the Isles have Pasturage and Employment for some particular Beasts more than other; and the Birds are incourag'd, by Woods for Shelter, and Maiz and Fruits for Food, to flock rather to some of the Islands (as to this of St. *Jago*) than to others.

St. *Jago* Road is one of the worst that I have been in. There is not clean Ground enough for above three Ships; and those also must lye very near each other. One even of these must lye close to the Shore, with a Land-fast there: And that is the best for a small Ship. I should not have come in here if I had not been told that it was a good secure Place; but I found it so much otherways, that I was in Pain to be gone. Captain *Barefoot*, who came to an Achor while I was here, in foul Ground, lost quickly 2 Anchors; and I had lost a small one. The Island *Fogo* shows its self from this Road very plain, at about 7 or 8 Leagues distance; and in the Night we saw the Flames of Fire issuing from its Top.

The A.'s Deliberation on the Sequel of his Voyage, and Departure from
St. Jago. *His Course, and the Winds,* &c. *in crossing the* Line. *He stands
away for the* Bay of All-Saints *in* Brazil; *and why. His Arrival on
that Coast and in the* Bay. *Of the several Forts, the Road, Situation, Town,
and Buildings of* Bahia: *Of its Governour, Ships and Merchants; and
Commodities to and from* Europe. *Claying of Sugar. The Season for the
European Ships, and* Coire *Cables: Of their Guinea-trade, and of the
Coasting-trade, and Whale-killing. Of the Inhabitants of* Bahia; *their
carrying in Hammocks; their Artificers, Crane for Goods, and Negro-
Slaves. Of the Country about* Bahia, *its Soil and Product. Its Timber
trees; the* Sapiera, Vermiatico, Comesserie, Guitteba, Serrie, *and*
Mangroves. *The Bastard-Coco, its Nuts and Cables; and the Silk-Cotton-
trees. The Brasilian Fruits, Oranges,* &c. *Of the* Sour-sops, Cashew's,
and Jennipah's. *Of their peculiar Fruits,* Arifah's, Mericasah's,
Petango's, Petumbo's, Mungaroo's, Muckishaw's, Ingwa's, Otee's,
and Musteran de ova's. *Of the Palm-berries, Physick-nuts,* Mendibee's,
&c. *and their Roots and Herbs,* &c. *Of their Wild-Fowl,* Maccaw's,
Parrots, &c. *The* Yemma, Carrion-crow, *and* Chattering-crow, Bill-
bird, Curreso, Turtle dove *and Wild-pigeons; the* Jenetee, Clocking-hen,
Crabcatcher, Galden, *and black* Heron: *The Ducks, Wigeon and Teal;
and Ostriches to the Southward, and of the Dungbill-fowls. Of their
Cattle, Horses,* &c. Leopards *and* Tiger's. *Of their Serpents; the Rattle-
Snake, small Green-Snake;* Amphisbæna, *small black and small Grey-
Snake; the great Land, and the great Water-Snake: And of the Water-
dog. Of their Sea-fish and Turtle; and of* St. Paul's-*Town.*

HAving dispatch'd my small Affairs at the *C.
Verd* Islands, I meditated on the Process of my
Voyage. I thought it requisite to touch once more at a
cultivated Place in these Seas, where my Men might be
refresh'd, and might have a Market wherein to furnish
themselves with Necessaries: For designing that my
next Stretch should be quite to *N. Holland,* and knowing
that after so long a Run nothing was to be expected
there but fresh Water, if I could meet even with that
there, I resolved upon putting in first at some Port of
Brazil, and to provide my self there with whatever I

might have further Occasion for. Beside the refreshing
and furnishing my Men, I aim'd also at the inuring them
gradually and by Intervals to the Fatigues that were to
be expected in the Remainder of the Voyage, which was
to be in a part of the World they were altogether Strangers to; none of them, except two young Men, having
ever cross'd the *Line*.

With this Design I sail'd from *St. Jago* on the 22d of
February, with the Winds at E. N. E. and N. E. fair
Weather, and a brisk Gale. We steered away S. S. E.
and S. S. E. half East, till in the Lat. of 7 deg. 50. min.
we met with many Riplings in the Sea like a Tide or
strong Current, which setting against the Wind caus'd
such a Ripling. We continu'd to meet these Currents
from that Lat. till we came into the Lat of 3 deg. 22 N.
when they ceased. During this Time we saw some
Boneta's, and Sharks; catching one of these. We had the
true general Trade-Wind blowing fresh at N. E. till in
the Lat. of 4 deg. 40 min. N. when the Wind varied, and
we had small Gales, with some Tornadoes. We were
then to the East of *St. Jago* 4 deg. 54 min. when we got
into Lat. 3 deg. 2 min. N. (where I said the Ripling
ceas'd) and Long. to the East of *St. Jago* 5 deg. 2 min.
we had the Wind whiffling between the S. by E. and
E. by N. small Gales, frequent Calms, very black Clouds,
with much Rain. In the Lat. of 3 deg. 8 min. N. and
Long. E. from *St. Jago* 5 deg. 8 min. we had the Wind
from the S. S. E. to the N. N. E. faint, and often interrupted with Calms. While we had Calms we had the
Opportunity of trying the Current we had met with
hitherto, and found that it set N. E. by E. half a Knot,
which is 12 Mile in 24 Hours: So that here it ran at the
Rate of half a Mile an Hour, and had been much
stronger before. The Rains held us by Intervals till the

Lat. of 1 deg. 0 min. N. with small Gales of Wind between S. S. E. and S. E. by E. and sometimes calm:
Afterwards we had the Wind between the S. and S. S. E.
till we cross'd the Line, small Winds, Calms, and pretty
fair Weather. We saw but few Fish beside Porposes; but
of them a great many, and struck one of them.

It was the 10th of *March*, about the Time of the
Equinox, when we cross'd the *Equator*, having had all
along from the Lat. of 4 deg. 40 min. N. where the true
Trade-Wind left us, a great Swell out of the S. E. and
but small uncertain Gales, mostly Southerly, so that we
crept to the Southward but slowly. I kept up against
these as well as I could to the Southward, and when we
had now and then a Flurry of Wind at E. I still went
away due South, purposely to get to the Southward as
fast as I could; for while near the *Line* I expected to
have but uncertain Winds, frequent Calms, Rains,
Tornadoes, &c. which would not only retard my Course,
but endanger Sickness also among my Men: especially
those who were ill provided with Cloaths, or were too
lazy to shift themselves when they were drench'd with
the Rains. The Heat of the Weather made them careless
of doing this; but taking a Dram of Brandy, which I
gave them when wet, with a Charge to shift themselves,
they would however lye down in their Hammocks with
their wet Cloaths; so that when they turn'd out they
caus'd an ill Smell where-ever they came, and their
Hammocks would stink sufficiently; that I think the
remedying of this is worth the Care of Commanders that
cross the *Line;* especially when they are, it may be, a
Month or more e'er they get out of the Rains, at sometimes of the Year, as in *June, July,* or *August.*

What I have here said about Currents, Winds,
Calms, &c. in this Passage, is chiefly for the farther

Illustration of what I have heretofore observ'd in general
about these Matters and especially as to crossing the
Line, in my *Discourse of the Winds*, &c. *in the Torrid
Zone:* [See Vol. II. p. 227.] Which Observations I
have had very much confirm'd to me in the Course of
this Voyage; and I shall particularize in several of the
chief of them as they come in my Way. And indeed I
think I may say this of the main of the Observations in
that *Treatise*, that the clear Satisfaction I had about
them, and how much I might rely upon them, was a
great Ease to my Mind during this vexatious Voyage;
wherein the Ignorance, and Obstinacy withal, of some
under me, occasion'd me a great deal of Trouble: Tho'
they found all along, and were often forc'd to acknowledge it, that I was seldom out in my Conjectures, when
I told them usually beforehand what Winds, *&c.* we
should meet with at such or such particular Places we
should come at.

Pernambuc was the Port that I designed for at my first
setting out from *St. Jago;* it being a Place most proper for
my Purpose, by Reason of its Situation, lying near the
Extremity of *C. St. Augustine*, the Easternmost Promontory of *Brazil;* by which means it not only enjoys the
greater Benefit of the Sea-breezes, and is consequently
more healthy than other Places to the Southward, but is
withal less subject to the Southerly Coasting-Trade-
winds, that blow half the Year on this Shore; which
were now drawing on, and might be troublesome to me:
So that I might both hope to reach soonest *Pernambuc*, as
most directly and nearest in my Run; and might thence
also more easily get away to the Southward than from
Bahia de Todos los Santos, or *Ria Janeira*.

But notwithstanding these Advantages I propos'd to
my self in going to *Pernambuc*, I was soon put by that

Design through the Refractoriness of some under me, and the Discontents and Backwardness of some of my Men. For the Calms and Shiftings of Winds which I met with, as I was to expect, in crossing the Line, made them, who were unacquainted with these Matters, almost heartless as to the Pursuit of the Voyage, as thinking we should never be able to weather Cape St. *Augustine:* And though I told them that by that Time we should get to about three Degrees South of the Line, we should again have a true brisk general Trade-Wind from the North-East, that would carry us to what part of *Brazil* we pleas'd, yet they would not believe it till they found it so. This, with some other unforeseen Accidents, not necessary to be mention'd in this Place, meeting with the Aversion of my Men to a long unknown Voyage, made me justly apprehensive of their Revolting, and was a great Trouble and Hindrance to me. So that I was obliged partly to alter my Measures, and met with many Difficulties, the Particulars of which I shall not trouble the Reader with: But I mention thus much of it in general for my own necessary Vindication, in my taking such Measures sometimes for prosecuting the Voyage as the State of my Ships Crew, rather than my own Judgment and Experience, determin'd me to. The Disorders of my Ship made me think at present that *Pernambuc* would not be so fit a Place for me; being told that Ships ride there 2 or 3 Leagues from the Town, under the Command of no Forts; so that whenever I should have been ashore it might have been easy for my discontented Crew to have cut or slipt their Cables, and have gone away from me: Many of them discovering already an Intention to return to *England,* and some of them declaring openly that they would go no further onwards than *Brazil.* I alter'd my Course therefore, and stood away for *Bahio de todos los Santos*, or the *Bay of all Saints*, where I hop'd to have the Governour's Help, if need should require, for securing my Ship from any such mutinous Attempt; being forced to keep my self all the way upon my Guard, and to lie with my Officers, such as I could trust, and with small Arms upon the Quarter-Deck; it scarce being safe for me to lie in my Cabbin, by Reason of the Discontents among my Men.

On the 23rd of *March* we saw the Land of *Brazil*; having had thither, from the Time when we came into the true Trade-wind again after crossing the Line, very fair Weather and brisk Gales, mostly at E. N. E. The Land we saw was about 20 Leagues to the North of *Bahia;* so I coasted along Shore to the Southward. This Coast is rather low than high, with Sandy-Bays all along by the Sea.

A little within Land are many very white Spots of Sand, appearing like Snow; and the Coast looks very pleasant, being checker'd with Woods and Savannahs. The Trees in general are not tall; but they are green and flourishing. There are many small Houses by the Sea-side, whose Inhabitants are chiefly Fishermen. They come off to Sea on Bark-logs, made of several Logs fasten'd Side to Side, that have one or two Masts with Sails to them. There are two Men in each Bark-log, one at either End, having small low Benches, raised a little above the Logs, to sit and fish on, and two Baskets hanging up at the Mast or Masts; one to put their Provisions in, the other for their Fish. Many of these were a-fishing now, and 2 of them came aboard, of whom I bought some Fish. In the Afternoon we sailed by one very remarkable Piece of Land, where, on a small pleasant Hill, there was a Church dedicated to the Virgin *Mary*. See a Sight of some Parts of this Coast [Table III.

N°. 1, 2, 3, 4, 5.] and of the Hill the Church stands on [Table III. N°. 1.]

I coasted along till the Evening, and then brought to, and lay by till the next Morning. About 2 Hours after we were brought to, there came a Sail out of the Offin (from Seaward) and lay by about a Mile to Windward of us, and so lay all Night. In the Morning upon speaking with her, she proved to be a *Portugueze* Ship bound to *Bahia*; therefore I sent my Boat aboard and desired to have one of his Mates to Pilot me in: He answer'd, that he had not a Mate capable of it, but that he would sail in before me, and shew me the way; and that if he went into the Harbour in the Night, he would hang out a Light for me. He said we had not far in, and might reach it before Night with a tolerable Gale; but that with so small an one as now we had we could not do it: So we jogg'd on till Night, and then he accordingly hung out his Light, which we steered after, sounding as we went in. I kept all my Men on Deck, and had an Anchor ready to let go on occasion. We had the Tide of Ebb against us, so that we went in but slowly; and it was about the Middle of the Night when we anchor'd. Immediately the *Portugueze* Master came aboard to see me, to whom I returned Thanks for his Civilities; and indeed I found much Respect, not only from this Gentleman, but from all of that Nation both here and in other Places, who were ready to serve me on all Occasions. The Place that we anchored in was about two Miles from the Harbour where the Ships generally ride; but the Fear I had lest my People should run away with the Ship, made me hasten to get a Licence from the Governour, to run up into the Harbour, and ride among their Ships, close by one of their Forts. So on the 25th of *March* about 10 a Clock in the Morning, the Tide serving, I went thither, being

D

piloted by the Super-intendant there, whose Business it is to carry up all the King of *Portugal*'s Ships that come hither, and to see them well moored. He brought us to an Anchor right against the Town, at the outer Part of the Harbour, which was then full of Ships, within 150 Yards of a small Fort that stands on a Rock half a Mile from the Shore. See a Prospect of the Harbour and the Town, as it appear'd to us while we lay at Anchor, [Table III. N°. 5.]

Bahia de todos los Santos lies in Lat. 13. deg. S. It is the most considerable Town in *Brazil*, whether in Respect of the Beauty of its Buildings, its Bulk, or its Trade and Revenue. It has the Convenience of a good Harbour that is capable of receiving Ships of the greatest Burthen: The Entrance of which is guarded with a strong Fort standing without the Harbour, call'd St. *Antonio:* A Sight of which I have given [Table III. N°. 4.] as it appeared to us the Afternoon before we came in; and its Lights (which they hang out purposely for Ships) we saw the same Night. There are other smaller Forts that command the Harbour, one of which stands on a Rock in the Sea, about half a Mile from the Shore. Close by this Fort all Ships must pass that anchor here, and must ride also within half a Mile of it at farthest between this and another Fort (that stands on a Point at the inner part of the Harbour and is called the *Dutch* Fort) but must ride nearest to the former, all along against the Town: Where there is good holding Ground, and less exposed to the Southerly Winds that blow very hard here. They commonly set in about *April*, but blow hardest in *May*, *June*, *July* and *August:* But the place where the Ships ride is exposed to these Winds not above 3 Points of the Compass.

Beside these, there is another Fort fronting the Har-

Table III.   Brazil

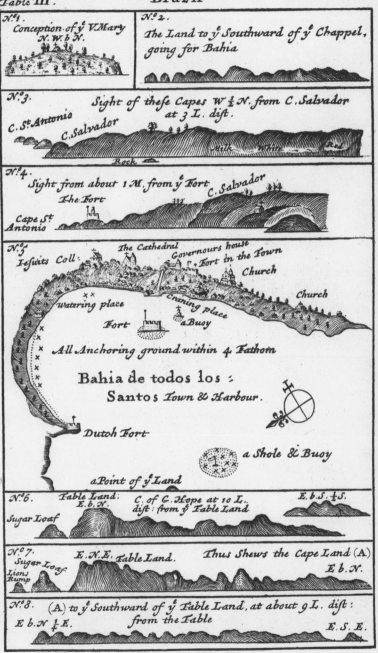

Nº 1.
Conception of yᵉ V.Mary
N. W. b N.

Nº 2.
The Land to yᵉ Southward of yᵉ Chappel,
going for Bahia

Nº 3.   Sight of these Capes W ½ N. from C. Salvador
at 3 L. dist.
C. Sᵗ Antonio
C. Salvador
Milk   White   Red
Rock

Nº 4.   Sight from about 1 M. from yᵉ Fort
The Fort   C. Salvador
Cape Sᵗ
Antonio

Nº 5.
Jesuits Coll.   The Cathedral   Governours house
Fort in the Town
Church
Church
watering place   Cuning place
Fort   a Buoy
All Anchoring ground within 4 Fathom
Bahia de todos los ⋮
Santos Town & Harbour.
Dutch Fort
a Point of yᵉ Land
a Shole & Buoy

Nº 6.   Table Land.
E. b. N.   C. of G. Hope at 10 L.   E. b. S. ½ S.
Sugar Loaf   dist: from yᵉ Table Land

Nº 7.
Sugar Loaf   E. N. E. Table Land.   Thus Shews the Cape Land (A)
Lions
Rump   E b. N.

Nº 8.   (A) to yᵉ Southward of yᵉ Table Land, at about 9 L. dist:
E b. N ½ E.   from the Table   E. S. E.

bour, and standing on the Hill upon which the Town stands. The Town it self consists of about 2000 Houses; the major part of which cannot be seen from the Harbour; but so many as appear in Sight, with a great Mixture of Trees between them, and all placed on a rising Hill, make a very pleasant Prospect; as may be judg'd by the Draught, [Table III. N°. 5.]

There are in the Town 13 Churches, Chapels, Hospitals, Convents, beside one Nunnery; *viz.* the *Ecclesia Major* or Cathedral, the Jesuits College, which are the chief, and both in Sight from the Harbour: *St. Antonio, Sta. Barbara*, both Parish-Churches; the *Franciscans* Church, and the *Dominicans*; and 2 Convents of *Carmelites*; a Chapel for Seamen close by the Sea-side, where Boats commonly land, and the Seamen go immediately to Prayers; another Chapel for poor People, at the farther End of the same Street, which runs along by the Shore; and a third Chapel for Soldiers, at the Edge of the Town remote from the Sea; and an Hospital in the Middle of the Town. The Nunnery stands at the outer-edge of the Town next the Fields, wherein by Report there are 70 Nuns. Here lives an Arch-bishop, who has a fine Palace in the Town; and the Governor's Palace is a fair Stone-building, and looks handsome to the Sea, tho' but indifferently furnish'd within: Both *Spaniards* and *Portugueze* in their Plantations abroad, as I have generally observ'd, affecting to have large Houses; but are little curious about Furniture, except Pictures some of them. The Houses of the Town are 2 or 3 Stories high, the Walls thick and strong, being built with Stone, with a Covering of Pantile; and many of them have Balconies. The principal Streets are large, and all of them pav'd or pitch'd with small Stones. There are also Parades in the most eminent Places of the Town, and many Gardens, as well

within the Town as in the Out-parts of it, wherein are
Fruit-trees, Herbs, Salladings and Flowers in great
Variety, but order'd with no great Care nor Art.

The Governour who resides here is call'd *Don John de
Lancastrio*, being descended, as they say, from our *English
Lancaster* Family; and he has a Respect for our Nation on
that Account, calling them his Country-men. I waited
on him several Times, and always found him very courteous and civil. Here are about 400 Soldiers in Garrison.
They commonly draw up and exercise in a large Parade
before the Governour's House; and many of them attend
him when he goes abroad. The Soldiers are decently clad
in brown Linnen, which in these hot Countries is far
better than Woollen; but I never saw any clad in Linnen
but only these. Beside the Soldiers in Pay, he can soon
have some Thousands of Men up in Arms on occasion.
The Magazine is on the Skirts of the Town, on a small
Rising between the Nunnery and the Soldiers Church.
'Tis big enough to hold 2 or 3000 Barrels of Powder; but
I was told it seldom has more than 100, sometimes but
80. There are always a Band of Soldiers to guard it, and
Centinels looking out both Day and Night.

A great many Merchants always reside at *Bahia*; for
'tis a Place of great Trade: I found here above 30 great
Ships from *Europe*, with 2 of the King of *Portugal*'s Ships
of War for their Convoy; beside 2 Ships that traded to
Africa only, either to *Angola*, *Gamba*, or other Places on
the Coast of *Guinea*; and Abundance of small Craft, that
only run to and fro on this Coast, carrying Commodities
from one Part of *Brazil* to another.

The Merchants that live here are said to be rich, and
to have many *Negro*-Slaves in their Houses, both of Men
and Women. Themselves are chiefly *Portugueze*, Foreigners having but little Commerce with them; yet here

was one Mr. *Cock* an *English* Merchant, a very civil Gentleman and of good Repute. He had a Patent to be our *English* Consul, but did not Care to take upon him any publick Character, because *English* Ships seldom come hither, here having been none in 11 or 12 Years before this Time. Here was also a *Dane*, and a *French* Merchant or two; but all have their Effects transported to and from *Europe* in *Portugueze* Ships, none of any other Nation being admitted to trade hither. There is a Custom-house by the Sea-side, where all Goods imported or exported are entred. And to prevent Abuses there are 5 or 6 Boats that take their Turns to row about the Harbour, searching any Boats they suspect to be running of Goods.

The chief Commodities that the *European* Ships bring hither, are Linnen-cloaths, both coarse and fine; some Woollens, also, as Bays, Searges, Perpetuana's, &c. Hats, Stockings, both of Silk and Thread, Bisket-bread, Wheatflower, Wine (chiefly *Port*) Oil-Olive, Butter, Cheese, &c. and Salt-beef and Pork would there also be good Commodities. They bring hither also Iron, and all Sorts of Iron-Tools; Pewter-Vessels of all Sorts, as Dishes, Plates, Spoons, &c. Looking-glasses, Beads, and other Toys; and the Ships that touch at *St. Jago* bring thence, as I said, Cotton-cloath, which is afterwards sent to *Angola*.

The *European* Ships carry from hence Sugar, Tobacco, either in Roll or Snuff, never in Leaf, that I know of: These are the Staple Commodities. Besides which, here are Dye-woods, as Fustick, &c. with Woods for other Uses, as speckled Wood, *Brazil*, &c. They also carry home raw Hides, Tallow, Train-Oil of Whales, &c. Here are also kept tame Monkeys, Parrots, Parrakites, &c. which the Seamen carry home.

The Sugar of this Country is much better than that

which we bring Home from our Plantations: For all the
Sugar that is made here is clay'd, which makes it whiter
and finer than our *Muscovada*, as we call our unrefin'd
Sugar. Our Planters seldom refine any with Clay, unless
sometimes a little to send Home as Presents for their
Friends in *England*. Their way of doing it is by taking
some of the whitest Clay and mixing it with Water, till
'tis like Cream. With this they fill up the Pans of Sugar,
that are sunk 2 or 3 Inches below the Brim by the drain-
ing of the Molosses out of it: First scraping off the thin
hard Crust of the Sugar that lies at the Top, and would
hinder the Water of the Clay from soaking through the
Sugar of the Pan. The refining is made by this Percola-
tion. For 10 or 12 Days Time that the clayish Liquor
lies soaking down the Pan, the white Water whitens the
Sugar as it passes thro' it; and the gross Body of the Clay
it self grows hard on the Top, and may be taken off at
Pleasure; when scraping off with a Knife the very upper-
part of the Sugar, which will be a little sullied, that
which is underneath will be white almost to the Bottom:
And such as is called *Brazil* Sugar is thus whiten'd.
When I was here this Sugar was sold for 50s. *per* 100 *lb.*
And the Bottoms of the Pots, which is very coarse Sugar,
for about 20s. *per* 100 *lb.* both Sorts being then scarce;
for here was not enough to lade the Ships, and therefore
some of them were to lye here till the next Season.

The *European* Ships commonly arrive here in *February*
or *March*, and they have generally quick Passages;
finding at that Time of the Year brisk Gales to bring
them to the Line, little Trouble, then, in crossing it, and
brisk E. N. E. Winds afterwards to bring them hither.
They commonly return from hence about the latter End
of *May*, or in *June*. 'Twas said when I was here that the
Ships would sail hence the 20th Day of *May;* and there-

fore they were all very busy, some in taking in their Goods, others in careening and making themselves ready. The Ships that come hither usually careen at their first coming; here being a Hulk belonging to the King for that Purpose. This Hulk is under the Charge of the Superintendent I spoke of, who has a certain Sum of Mony for every Ship that careens by her. He also provides Firing and other Necessaries for that Purpose: And the Ships do commonly hire of the Merchants here each 2 Cables to moor by all the Time they lye here, and so save their own Hempen Cables; for these are made of a Sort of Hair, that grows on a certain Kind of Trees, hanging down from the Top of their Bodies, and is very like the black *Coyre* in the *East-Indies*, if not the same. These Cables are strong and lasting: And so much for the *European* Ships.

The Ships that use the *Guinea*-Trade are small Vessels in Comparison of the former. They carry out from hence Rum, Sugar, the Cotton-cloaths of St. *Jago*, Beads, &c. and bring in Return, Gold, Ivory, and Slaves; making very good Returns.

The small Craft that belong to this Town are chiefly imployed in carrying *European* Goods from *Bahia*, the Center of the *Brasilian* Trade, to the other Places on this Coast; bringing back hither Sugar, Tobacco, &c. They are sailed chiefly with Negro-Slaves; and about *Christmas* these are mostly imployed in Whale-killing: For about that Time of the Year a Sort of Whales, as they call them, are very thick on this Coast. They come in also into the Harbours and inland Lakes, where the Seamen go out and kill them. The Fat of them is boiled to Oil; the Lean is eaten by the Slaves and poor People: And I was told by one that had frequently eaten of it, that the Flesh was very sweet and wholsome. These are said to be but small Whales; yet here are so many, and so easily kill'd, that they get a great deal of Money by it. Those that strike them buy their Licence for it of the King: And I was inform'd that he receives 30000 Dollars *per Annum* for this Fishery. All the small Vessels that use this Coasting-Traffick are built here; and so are some Men of War also for the King's Service. There was one a building when I was here, a Ship of 40 or 50 Guns: And the Timber of this Country is very good and proper for this Purpose. I was told it was very strong, and more durable than any we have in *Europe;* and they have enough of it. As for their Ships that use the *European* Trade, some of them that I saw there were *English* built, taken from us by the *French*, during the late War, and sold by them to the *Portugueze*.

Besides Merchants and others that trade by Sea from this Port, here are other pretty wealthy Men, and several Artificers and Trades-men of most Sorts, who by Labour and Industry maintain themselves very well; especially such as can arrive at the Purchase of a Negro-Slave or two. And indeed, excepting People of the lowest Degree of all, here are scarce any but what keep Slaves in their Houses. The richer Sort, besides the Slaves of both Sexes whom they keep for servile Uses in their Houses, have Men slaves who wait on them abroad, for State; either running by their Horse-sides when they ride out, or to carry them to and fro on their Shoulders in the Town when they make short Visits near Home. Every Gentleman or Merchant is provided with Things necessary for this Sort of Carriage. The main Thing is a pretty large Cotton Hammock of the *West-India* Fashion, but mostly died blue, with large Fringes of the same, hanging down on each Side. This is carried on the *Negro*'s Shoulders by the help of a Bambo about

12 or 14 Foot long, to which the Hammock is hung; and a Covering comes over the Pole, hanging down on each Side like a Curtain: So that the Person so carry'd cannot be seen unless he pleases; but may either lye down, having Pillows for his Head; or may sit up by being a little supported with these Pillows, and by letting both his Legs hang out over one Side of the Hammock. When he hath a Mind to be seen he puts by his Curtain, and salutes every one of his Acquaintance whom he meets in the Streets; for they take a Piece of Pride in greeting one another from their Hammocks, and will hold long Conferences thus in the Street: But then their 2 Slaves who carry the Hammock have each a strong well-made Staff, with a fine Iron Fork at the upper End, and a sharp Iron below, like the Rest for a Musket, which they stick fast in the Ground, and let the Pole or Bambo of the Hammock rest upon them, till their Master's Business or the Complement is over. There is scarce a Man of any Fashion, especially a Woman, will pass the Streets but so carried in a Hammock. The chief Mechanick Traders here, are Smiths, Hatters, Shoemakers, Tanners, Sawyers, Carpenters, Coopers, &c. Here are also Taylors, Butchers, &c. which last kill the Bullocks very dexterously, sticking them at one Blow with a sharp-pointed Knife in the Nape of the Neck, having first drawn them close to a Rail; but they dress them very slovenly. It being *Lent* when I came hither, there was no buying any Flesh till *Easter*-Eve, when a great Number of Bullocks were kill'd at once in the Slaughter-houses within the Town, Men, Women and Children flocking thither with great Joy to buy, and a Multitude of Dogs, almost starv'd, following them; for whom the Meat seem'd fittest, it was so lean. All these Trades-men buy *Negroes*, and train them up to their several Employ-

ments, which is a great Help to them; and they having
so frequent Trade to *Angola*, and other Parts of *Guinea*,
they have a constant Supply of Blacks both for their
Plantations and Town. These Slaves are very useful in
this Place for Carriage, as Porters; for as here is a great
Trade by Sea, and the Landing-place is at the Foot of a
Hill, too steep for drawing with Carts, so there is great
need of Slaves to carry Goods up into the Town, especially for the inferiour Sort: But the Merchants have also
the Convenience of a great Crane that goes with Ropes
or Pullies, one End of which goes up while the other goes
down. The House in which this Crane is, stands on the
Brow of the Hill towards the Sea, hanging over the
Precipice; and there are Planks set shelving against the
Bank from thence to the Bottom, against which the
Goods lean or slide as they are hoisted up or let down.
The *Negro*-Slaves in this Town are so numerous, that
they make up the greatest Part or Bulk of the Inhabitants: Every House, as I said, having some, both Men
and Women, of them. Many of the *Portugueze*, who are
Batchelors, keep of these black Women for Misses, tho'
they know the Danger they are in of being poyson'd by
them, if ever they give them any Occasion of Jealousy.
A Gentleman of my Acquaintance, who had been
familiar with his Cook-maid, lay under some such
Apprehensions from her when I was there. These Slaves
also of either Sex will easily be engaged to do any Sort
of Mischief; even to Murder, if they are hired to do it,
especially in the Night; for which Reason, I kept my
Men on board as much as I could; for one of the *French*
King's Ships being here, had several Men murther'd by
them in the Night, as I was credibly inform'd.

Having given this Account of the Town of *Bahia*, I
shall next say somewhat of the Country. There is a

Salt-water Lake runs 40 Leagues, as I was told, up the
Country, N. W. from the Sea, leaving the Town and
Dutch Fort on the Starboard Side. The Country all
around about is for the most part a pretty flat even
Ground, not high, nor yet very low: It is well water'd
with Rivers, Brooks and Springs; neither wants it for
good Harbours, navigable Creeks, and good Bays for
Ships to ride in. The Soil in general is good, naturally
producing very large Trees of divers Sorts, and fit for
any Uses. The Savannahs also are loaden with Grass,
Herbs, and many Sorts of smaller Vegetables; and being
cultivated, produce any Thing that is proper for those
hot Countries, as Sugar-Canes, Cotton, Indico, Tobacco,
Maiz, Fruit-Trees of several Kinds, and eatable Roots of
all Sorts. Of the several Kinds of Trees that are here,
I shall give an Account of some, as I had it partly from
an Inhabitant of *Bahia*, and partly from my Knowledge
of them otherwise, *viz. Sapiera, Vermiatico, Comesserie,
Guitteba, Serrie,* as they were pronounc'd to me, three
Sorts of *Mangrove,* speckled Wood, Fustick, Cotton-
Trees of 3 Sorts, *&c.* together with Fruit-Trees of divers
Sorts that grow wild, beside such as are planted.

Of Timber-Trees, the *Sapiera* is said to be large and
tall; it is very good Timber, and is made use of in
building of Houses; so is the *Vermiatico,* a tall streight-
bodied Tree, of which they make Plank 2 Foot broad;
and they also make Canoa's with it. *Comesserie* and
Guitteba are chiefly used in building Ships; these are as
much esteem'd here as Oaks are in *England,* and they say
either Sort is harder and more durable than Oak. The
Serrie is a Sort of Tree much like Elm, very durable in
Water. Here are also all the three Sorts of *Mangrove*
Trees, *viz.* the Red, the White, and the Black, which I
have described [Vol. I. p. 46.] The Bark of the red Man-

grove, is here us'd for tanning of Leather, and they have great Tan-pits for it. The black Mangrove grows larger here than in the *West-Indies*, and of it they make good Plank. The white Mangrove is larger and tougher than in the *West-Indies;* of these they make Masts and Yards for Barks.

There grow here wild or bastard Coco-Nut Trees, neither so large nor so tall as the common ones in the *East* or *West-Indies*. They bear Nuts as the others, but not a quarter so big as the right Coco-Nuts. The Shell is full of Kernel, without any hollow Place or Water in it; and the Kernel is sweet and wholsome, but very hard both for the Teeth and for Digestion. These Nuts are in much Esteem for making Beads for *Pater noster*'s, Boles of Tobacco-Pipes, and other Toys: and every small Shop here has a great many of them to sell. At the Top of these Bastard Coco-trees, among the Branches, there grows a Sort of long black Thread like Horsehair, but much longer, which by the *Portugueze* is called *Tresabo*. Of this they make Cables which are very serviceable, strong and lasting; for they will not rot as Cables made of Hemp, tho' they lye exposed both to Wet and Heat. These are the Cables which I said they keep in their Harbours here, to let to hire to *European* Ships, and resemble the *Coyre-*Cables.

Here are 3 Sorts of Cotton-Trees that bear Silk-Cotton. One Sort is such as I have formerly describ'd, [Vol. I. p. 118.] by the Name of the Cotton-tree. The other 2 Sorts I never saw any where but here. The Trees of these latter Sorts are but small in Comparison of the former, which are reckon'd the biggest in all the *West-India* Woods; yet are however of a good Bigness and Heighth. One of these last Sorts is not so full of Branches as the other of them; neither do they produce their Fruit the same Time of the Year: For one Sort had its Fruit just ripe, and was shedding its Leaves while the other Sort was yet green, and its Fruit small and growing, having but newly done blossoming; the Tree being as full of young Fruit as an Apple-Tree ordinarily in *England*. These last yield very large Pods, about 6 Inches long, and as big as a Man's Arm. It is ripe in *September* and *October;* then the Pod opens, and the Cotton bursts out in a great Lump as big as a Man's Head. They gather these Pods before they open; otherways it would fly all away. It opens as well after 'tis gathered; and then they take out the Cotton, and preserve it to fill Pillows and Bolsters, for which use 'tis very much esteemed: But 'tis fit for nothing else, being so short that it cannot be spun. 'Tis of a tawney Colour; and the Seeds are black, very round, and as big as a white Pea. The other Sort is ripe in *March* or *April*. The Fruit or Pod is like a large Apple, and very round. The out-side Shell is as thick as the Top of one's Finger. Within this there is a very thin whitish Bag or Skin which incloseth the Cotton. When the Cotton-Apple is ripe, the outer thick green Shell splits it self into 5 equal Parts from Stemb to Tail, and drops off, leaving the Cotton hanging upon the Stemb, only pent up in its fine Bag. A Day or two afterwards the Cotton swells by the Heat of the Sun, breaks the Bag and bursts out, as big as a Man's Head: And then as the Wind blows 'tis by Degrees driven away, a little at a Time, out of the Bag that still hangs upon the Stemb, and is scatter'd about the Fields; the Bag soon following the Cotton, and the Stemb the Bag. Here is also a little of the right *West-India* Cotton Shrub: but none of the Cotton is exported, nor do they make much Cloth of it.

This Country produces great Variety of fine Fruits, as very good Oranges of 3 or 4 Sorts; (especially one

Sort of *China* Oranges;) Limes in Abundance, Pomegranates, Pomecitrons, Plantains, Bonano's, right Coco-
nuts, Guava's, Coco-plumbs, (call'd here *Munsheroo's*)
Wild-Grapes, such as I have describ'd [Vol. II. p. 160.]
beside such Grapes as grow in *Europe*. Here are also
Hog-plumbs, Custard-Apples, *Sour-sops*, *Cashews*, *Papah's*
(called here *Mamoons*) *Jennipah's* (called here *Jennipapah's*) Manchineel-Apples and Mango's. Mango's are
yet but rare here: I saw none of them but in the *Jesuit's*
Garden, which has a great many fine Fruits, and some
Cinnamon-trees. These, both of them, were first brought
from the *East-Indies*, and they thrive here very well: So
do Pumplemusses, brought also from thence; and both
China and *Sevil* Oranges are here very plentiful as well as
good.

The *Sour-sop* (as we call it) is a large Fruit as big as a
Man's Head, of a long or oval Shape, and of a green
Colour; but one Side is yellowish when ripe. The out-
side Rind or Coat is pretty thick, and very rough, with
small sharp Knobs; the Inside is full of spungy Pulp,
within which also are many black Seeds or Kernels, in
Shape and Bigness like a Pumpkin-seed. The Pulp is very
juicy, of a pleasant Taste, and wholesome. You suck the
Juice out of the Pulp, and so spit it out. The Tree or
Shrub that bears this Fruit grows about 10 or 12 Foot
high, with a small short Body; the Branches growing
pretty strait up; for I did never see any of them spread
abroad. The Twigs are slender and tough; and so is the
Stemb of the Fruit. This Fruit grows also both in the
East and *West-Indies*.

The *Cashew* is a Fruit as big as a Pippin, pretty long,
and bigger near the Stemb than at the other End,
growing tapering. The Rind is smooth and thin, of a
red and yellow Colour. The Seed of this Fruit grows at

the End of it; 'tis of an Olive Colour shaped like a Bean, and about the same Bigness, but not altogether so flat. The Tree is as big as an Apple-Tree, with Branches not thick, yet spreading off. The Boughs are gross, the Leaves broad and round, and in Substance pretty thick. This Fruit is soft and spongy when ripe, and so full of Juice that in biting it the Juice will run out on both Sides of one's Mouth. It is very pleasant, and gratefully rough on the Tongue; and is accounted a very wholesome Fruit. This grows both in the *East* and *West-Indies*, where I have seen and eaten of it.

The *Jennipah* or *Jennipapah* is a Sort of Fruit of the Calabash or Gourd-kind. It is about the Bigness of a Duck-Egg, and somewhat of an Oval Shape; and is of a grey Colour. The Shell is not altogether so thick nor hard as a Calabash: 'Tis full of whitish Pulp mixt with small flat Seeds; and both Pulp and Seeds must be taken into the Mouth, where sucking out the Pulp, you spit out Seeds. It is of a sharp and pleasing Taste, and is very innocent. The Tree that bears it is much like an Ash, streight-bodied, and of a good Height; clean from Limbs till near the Top, where there Branches forth a small Head. The Rind is of a pale grey, and so is the Fruit. We us'd of this Tree to make Helves or Handles for Axes (for which it is very proper) in the Bay of *Campeachy;* where I have seen of them, and no where else but here.

Besides these, here are many Sorts of Fruits which I have not met with any where but here; as *Arisah*'s, *Mericasah*'s, *Petango*'s, &c. *Arisah*'s are an excellent Fruit, not much bigger than a large Cherry; shaped like a Catherine-Pear, being small at the Stemb, and swelling bigger towards the End. They are of a greenish Colour, and have small Seeds as big as Mustard Seeds; they are somewhat tart, yet pleasant, and very wholsome, and may be eaten by sick People.

Mericasah's, are an excellent Fruit, of which there are 2 Sorts; one growing on a small Tree or Shrub, which is counted the best; the other growing on a Kind of Shrub like a Vine, which they plant about Arbours to make a Shade, having many broad Leaves. The Fruit is as big as a small Orange, round and green. When they are ripe they are soft and fit to eat; full of white Pulp mixt thick with little black Seeds, and there is no separating one from the other, till they are in your Mouth; when you suck in the white Pulp and spit out the Stones. They are tart, pleasant, and very wholsome.

Petango's, are a small red Fruit, that grow also on small Trees, and are as big as Cherries, but not so globular, having one flat Side, and also 5 or 6 small protulerant Ridges. 'Tis a very pleasant tart Fruit, and has a pretty large flattish Stone in the Middle.

Petumbo's, are a yellow Fruit (growing on a Shrub like a Vine) bigger than Cherries, with a pretty large Stone: These are sweet, but rough in the Mouth.

Mungaroo's, are a Fruit as big as Cherries, red on one Side and white on the other Side: They are said to be full of small Seeds, which are commonly swallowed in eating them.

Muckishaw's, are said to be a Fruit as big as Crab-Apples, growing on large Trees. They have also small Seeds in the Middle, and are well tasted.

Ingwa's, are a Fruit like the Locust-Fruit, 4 Inches long, and one broad. They grow on high Trees.

Otee, is a Fruit as big as a large Coco-Nut. It hath a Husk on the outside, and a large Stone within, and is accounted a very fine Fruit.

Musteran-de-ova's, are a round Fruit as big as large

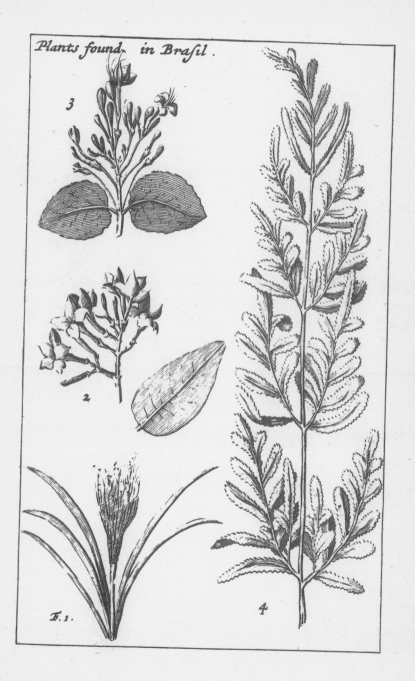

Plants found in Brasil.

Hazel-Nuts, cover'd with thin brittle Shells of a blackish
Colour: They have a small Stone in the middle, inclosed
within a black pulpy Substance, which is of a pleasant
Taste. The outside Shell is chewed with the Fruit, and
spit out with the Stone, when the Pulp is suck'd from
them. The Tree that bears this Fruit is tall, large, and
very hard Wood. I have not seen any of these five last
named Fruits, but had them thus described to me by
an *Irish* Inhabitant of *Bahia*; tho' as to this last, I am apt
to believe, I may have both seen and eaten of them in
Achin in *Sumatra*.

Palm-berries (called here *Dendees*) grow plentifully
about *Bahia*; the largest are as big as Wall-nuts; they
grow in Bunches on the top of the Body of the Tree,
among the Roots of the Branches or Leaves, as all Fruits
of the Palm-kind do. These are the same kind of Berries
or Nuts as those they make the Palm-Oyl with on the
Coast of *Guinea*, where they abound: And I was told that
they make Oyl with them here also. They sometimes
roast and eat them; but when I had one roasted to prove
it, I did not like it.

Physick-Nuts, as our Seamen call them, are called here
Pineon; and *Agnus Castus* is called here *Carrepat:* These
both grow here: So do *Mendibees*, a Fruit like *Physick-
Nuts*. They scorch them in a Pan over the Fire before
they eat them.

Here are also great plenty of Cabbage-Trees, and
other Fruits, which I did not get information about, and
which I had not the Opportunity of seeing; because this
was not the Season, it being our Spring, and consequently their Autumn, when their best Fruits were gone,
tho' some were left. However I saw abundance of wild
Berries in the Woods and Fields, but I could not learn
their Names or Nature.

E

They have withal good plenty of ground Fruit, as *Callavances*, Pine-Apples, Pumkins, Water-Melons, Musk-Melons, Cucumbers, and Roots; as Yams, Potato's Cassava's, &c. Garden-Herbs also good store; as Cabbages, Turnips, Onions, Leeks, and abundance of other Sallading, and for the Pot. Drugs of several sorts, *viz.* Sassafras, Snake-Root, &c. Beside the Woods I mentioned for Dying, and other Uses, as Fustick, Speckled-wood, &c.

I brought home with me from hence a good Number of Plants, dried between the Leaves of Books; of some of the choicest of which, that are not spoil'd, I may give a Specimen at the *End* of the *Book*.

Here are said to be great plenty and variety of Wild-Fowl, *viz. Yemma's, Maccaw's* (which are called here *Jackoo's,* and are a larger sort of Parrots, and scarcer), Parrots, Parakites, Flamingo's, Carrion-Crows, Chattering-Crows, Cockrecoes, Bill-Birds finely painted, Corresoes, Doves, Pidgeons, *Jenetees,* Clocking-Hens, Crab-Catchers, Galdens, Currecoo's, Muscovy Ducks, common Ducks, Widgeons, Teal, Curlews, Men of War Birds, Booby's, Noddy's, Pelicans, &c.

The *Yemma* is bigger than a Swan, grey-feathered, with a long thick sharp-pointed Bill.

The Carrion-Crow and Chattering-Crows, are called here *Mackeraw's,* and are like those I described in the *West-Indies,* [Vol. II. p. 172.] The Bill of the Chattering-Crow is black, and the Upper-Bill is round, bending downwards like a Hawks-Bill, rising up in a Ridge almost Semi-circular, and very sharp, both at the Ridge or Convexity, and at the Point or Extremity: The Lower-Bill is flat and shuts even with it. I was told by a *Portugueze* here, that their *Negro*-Wenches make Love-Potions with these Birds. And the *Portugueze* care not to let them have any of these Birds, to keep them from that Superstition: As I found one Afternoon when I was in the Fields with a Padre and another, who shot two of them, and hid them, as they said, for that Reason. They are not good Food, but their Bills are reckoned a good Antidote against Poison.

The *Bill-Birds* are so called by the *English*, from their monstrous Bills, which are as big as their Bodies. I saw none of these Birds here, but saw several of the Breasts flea'd off and dried, for the Beauty of them; the Feathers were curiously colour'd with Red, Yellow, and Orange-colour.

The *Curreso*'s (called here *Mackeraw*'s) are such as are in the Bay of *Campeachy* [Vol. II. p. 172.]

Turtle-Doves are in great plenty here; and two sorts of Wild Pidgeons; the one sort Blackish, the other a light Grey: The Blackish or dark Grey are the Bigger, being as large as our Wood-Quests, or Wood-Pidgeons in *England*. Both sorts are very good Meat; and are in such plenty from *May* till *September*, that a Man may shoot 8 or 10 Dozen in several Shots at one standing, in a close misty Morning, when they come to feed on Berries that grow in the Woods.

The *Jenetee* is a Bird as big as a Lark, with blackish Feathers, and yellow Legs and Feet. 'Tis accounted very wholsome Food.

Clocking-Hens, are much like the Crab-catchers, which I have described [Vol. II. p. 175.] but the Legs are not altogether so long. They keep always in swampy wet Places, tho' their Claws are like Land-Fowls Claws. They make a Noise or *Cluck* like our Brood-Hens, or Dunghil-Hens, when they have Chickens, and for that Reason they are called by the *English*, Clocking-Hens. There are many of them in the Bay of

Campeachy (tho' I omitted to speak of them there) and elsewhere in the *West-Indies*. There are both here and there four sorts of these long-legg'd Fowls, near a-kin to each other, as so many *Sub-Species* of the same Kind; *viz.* Crab-catchers, Clocking-Hens, Galdens (which three are in shape and Colour like Herons in *England*, but less; the *Galden*, the biggest of the three, the Crab-catcher the smallest;) and a fourth sort which are Black, but shaped like the other, having long Legs and short Tails; these are about the bigness of *Crab-catchers*, and feed as they do.

Currecoos, are Water Fowls, as big as pretty large Chickens, of a bluish Colour, with short Legs and Tail; they feed also in swampy Ground, and are very good Meat. I have not seen of them elsewhere.

The Wild-Ducks here are said to be of two sorts, the *Muscovy*, and the common-Ducks. In the wet Season here are abundance of them, but in the dry Time but few. Wigeon and Teal also are said to be in great plenty here in the wet Season.

To the Southward of *Bahia* there are also Ostridges in great plenty, tho' 'tis said, they are not so large as those of *Africa:* They are found chiefly in the Southern Parts of *Brazil*, especially among the large Savannahs near the River of *Plate*; and from thence further South towards the Streights of *Magellan*.

As for Tame Fowl at *Bahia*, the chief beside their Ducks, are Dunghil-Fowls, of which they have two sorts; one sort much of the size of our Cocks and Hens; the other very large: And the Feathers of these last are a long time coming forth: so that you see them very naked when half grown; but when they are full grown and well feathered, they appear very large Fowls, as indeed they are; neither do they want for Price; for they are sold at

Bahia for half a Crown or three Shillings apiece, just as they are brought first to Market out of the Country, when they are so lean as to be scarce fit to eat.

The Land Animals here are Horses, black Cattle, Sheep, Goats, Rabbits, Hogs, Leopards, Tygers, Foxes, Monkeys, Pecary (a sort of wild Hogs, called here *Pica*) Armadillo, Alligators, Guano's (call'd *Quittee*) Lizards, Serpents, Toads, Frogs, and a sort of amphibious Creatures called by the *Portugueze Cachora's de agua*, in *English* Water-Dogs.

The Leopards and Tygers of this Country are said to be large and very fierce: But here on the Coast they are either destroyed, or driven back towards the Heart of the Country; and therefore are seldom found but in the Borders and Out-plantations, where they oftentimes do Mischief. Here are three or four sorts of Monkeys, of different Sizes and Colours. One sort is very large; and another sort is very small: These last are ugly in Shape and Feature, and have a strong Scent of Musk.

Here are several sorts of Serpents, many of them vastly great, and most of them very venomous: As the Rattle-snake for one: And for Venom, a small Green Snake is bad enough, no bigger than the Stemb of a Tobacco-pipe, and about 18 Inches long, very common here.

They have here also the *Amphisbæna*, or Two-headed Snake, of a grey Colour, mixt with blackish Stripes, whose Bite is reckon'd to be incurable. 'Tis said to be blind, tho' it has two small Specks in each Head like Eyes: But whether it sees or not I cannot tell. They say it lives like a Mole, mostly under Ground; and that when it is found above Ground it is easily kill'd, because it moves but slowly: Neither is its Sight (if it hath any) so good as to discern any one that comes near to kill it: as few of these Creatures fly at a Man, or hurt him but when he comes in their way. 'Tis about 14 Inches long, and about the bigness of the inner Joint of a Man's middle Finger; being of one and the same bigness from one End to the other, with a Head at each End, (as they said; for I cannot vouch it, for one I had was cut short at one End) and both alike in shape and bigness; and 'tis said to move with either Head foremost, indifferently; whence 'tis called by the *Portugueze, Cobra de dos Cabesas,* the Snake with two Heads.

The small black Snake is a very venomous Creature.

There is also a grey Snake, with red and brown Spots all over its back. 'Tis as big as a Man's Arm, and about 3 Foot long, and is said to be venomous. I saw one of these.

Here are two sorts of very large Snakes or Serpents: One of 'em a Land-snake, the other a Water-snake. The Land-snake is of a grey Colour, and about 18 or 20 Foot long: Not very venomous, but ravenous. I was promised the sight of one of their Skins, but wanted Opportunity.

The Water-snake is said to be near 30 Foot long. These live wholly in the Water, either in large Rivers, or great Lakes, and prey upon any Creature that comes within their Reach, be it Man or Beast. They draw their Prey to them with their Tails: for when they see any thing on the Banks of the River or Lake where they lurk, they swing about their Tails 10 or 12 Foot over the Bank; and whatever stands within their Sweep is snatch'd with great Violence into the River, and drowned by them. Nay 'tis reported very credibly that if they see only a shade of any Animal at all on the Water, they will flourish their Tails to bring in the Man or Beast whose Shade they see, and are oftentimes too successful in it. Wherefore Men that have Business near any Place where these Water-Monsters are suspected to lurk, are always provided with a Gun, which they often fire, and that scares them away, or keeps them quiet. They are said to have great Heads, and strong Teeth about 6 Inches long. I was told by an *Irish* Man who lived here, that his Wife's Father was very near being taken by one of them about this Time of my first Arrival here, when his Father was with him up in the Country: For the Beast flourish'd his Tail for him, but came not nigh enough by a Yard or two; however it scared him sufficiently.

The amphibious Creatures here which I said are called by the *Portugueze Cuchora*'s *de Agua*, or Water-dogs, are said to be as big as small Mastiffs, and are all hairy and shaggy from Head to Tail. They have 4 short Legs, a pretty long Head and short Tail; and are of a blackish Colour. They live in fresh Water-ponds, and oftentimes come ashore and Sun themselves; but retire to the Water if assaulted. They are eaten, and said to be good Food. Several of these Creatures which I have now spoken of I have not seen, but inform'd my self about them while I was here at *Bahia*, from sober and sensible Persons among the Inhabitants, among whom I met with some that could speak *English*.

In the Sea upon this Coast there is great Store and Diversity of Fish, *viz.* Jew-fish, for which there is a great Market at *Bahia* in *Lent:* Tarpoon's, Mullets, Groopers, Snooks, Gar-fish (called here *Goolion*'s,) *Gorasses*, Bar-rama's, Coquinda's, Cavallie's, Cuchora's (or Dog-fish) Conger-Eels, Herrings (as I was told) the *Serrew,* the *Olio de Boy,* (I write and spell them just as they were named to me) Whales, &c.

Here is also Shell-fish (tho' in less Plenty about *Bahia* than on other Parts of the Coast,) *viz.* Lobsters, Craw-

fish, Shrimps, Crabs, Oysters of the common Sort,
Conchs, Wilks, Cockles, Muscles, Perriwinkles, &c. Here
are three Sorts of Sea-Turtle, viz. Hawksbill, Loggerhead, and Green: But none of them are in any esteem,
neither Spaniards nor Portugueze loving them: Nay they
have a great Antipathy against them, and would much
rather eat a Porpoise, tho' our English count the green
Turtle very extraordinary Food. The Reason that is
commonly given in the West-Indies for the Spaniards not
caring to eat of them, is the Fear they have lest, being
usually foul-bodied, and many of them pox'd (lying, as
they do, so promiscuously with their Negrines and other
She-slaves) they should break out loathsomely like
Lepers; which this Sort of Food, 'tis said, does much
encline Men to do, searching the Body, and driving out
any such gross Humours: For which Cause many of our
English Valetudinarians have gone from Jamaica (tho'
there they have also Turtle) to the I. Caimanes, at the
Laying-time, to live wholly upon Turtle that then
abound there; purposely to have their Bodies scoured by
this Food, and their Distempers driven out; and have
been said to have found many of them good Success in it.
But this by the way. The Hawks-bill-Turtle on this
Coast of Brazil is most sought after of any, for its Shell;
which by Report of those I have convers'd with at
Bahia, is the clearest and best clouded Tortoise-shell in
the World. I had some of it shewn me, which was indeed
as good as I ever saw. They get a pretty deal of it in
some Parts on this Coast; but 'tis very dear.

Beside this Port of Bahia de todos los Santos, there are 2
more principal Ports on Brazil, where European Ships
Trade, viz. Pernambuc and Ria Janeira; and I was told
that there go as many Ships to each of these Places as
to Bahia, and 2 Men of War to each Place for their

Convoys. Of the other Ports in this Country none is of greater Note than that of St. *Paul*'s, where they gather much Gold; but the Inhabitants are said to be a Sort of *Banditti*, or loose People that live under no Government: But their Gold brings them all Sorts of Commodities that they need, as Clothes, Arms, Ammunition, *&c*. The Town is said to be large and strong.

CHAP. III

The A.'s Stay and Business at Bahia: *Of the Winds and Seasons of the Year there. His Departure for* N. Holland, C. Salvadore. *The Winds on the* Brasilian *Coast*; *and Abrohlo Shoal*; *Fish, and Birds: The Shear-water Bird, and Cooking of Sharks. Excessive Number of Birds about a dead Whale; of the Pintado-bird, and the Petrel,* &c. *Of a Bird that shews the* C. *of* G. Hope *to be near: Of the Sea-reckonings, and Variations: And a Table of all the* Variations *observ'd in this Voyage. Occurrences near the* Cape; *and the A.'s passing by it. Of the Westerly Winds beyond it: A Storm, and its Presages. The A.'s Course to* N. Holland; *and Signs of approaching it. Another* Abrohlo *Shole and Storm, and the A.'s Arrival on part of* N. Holland. *That part describ'd; and* Shark's *Bay, where he first anchors. Of the Land there, Vegetables, Birds,* &c. *A particular Sort of* Guano: *Fish, and beautiful Shells; Turtle, large Shark, and Water-Serpents. The A.'s removing to another part of* N. Holland: *Dolphins, Whales, and more Sea-Serpents: and of a* Passage *or* Streight *suspected here: Of the Vegetables, Birds, and Fish. He anchors on a third Part of* N. Holland, *and digs Wells, but brackish. Of the Inhabitants there, the great Tides, the Vegetables and Animals,* &c.

MY Stay here at *Bahia* was about a Month; during which Time the Vice-Roy of *Goa* came hither from thence in a great Ship, said to be richly laden with all Sorts of *India* Goods; but she did not break Bulk here, being bound Home for *Lisbon*; only the Vice-Roy intended to refresh his Men (of whom he had lost many, and most of the rest were very sickly, having been 4 Months in their Voyage hither) and so to take in Water, and depart for *Europe*, in Company with the other *Portugueze* Ships thither bound; who had Orders to be ready to sail by the twentieth of *May*. He desir'd me to carry a Letter for him, directed to his Successor the new Vice-Roy of *Goa*; which I did, sending it thither afterwards by Captain *Hammond*, whom I found near the *Cape of Good Hope*. The refreshing my Men, and taking in Water, was the main also of my Business here; beside the having the better Opportunity to compose the Disorders among my Crew: Which, as I have before related, were grown to so great a Heighth, that they could not without great Difficulty be appeased: However, finding Opportunity, during my Stay in this Place, to allay in some Measure the Ferment that had been raised among my Men, I now set my self to provide for the carrying on of my Voyage with more Heart than before, and put all Hands to work, in order to it, as fast as the Backwardness of my Men would permit; who shew'd continually their Unwillingness to proceed farther. Besides, their Heads were generally fill'd with strange Notions of Southerly Winds that were now setting in (and there had been already some Flurries of them) which, as they surmis'd, would hinder any farther Attempts of going on to the Southward, so long as they should last.

The Winds begin to shift here in *April* and *September*, and the Seasons of the Year (the Dry and the Wet) alter with them. In *April* the Southerly Winds make their Entrance on this Coast, bringing in the wet Season, with violent Tornado's, Thunder and Lightening, and much Rain. In *September* the other Coasting Trade, at East North-East comes in, and clears the Sky, bringing fair Weather. This, as to the Change of Wind, is what I have observ'd [Vol. II. p. 240.] but as to the Change of Weather accompanying it so exactly here at *Bahia*, this is a particular Exception to what I have experienc'd in all other Places of South Latitudes that I have been in between the *Tropicks*, or those I have heard of; for there the dry Seasons sets in, in *April*, and the Wet about *October* or *November*, sooner or later (as I have said that they are, in South Latitudes, the Reverse of the Seasons, or Weather, in the same Months in N. Latitudes, [Vol. II. p. 274.]) whereas on this Coast of *Brazil*,

the wet Season comes in in *April*, at the same Time that
it doth in N. Latitudes, and the dry (as I have said
here) in *September*; the Rains here not lasting so far in
the Year as in other Places; For in *September* the Weather
is usually so fair, that in the latter part of that Month
they begin to cut their Sugar-Canes here, as I was told;
for I enquired particularly about the Seasons: Though
this, as to the Season of cutting of Canes, which I was
now assur'd to be in *September*, agrees not very well with
what I was formerly told [Vol. II. p. 279.] that in
Brazil they cut the Canes in *July*. And so, as to what is
said a little lower in the same Page, that in managing
their Canes they are not confin'd to the Seasons, this
ought to have been express'd only of planting them; for
they never cut them but in the dry Season.

But to return to the Southerly Winds, which came in
(as I expected they would) while I was here: These
daunted my Ship's Company very much, tho' I had
told them they were to look for them: But they being
ignorant as to what I told them farther, that these were
only Coasting-Winds, sweeping the Shore to about 40
or 50 Leagues in Breadth from it, and imagining that
they had blown so all the Sea over, between *America* and
Africa; and being confirm'd in this their Opinion by the
Portugueze Pilots of the *European* Ships, with whom several
of my Officers conversed much, and who were themselves as ignorant that these were only Coasting Trade-
Winds (themselves going away before them, in their
Return homewards, till they cross the Line, and so
having no Experience of the Breadth of them) being
thus possess'd with a Conceit that we could not sail
from hence till *September*; this made them still the more
remiss in their Duties, and very listless to the getting
Things in a Readiness for our Departure. However I

was the more diligent my self to have the Ship scrubb'd, and to send my Water-Casks ashore to get them trimm'd, my Beer being now out. I went also to the Governour to get my Water fill'd; for here being but one Watering-place (and the Water running low, now at the End of the dry Season) it was always so crouded with the *European* Ships Boats, who were preparing to be gone, that my Men could seldom come nigh it, till the Governour very kindly sent an Officer to clear the Water-place for my Men, and to stay there till my Water-Casks were all full, whom I satisfied for his Pains. Here I also got aboard 9 or 10 Ton of Ballast, and made my Boatswain fit the Rigging that was amiss: and I enquired also of my particular Officers whose Business it was, whether they wanted any Stores, especially Pitch and Tar; for that here I would supply my self before I proceeded any farther; but they said they had enough, tho' it did not afterwards prove so.

I commonly went ashore every Day, either upon Business, or to recreate my self in the Fields, which were very pleasant, and the more for a Shower of Rain now and then, that ushers in the wet Season. Several Sorts of good Fruits were also still remaining, especially Oranges, which were in such Plenty, that I and all my Company stocked our selves for our Voyage with them, and they did us a great Kindness; and we took in also a good Quantity of Rum and Sugar: But for Fowls they being here lean and dear, I was glad I had stock'd my self at St. *Jago*. But by the little Care my Officers took for fresh Provisions, one might conclude, they did not think of going much farther. Besides, I had like to have been imbroiled with the Clergy here (of the *Inquisition*, as I suppose) and so my Voyage might have been hindred. What was said to them of me, by some of my Company that went ashore, I know not; but I was assured by a Merchant there, that if they got me into their Clutches (and it seems, when I was last ashore they had narrowly watch'd me) the Governour himself could not release me. Besides I might either be murther'd in the Streets, as he sent me Word, or poisoned, if I came ashore any more; and therefore he advised me to stay aboard. Indeed I had now no further Business ashore but to take leave of the Governour, and therefore took his Advice.

Our Stay here was till the 23d of *April*. I would have gone before if I could sooner have fitted my self; but was now earnest to be gone, because this Harbour lies open to the S. and S. S. W. which are raging Winds here, and now was the Season for them. We had 2 or 3 Touches of them; and one pretty severe, and the Ships ride there so near each other, that if a Cable should fail, or an Anchor start, you are instantly aboard of one Ship or other: And I was more afraid of being disabled here in Harbour by these blustring Winds, than discouraged by them, as my People were, from prosecuting the Voyage; for at present I even wish'd for a brisk Southerly Wind as soon as I should be once well out of the Harbour, to set me the sooner into the true General Trade-Wind.

The Tide of Flood being spent, and having a fine Land-Breeze on the 23d in the Morning. I went away from the Anchoring place before 'twas light; and then lay by till Day-light that we might see the better how to go out of the Harbour. I had a Pilot belonging to Mr. *Cock*, who went out with me, to whom I gave 3 Dollars; but I found I could as well have gone out my self, by the Soundings I made at coming in. The Wind was E. by N. and fair Weather. By 10 a Clock I was got past all Danger, and then sent away my Pilot. At 12 Cape

Salvadore bore N. distant 6 Leagues, and we had the Winds between the E. by N. and S. E. a considerable Time, so that we kept along near the Shore, commonly in Sight of it. The Southerly Blasts had now left us again; for they come at first in short Flurries, and shift to other Points (for 10 or 12 Days sometimes) before they are quite set in: And we had uncertain Winds, between Sea and Land-Breezes, and the Coasting-Trade, which was its self unsettled.

The Easterly Winds at present made me doubt I should not weather a great Shoal which lies in Lat. betwen 18 deg. and 19 deg. S. and runs a great way into the Sea, directly from the Land, Easterly. Indeed the Weather was fair (and continued so a good while) so that I might the better avoid any Danger from it: And if the Wind came to the Southward I knew I could stretch off to Sea; so that I jogg'd on couragiously. The 27th of *April* we saw a small Brigantine under the Shore plying to the Southward. We also saw many Men of War-birds and Boobies, and Abundance of *Albicore*-Fish. Having still fair Weather, small Gales, and some Calms, I had the Opportunity of trying the Current, which I found to set sometimes Northerly and sometimes Southerly: And therefore knew I was still within the Verge of the Tides. Being now in the Lat. of the *Abrohlo* Shoals, which I expected to meet with, I sounded, and had Water lessening from 40 to 33, and so to 25 Fathom: But then it rose again to 33, 35, 37, &c. all Coral Rocks. Whilst we were on this Shoal (which we cross'd towards the further part of it from Land, where it lay deep, and so was not dangerous) we caught a great many Fish with Hook and Line: and by evening Amplitude we had 6 deg. 38 min. East Variation. This was the 27th of *April*; we were then in Lat. 18 deg. 13 min. S. and East

Longitude from Cape *Salvadore* 31 min. On the 29th, being then in Lat. 18 deg. 39 min. S. we had small Gales from the W. N. W. to the W. S. W. often shifting. The 30th we had the Winds from W. to S. S. E. Squalls and Rain: And we saw some Dolphins and other Fish about us. We were now out of Sight of Land, and had been so 4 or 5 Days: But the Winds now hanging in the South was an apparent Sign that we were still too nigh the Shore to receive the true General East-Trade; as the Easterly Winds we had before shew'd that we were too far off the Land to have the Benefit of the Coasting South-Trade: and the Faintness of both these Winds, and their often shifting from the S. S. W. to the S. E. with Squalls, Rain and small Gales, were a Confirmation of our being between the Verge of the S. Coasting-Trade, and that of the true Trade; which is here, regularly, S. E.

The 3d of *May* being in Lat 20 deg. 00 min. and Merid. distance West from Cape *Salvadore* 234 Miles, the Variation was 7 deg. 00 min. We saw no Fowl but Shear-waters, as our Sea-men call them, being a small black Fowl that sweep the Water as they fly, and are much in the Seas that lie without either of the *Tropicks:* they are not eaten. We caught 3 small Sharks, each 6 Foot 4 Inches long; and they were very good Food for us. The next Day we caught 3 more Sharks of the same Size, and we eat them also, esteeming them as good Fish boil'd and press'd, and then stew'd with Vinegar and Pepper.

We had nothing of Remark from the 3d of *May* to the 10th, only now and then seeing a small Whale spouting up the Water. We had the Wind Easterly, and we ran with it to the Southward, running in this Time from the Lat. of 20 deg. 00 m. to 29 deg. 5 min. S. and having then 7 d. 3 m. E. Long. from C. *Salvadore*; the Variation increasing upon us, at present, notwithstanding we went

East. We had all along a great Difference between the Morning and Evening Amplitudes; usually a Degree or two, and sometimes more. We were now in the true Trade, and therefore made good Way to the Southward, to get without the Verge of the General Trade-Wind into a Westerly Wind's way, that might carry us towards the Cape of *Good Hope*. By the 12th of *May*, being in Lat. 31 Deg. 10 min. we began to meet with Westerly Winds, which freshned on us, and did not leave us till a little before we made the Cape. Sometimes it blew so hard that it put us under a Fore-course; especially in the Night; but in the Day-time we had commonly our Main Top-sail rift. We met with nothing of Moment; only we past by a dead Whale, and saw Millions (as I may say) of Sea-Fowls about the Carcass (and as far round about it as we could see) some feeding, and the rest flying about, or sitting on the Water, waiting to take their Turns. We first discovered the Whale by the Fowls; for indeed I did never see so many Fowls at once in my Life before, their Numbers being inconceivably great: They were of divers Sorts, in Bigness, Shape and Colour. Some were almost as big as Geese, of a grey Colour, with white Breasts, and with such Bills, Wings, and Tails. Some were *Pintado*-Birds, as big as Ducks, and speckled black and white. Some were Shear-waters; some Petrels; and there were several Sorts of large Fowls. We saw of these Birds, especially the *Pintado*-birds, all the Sea over from about 200 Leagues distant from the Coast of *Brazil*, to within much the same Distance of *New-Holland*. The *Pintado* is a Southern Bird, and of that temperate Zone; for I never saw of them much to the Norward of 30 deg. S. The *Pintado*-Bird is as big as a Duck; but appears, as it flies, about the Bigness of a tame Pidgeon, having a short Tail, but the Wings very long, as most Sea-Fowls have;

F

especially such as these that fly far from the Shore, and
seldom come nigh it; for their Resting is sitting afloat
upon the Water; but they lay, I suppose, ashore. There
are three Sorts of these Birds, all of the same Make and
Bigness, and are only different in Colour. The first is
black all over: The second Sort are grey, with white
Bellies and Breasts. The third Sort, which is the true
Pintado, or Painted-Bird, is curiously spotted white and
black. Their Heads, and the Tips of their Wings and
Tails, are black for about an Inch; and their Wings are
also edg'd quite round with such a small black List;
only within the black on the Tip of their Wings there is a
white Spot seeming as they fly (for then their Spots are
best seen) as big as a Half-crown. All this is on the Out-
side of the Tails and Wings; and as there is a white Spot
in the black Tip of the Wings, so there is in the Middle
of the Wings which is white, a black Spot; but this,
towards the Back of the Bird, turns gradually to a dark
grey. The Back its self, from the Head to the Tip of the
Tail, and the Edge of the Wings next to the Back, are all
over-spotted with fine small, round, white and black
Spots, as big as a Silver Two-pence, and as close as they
can stick one by another: The Belly, Thighs, Sides, and
inner-part of the Wings, are of a light grey. These Birds,
of all these Sorts, fly many together, never high, but
almost sweeping the Water. We shot one a while after on
the Water in a Calm, and a Water-Spaniel we had with
us brought it in: I have given a Picture of it [See *Birds*,
Fig. 1.] but it was so damaged, that the Picture doth not
shew it to Advantage; and its Spots are best seen when
the Feathers are spread as it flies.

The Petrel is a Bird not much unlike a Swallow, but
smaller, and with a shorter Tail. 'Tis all over black, except a white Spot on the Rump. They fly sweeping like

F. 2.

This very much resembles the Guarauna, described, and figured by Piso.

F. 1.

The Pintado Bird.

Swallows, and very near the Water. They are not so often seen in fair Weather; being Foul-weather Birds, as our Seamen call them, and presaging a Storm when they come about a Ship; who for that Reason don't love to see them. In a Storm they will hover close under the Ship's Stern, in the Wake of the Ship (as 'tis call'd) or the Smoothness which the Ship's passing has made on the Sea; And there as they fly (gently then) they pat the Water alternately with their Feet, as if they walk'd upon it; tho' still upon the Wing. And from hence the Seamen give them the Name of *Petrels*, in Allusion to St. *Peter*'s walking upon the Lake of *Gennesareth*.

We also saw many Bunches of Sea-weeds in the Lat. of 39. 32. and by Judgment, near the Meridian of the Island *Tristian d' Aconha:* And then we had about 2 d. 20 min. East Variation: which was now again decreasing as we ran to the Eastward, till near the Meridian of *Ascention*; where we found little or no Variation: But from thence, as we ran farther to the East, our Variation increased Westerly.

Two Days before I made the Cape of *G. Hope*, my Variation was 7 deg. 58 min. West. I was then in 43 deg. 27 min. East Longit. from C. *Salvador*, being in Lat. 35 deg. 30 min. this was the first of *June*. The second of *June* I saw a large black Fowl, with a whitish flat Bill, fly by us; and took great Notice of it, because in the *East-India* Waggoner, or Pilot-book, there is mention made of large Fowls, as big as Ravens, with white flat Bills and black Feathers, that fly not above 30 Leagues from the *Cape*, and are look'd on as a Sign of ones being near it. My Reckoning made me then think my self above 90 Leagues from the *Cape*, according to the Longitude which the *Cape* hath in the common Sea-Charts: So that I was in some doubt, whether these were the right Fowls spoken of in the Waggoner; or whether those Fowls might not fly farther off Shore than is there mentioned; or whether, as it prov'd, I might not be nearer the *Cape* than I reckoned myself to be; for I found, soon after, that I was not then above 25 or 30 Leagues at most from the Cape. Whether the Fault were in the Charts laying down the *Cape* too much to the East from *Brazil*, or were rather in our Reckoning, I could not tell: But our Reckonings are liable to such Uncertainties from Steerage, Log, Currents, Half-Minute-Glasses; and sometimes want of Care, as in so long a Run cause often a Difference of many Leagues in the whole Account.

Most of my Men that kept Journals imputed it to the Half-Minute-Glasses: and indeed we had not a good Glass in the Ship beside the Half-watch or Two-Hour-Glasses. As for our Half-Minute-Glasses we tried them all at several Times, and we found those that we had used from *Brazil* as much too short, as others we had used before were too long; which might well make great Errors in those several Reckonings. A Ship ought therefore to have its Glasses very exact; and besides, an extraordinary Care ought to be used in heaving the Log, for Fear of giving too much Stray-Line in a moderate Gale; and also to stop quickly in a brisk Gale, for when a Ship runs 8, 9 or 10 Knots, half a Knot or a Knot is soon run out, and not heeded: But to prevent Danger, when a Man thinks himself near Land, the best way is to look out betimes, and lye by in the Night, for a Commander may err easily himself; beside the Errors of those under him, tho' never so carefully eyed.

Another Thing that stumbled me here was the *Variation*, which, at this Time, by the last Amplitude I had I found to be but 7 deg. 58 min. W. whereas the Variation at the *Cape* (from which I found my self not 30 Leagues distant) was then computed, and truly, about 11 deg. or more: And yet a while after this, when I was got 10 Leagues to the Eastward of the *Cape*, I found the Variation but 10 deg. 40 min. W. whereas it should have been rather more than at the *Cape*. These Things, I confess, did puzzle me: Neither was I fully satisfied as to the Exactness of the taking the Variation at Sea: For in a great Sea, which we often meet with, the Compass will traverse with the Motion of the Ship; besides the Ship may and will deviate somewhat in steering, even by the best Helmsmen: And then when you come to take an *Azimuth*, there is often some Difference between him that looks at the Compass, and the Man that takes the Altitude heighth of the Sun; and a small Error in each, if the Error of both should be one way, will make it wide of any great Exactness. But what was most shocking to me, I found that the Variation did not always increase or decrease in Proportion to the Degrees of Longitude East or West; as I had a Notion they might do to a certain Number of Degrees of Variation East or West, at such or such particular Meridians. But finding in this Voyage that the Difference of Variation did not bear a regular Proportion to the Difference of Longitude, I was much pleas'd to see it thus observ'd in a Scheme shewn me after my Return home, wherein are represented the several Variations in the *Atlantick* Sea, on both Sides the Equator; and there, the Line of no Variation in that Sea is not a Meridian Line, but goes very oblique, as do those also which shew the Increase of Variation on each Side of it. In that Draught there is so large an Advance made as well towards the accounting for those seemingly irregular Increases and Decreases of Variation towards the S. E. Coast of *America*, as towards the fixing a general Scheme or System of the Variation every where, which would be of such great Use in Navigation, that I cannot but hope that the ingenious Author, Capt. *Hally*, who to his profound Skill in all Theories of these kinds, hath added and is adding continually Personal Experiments, will e'er long oblige the World with a fuller Discovery of the Course of the Variation, which hath hitherto been a Secret. For my Part I profess my self unqualified for offering at any thing of a General Scheme; but since Matter of Fact, and whatever increases the History of the Variation, may be of use towards the settling or confirming the Theory of it, I shall here once for all insert a *Table* of all the *Variations* I observed beyond the *Equator* in this Voyage, both in going out, and returning back; and what Errors there may be in it, I shall leave to be corrected by the Observations of others.

A Table of Variations

1699.		D. M. S.Lat.		D. M. Longit.		D. M. Variat.	
Mar.	14	6	15	1	47 *a*	3	27 E
	21	12	45	12	9	3	27
Apr.	25	14	49	00	10 *b*	7	0
	28	18	13	00	31	6	38
	30	19	00	2	20	6	30
May.	2	19	22	3	51	8	15
	3	20	1	3	40	7	0
	5	22	47	3	48	9	40
	6	24	23	3	53	7	36
	7	25	44	3	53	10	15
	8	26	47	4	35	7	14
	9	28	9	5	50	9	45
	10	29	5	7	3	11	41
	11	29	23	7	38	12	47

a W. from St. *Jago*.
b E. from C. *Salvador* in *Brazil*.

1699.	D. M. S.Lat.		D. M. Longit.		D. M. Variat.	
May. 17	34	58	18	43	5	40 E
18	34	54	19	06	6	19
19	35	48	19	45	5	6
23	39	42	27	1	2	55
25	39	11	31	35	2	0
June. 1	35	30	43	27	7	58 W
5	35	8	00	23 c	10	40
6	36	7	3	6	11	10
8	36	17	10	3	15	00
9	35	59	12	0	19	38
12	35	20	20	18	21	35
14	35	5	26	13	23	50
15	34	51	29	24	25	56
17	34	27	36	8	24	54
19	34	17	39	24	25	29
20	34	15	42	25	24	22
22	33	34	45	41	22	15
25	35	8	45	28	24	30
28	36	40	49	33	22	50
29	36	40	53	12	22	44
30	36	15	56	22	21	40
July. 1	35	35	58	44	19	45
4	33	32	66	22	16	40
6	31	30	68	34	12	20
7	31	45	69	00	12	2
10	32	39	70	21	13	36
11	33	4	72	00	12	29
13	21	17	74	43	10	0
15	29	20	75	25	10	28
18	28	16	78	29	9	51
23	26	43	84	19	9	11
24	26	28	85	20	8	9
25	26	14	85	52	8	40
26	25	36	86	21	8	20

c E. from C. *G. Hope*.

1699.	D. M. S.Lat.		D. M. Longit.		D. M. Variat.	
July. 27	26	43	86	16	7	0 W
29	27	38	87	25	8	20
31	26	54	88	1	9	0
Aug. 5	25	30	86	3	7	24
15	24	41	86	2 d	6	6
17	23	2	00	22	7	6
20	19	37	3	00	7	00
24	19	52	4	41	7	7
25	19	45	5	10	6	40
27	19	24	6	11	5	18
28	18	38	6	57	6	12
Sept. 6	17	16	9	18	4	3
7	16	9	8	57	2	7
8	15	37	9	34	2	20
10	13	55	10	55	1	47
11	13	12	11	42	1	47
Dec. 29	5	1	6	34 e	1	2 E
1700. Jan. 3	1	32	6	53	4	8
Feb. 13	0	9	2	48 f	4	0
16	0	12	7	31	6	26
21	0	12	15	23	8	45
23	0	43	18	00	8	45
27	2	43	19	41	9	50
Mar. 10	5	10	00	5 g	1	0
13	5	35	00	44 h	9	0
30	5	15	6	4	8	25 W
Apr. 6	3	32	8	25	7	66
22	1	32	00	37 i	3	00

d E. from *Sharks-Bay* in *N. Holland*.
e E. from *Babao-Bay* in *J. Timor*.
f E. from C. *Mabo* in *N. Guinea*.
g E. from C. *St. George* on I. *N. Britannia*.
h W. from *ditto*.
i W. from C. *Maba*.

1700.	D. M. S. Lat.		D. M. Longit.		D. M. Variat.	
May. 1	3	00		*k*	2	15 E
24	9	59	00	25 *l*	0	15 W
27	14	33	3	30	1	25
June. 2	19	44	8	7	5	38
3	19	51	9	58	6	10
4	19	46	11	6	6	20
5	20	00	12	22	4	58
6	20	00	14	17	7	20
9	19	59	16	01	6	32
11	9	57	17	42	8	1
12	19	48	19	0	6	0
Nov. 7	21	26		*m*	9	0
14	27	1	35	35	16	50
15	27	10	36	34	18	57
16	27	11	37	54	17	24
19	28	14	41	40	19	39
21	29	24	44	47	20	50
23	29	42	47	34	21	38
24	30	16	49	26	26	00
25	30	40	51	24	22	38
27	31	51	55	5	22	40
29	32	55	56	28	27	10
30	31	55	57	25	27	10
Dec. 1	31	57	58	17	24	30
2	31	57	59	33	27	57
4	32	3	61	45	24	50
6	32	15	66	00	23	30
7	37	28	68	36	24	48
8	33	49	64	38	21	53
9	32	49	70	09	24	00
11	32	50	71	45	21	15

k At Anchor off I. *Ceram.*

l W. from *Baba*-Bay.

m W. from *Princes* Isle by *Java*-Head.

1700.	D. M. S.Lat.		D. M. Longit.		D. M. Variat.	
Dec. 13	31	55	72	32	20	16 W
14	31	35	73	39	20	00
15	32	21	75	22	20	00
17	33	5	79	39	18	42
18	33	0	80	39	17	15
21	34	39	82	46	16	41
22	34	36	83	19	14	36
23	34	21	83	42	14	00
25	34	38	84	21	14	00
1701. *Jan.* 15	31	25	2	32 *n*	10	20
16	30	5	4	42	9	36
17	28	46	6	8	8	25
18	27	26	7	32	7	40
19	26	11	9	9	7	30
20	25	00	10	49	7	9
21	23	42	12	34	6	55
22	22	51	14	10	5	56
23	21	48	15	17	5	32
24	21	24	15	51	4	56
26	19	57	16	48	4	20
27	19	10	17	22	3	24
28	18	13	18	23	4	00
29	17	22	19	29	2	00
Feb. 16	12	52	3	8 *o*	1	50
17	11	55	4	42	1	10
18	11	17	5	30	0	20
19	10	22	6	32	1	10
21	We made the I. *Ascention.*					

n W. from the *Table* Land at C. *G. Hope.*
o W. *Santa Helena.*

But to return from this Digression: Having fair Weather, and the Winds hanging Southerly, I jog'd on to the Eastward, to make the *Cape*. On the third of *June* we saw a Sail to Leeward of us, shewing *English* Colours. I bore away to speak with her, and found her to be the *Antelope* of *London*, commanded by Captain *Hammond*, and bound for the Bay of *Bengal* in the Service of the *New-East-India* Company. There were many Passengers aboard, going to settle there under Sir *Edward Littleton*, who was going Chief thither: I went aboard, and was known by Sir *Edward* and Mr. *Hedges*, and kindly received and treated by them and the Commander; who had been afraid of us before, tho' I had sent one of my Officers aboard. They had been in at the *Cape*, and came from thence the Day before, having stocked themselves with Refreshments. They told me that they were by Reckoning, 60 Miles to the West of the *Cape*. While I was aboard them, a fine small Westerly Wind sprang up; therefore I shortned my stay with them, because I did not design to go into the *Cape*. When I took leave I was presented with half a Mutton, 12 Cabbages, 12 Pumkins, 6 Pound of Butter, 6 Couple of Stock-fish, and a quantity of Parsnips; sending them some Oatmeal, which they wanted.

From my first setting out from *England*, I did not design to touch at the *Cape*; and that was one Reason why I touch'd at *Brazil*, that there I might refresh my Men, and prepare them for a long Run to *New Holland*. We had not yet seen the Land; but about 2 in the Afternoon we saw the *Cape*-Land bearing East, at about 16 Leagues distance: And Captain *Hammond* being also bound to double the *Cape*, we jog'd on together this Afternoon and the next Day, and had several fair Sights of it; which may be seen [*Table* III. N°. 6, 7, 8.]

To proceed: Having still a Westerly Wind, I jog'd
on in company with the *Antelope*, till *Sunday June* the 4th
at 4 in the Afternoon, when we parted; they steering
away for the *East-Indies*, and I keeping an E. S. E.
Course, the better to make my way for *New Holland*: For
tho' *New Holland* lies North-Easterly from the *Cape*, yet
all Ships bound towards that Coast, or the Streights of
Sundy, ought to keep for a while in the same Parallel, or
in a Lat. between 35 and 40. at least a little to the S. of
the East. that they may continue in a variable Winds
way; and not venture too soon to stand so far to the
North, as to be within the Verge of the Trade-Wind,
which will put them by their Easterly Course. The
Wind increased upon us; but we had yet sight of the
Antelope, and of the Land too, till *Tuesday* the 6th of *June*:
And then we saw also by us an innumerable Company
of Fowls of divers sorts; so that we look'd about to see if
there were not another dead Whale, but saw none.

The Night before, the Sun set in a black Cloud, which
appeared just like Land; and the Clouds above it were
gilded of a dark red Colour. And on the *Tuesday*, as the
Sun drew near the Horizon, the Clouds were gilded
very prettily to the Eye, tho' at the same time my Mind
dreaded the Consequences of it. When the Sun was now
not above 2 deg. high, it entered into a dark Smoaky-
coloured Cloud that lay parallel with the Horizon, from
whence presently seem'd to issue many dusky blackish
Beams. The Sky was at this time covered with small hard
Clouds (as we call such as lye scattering about, not
likely to Rain) very thick one by another; and such of
them as lay next to the Bank of Clouds at the Horizon,
were of a pure Gold Colour to 3 or 4 deg. high above the
Bank: From these to about 10 deg. high they were
redder, and very bright; above them they were of a

darker Colour still, to about 60 or 70 deg. high; where the Clouds began to be of their common Colour. I took the more particular Notice of all this, because I have generally observed such colour'd Clouds to appear before an approaching Storm: And this being Winter here, and the time for bad Weather, I expected and provided for a violent blast of Wind, by riffing our Topsails, and giving a strict charge to my Officers to hand them or take them in, if the Wind should grow stronger. The Wind was now at W. N. W. a very brisk Gale. About 12 a Clock at Night we had a pale whitish Glare in the N. W. which was another Sign, and intimated the Storm to be near at hand; and the Wind increasing upon it, we presently handed our Top-sails, furled the Main-sail, and went away only with our Fore-sail. Before 2 in the Morning it came on very fierce, and we kept right before Wind and Sea, the Wind still encreasing: But the Ship was very governable, and steered incomparably well. At 8 in the Morning we settled our Fore-yard, lowering it 4 or 5 Foot, and we ran very swiftly; especially when the Squalls of Rain or Hail, from a black Cloud, came over Head, for then it blew excessive hard. These, tho' they did not last long, yet came very thick and fast one after another. The Sea also ran very high; But we running so violently before Wind and Sea, we ship'd little or no Water; tho' a little wash'd into our upper Deck-Ports; and with it a Scuttle or Cuttle-Fish was cast upon the Carriage of a Gun.

The Wind blew extraordinary hard all *Wednesday*, the 7th of *June*, but abated of its fierceness before Night: Yet it continued a brisk Gale till about the 16th, and still a moderate one till the 19th Day; by which time we had run about 600 Leagues: For the most part of which time the Wind was in some point of the West, *viz*. from

the W. N. W. to the S. by W. It blew hardest when at W.
or between the W. and S. W. but after it veered more
Southerly the foul Weather broke up: This I observed
at other times also in these Seas, that when the Storms
at West veered to the Southward they grew less; and
that when the Wind came to the E. of the S. we had still
smaller Gales, Calms, and fair Weather. As for the
Westerly Winds on that side the *Cape*, we like them never
the worse for being violent, for they drive us the faster
to the Eastward; and are therefore the only Winds
coveted by those who Sail towards such parts of the
East-Indies, as lye South of the Equator; as *Timor*, *Java*,
and *Sumatra*; and by the Ships bound for *China*, or any
other that are to pass through the Streights of *Sundy*.
Those Ships having once past the *Cape*, keep commonly
pretty far Southerly, on purpose to meet with these West-
winds, which in the Winter Season of these Climates
they soon meet with; for then the Winds are generally
Westerly at the *Cape*, and especially to the Southward of
it: But in their Summer Months they get to the Southward of 40 deg. usually e're they meet with the Westerly
Winds. I was not at this time in a higher Lat. than 36
deg. 40 min. and oftentimes was more Northerly, altering
my Latitude often as Winds and Weather required;
for in such long Runs 'tis best to shape one's Course
acording to the Winds. And if in steering to the East, we
should be obliged to bear a little to the N. or S. of it, 'tis
no great Matter; for 'tis but sailing 2 or 3 Points from the
Wind, when 'tis either Northerly or Southerly; and this
not only easeth the Ship from straining, but shortens the
way more than if a Ship was kept close on a Wind, as
some Men are fond of doing.

The 19th of *June*, we were in Lat. 34 deg. 17 min. S.
and Long. from the *Cape* 39 deg. 24 min. E. and had

small Gales and Calms. The Winds were at N. E. by E. and continued in some Part of the E. till the 27th Day. When it having been some Time at N. N. E. it came about at N. and then to the W. of the N. and continued in the West-board (between the N. N. W. and S. S. W.) till the 4th of *July*; in which Time we ran 782 Miles; then the Winds came about again to the East, we reckoning our selves to be in a Meridian 1100 L. East of the *Cape*; and having fair Weather, sounded, but had no Ground.

We met with little of Remark in this Voyage, besides being accompanied with Fowls all the way, especially Pintado-Birds, and seeing now and then a Whale: But as we drew nigher the Coast of *New-Holland*, we saw frequently 3 or 4 Whales together. When we were about 90 Leagues from the Land we began to see Sea-weeds, all of one Sort; and as we drew nigher the Shore we saw them more frequently. At about 30 Leagues distance we began to see some Scuttle-bones floating on the Water; and drawing still nigher the Land we saw greater Quantities of them.

July 25. being in Lat. 26. deg. 14 min. S. and Longitude E. from the C. of *Good Hope* 85 deg. 52 min. we saw a large Gar-fish leap 4 Times by us, which seemed to be as big as a Porpose. It was now very fair Weather, and the Sea was full of a Sort of very small Grass or Moss, which as it floated in the Water seem'd to have been some Spawn of Fish; and there was among it some small Fry. The next Day the Sea was full of small round Things like Pearl, some as big as white Peas; they were very clear and transparent, and upon crushing any of them a Drop of Water would come forth: The Skin that contain'd the Water was so thin that it was but just discernable. Some Weeds swam by us, so that we did not doubt but we should quickly see Land. On the 27th also, some Weeds swam by us, and the Birds that had flown along with us all the way almost from *Brazil*, now left us, except only 2 or 3 Shear-waters. On the 28th we saw many Weeds swim by us, and some Whales, blowing. On the 29th we had dark cloudy Weather, with much Thunder, Lightning, and violent Rains in the Morning; but in the Evening it grew fair. We saw this Day a Scuttle-bone swim by us, and some of our young Men a Seal, as it should seem by their Description of its Head. I saw also some Boneta's, and some Skipjacks, a Fish about 8 Inches long, broad, and sizeable, not much un-like a Roach; which our Seamen call so from their leap-ing about.

The 30th of *July*, being still nearer the Land, we saw Abundance of Scuttle-bones and Sea-weed, more Tokens that we were not far from it; and saw also a Sort of Fowls, the like of which we had not seen in the whole Voyage, all the other Fowls having now left us. These were as big as Lapwings; of a grey Colour, black about their Eyes, with red sharp Bills, long Wings, their Tails long and forked like Swallows; and they flew flapping their Wings like Lapwings. In the Afternoon we met with a Ripling like a Tide or Current, or the Water of some Shoal or Over-fall; but were past it before we could sound. The Birds last mention'd and this were further Signs of Land. In the Evening we had fair Weather, and a small Gale at West. At 8 a Clock we sounded again; but had no Ground.

We kept on still to the Eastward, with an easy Sail, looking out sharp: For by the many Signs we had, I did expect that we were near the Land. At 12 a Clock in the Night I sounded, and had 45 Fathom, coarse Sand and small white Shells. I presently clapt on a Wind and

stood to the South, with the Wind at W. because I
thought we were to the South of a Shoal call'd the
Abrohles (an Appellative Name for Shoals, as it seems to
me) which in a Draught I had of that Coast is laid down
in 27 deg. 28 min. Lat. stretching about 7 Leagues into
the Sea. I was the Day before in 27 deg. 38 min. by
Reckoning. And afterwards steering E. by S. purposely
to avoid it, I thought I must have been to the South of it:
But sounding again, at 1 a Clock in the Morning, *Aug.* the
first, we had but 25 Fathom, Coral Rocks; and so found
the Shoal was to the South of us. We presently tack'd
again, and stood to the North, and then soon deepned
our Water; for at 2 in the Morning we had 26 Fathom
Coral still: At 3 we had 28 Coral-ground: At 4 we had 30
Fathom, coarse Sand, with some Coral: At 5 we had 45
Fathom, coarse Sand and Shells; being now off the Shoal,
as appear'd by the Sand and Shells, and by having left
the Coral. By all this I knew we had fallen into the
North of the Shoal, and that it was laid down wrong in
my Sea-Chart: For I found it lye in about 27 deg. Lat.
and by our Run in the next Day, I found that the Out-
ward-edge of it, which I sounded on, lies 16 Leagues off
Shore. When it was Day we steered in E. N. E. with a
fine brisk Gale; but did not see the Land till 9 in the
Morning, when we saw it from our Topmast-head, and
were distant from it about 10 Leagues; having then 40
Fathom-water, and clean Sand. About 3 Hours after we
saw it on our Quarter-Deck, being by Judgment about 6
Leagues off, and we had then 40 Fathom, clean Sand.
As we ran in, this Day and the next, we took several
Sights of it, at different Bearings and Distances; from
which it appear'd as you see in [*Table* IV. N°. 1, 2, 3, 4,
5.] And here I would note once for all, that the Latitudes
mark'd in the Draughts, or Sights here given, are not the

G

Latitude of the Land, but of the Ship when the Sight was taken. This Morning, *August* the first, as we were standing in we saw several large Sea-fowls, like our Gannets on the Coast of *England*, flying 3 or 4 together; and a Sort of white Sea-Mews, but black about the Eyes, and with forked Tails. We strove to run in near the Shore to seek for a Harbour to refresh us after our tedious Voyage; having made one continued Stretch from *Brazil* hither of about 114 deg. designing from hence also to begin the Discovery I had a Mind to make on *N. Holland* and *N. Guinea*. The Land was low, and appear'd even, and as we drew nearer to it, it made (as you see in *Table* IV. N°. 3, 4, 5.) with some red and some white Clifts; these last in Lat. 26. 10 S. where you will find 54 Fathom, within 4 Miles of the Shore.

About the Lat. of 26 deg. S. we saw an Opening, and ran in, hoping to find a Harbour there: But when we came to its Mouth, which was about 2 Leagues wide, we saw Rocks and foul Ground within, and therefore stood out again: There we had 20 Fathom-water within 2 Mile of the Shore. The Land every where appear'd pretty low, flat and even; but with steep Cliffs to the Sea; and when we came near it there were no Trees, Shrubs or Grass to be seen. The Soundings in the Lat. of 26 deg. S. from about 8 or 9 Leagues off till you come within a League of the Shore, are generally about 40 Fathom; differing but little, seldom above 3 or 4 Fathom. But the Lead brings up very different Sorts of Sand, some coarse, some fine; and of several Colours, as Yellow, White, Grey, Brown, Blueish and Reddish.

When I saw there was no Harbour here, nor good anchoring, I stood off to Sea again, in the Evening of the second of *August*, fearing a Storm on a Leeshore, in a Place where there was no Shelter, and desiring at least to

Table IV.

New Holland

N.º 1.
N, Holland, from Top-mast head in y.ᵉ Lat: 27 D. 30 M. S. at these Bearings:
E. b. N.   E. S. E.   dist: 10 L.

N.º 2.
N, Holland, the same Coast from 8 L. dist: Lat: 27 D. 28 M. S
N. E. b. N.
East

N.º 3.
N ½ W.   N, Holland, at 5 L. dist: in Lat: 26–46 S.
S. E. b. S.
Reddish Land

N.º 4.
N, Holland, at 6 L. dist: in Lat: 26–35 S.
N. N. E. ½ E.   N. E.
Reddish Land

N.º 5.
N, Holland, from Lat: 26–10. 8 L. from y.ᵉ white Hills
N. b. E.   N. E. ½ N.
white Hills   Reddish Land

N.º 6.

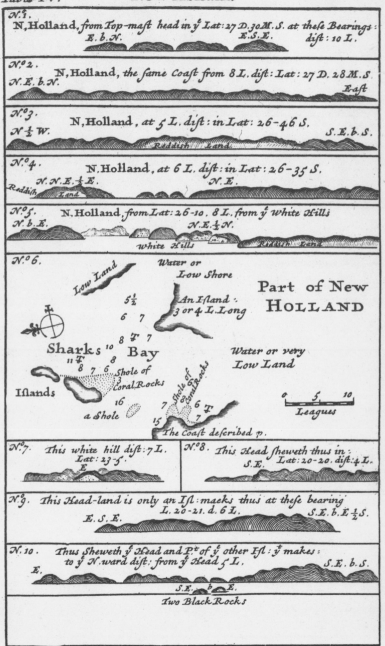

Low Land
Water or
Low Shore
5½
6   7
An Island
3 or 4 L. Long
Part of New
HOLLAND
8   T   7
Sharks   10   Bay
11   T
8   8
8   7   6   Shole of
3   Coral Rocks
Water or very
Low Land
Islands
16
7   8
a Shole   15
Shole of Coral Rocks
6   T
7
The Coast described p.
0   5   10
Leagues

N.º 7.   This white hill dist: 7 L.
Lat: 23–5.
E

N.º 8.   This Head sheweth thus in:
S. E.   Lat: 20–20. dist: 4 L.

N.º 9.   This Head-land is only an Isl: maeks thus at these bearing
L. 20–21. d. 6 L.
E. S. E.   S. E. b. E. ½ S.

N. 10.   Thus Sheweth y.ᵉ Head and P.ᵗ of y.ᵉ other Isl: y.ᵗ makes:
to y.ᵉ N. ward dist: from y.ᵉ Head 5 L.
E.   S. E. b. S.

S. E.   b.   E.
Two Black Rocks

have Sea-room: For the Clouds began to grow thick in the Western-board, and the Wind was already there, and began to blow fresh almost upon the Shore; which at this Place lies along N. N. W. and S. S. E. By 9 a Clock at Night we had got a pretty good Offin; but the Wind still increasing, I took in my Main Top-sail, being able to carry no more Sail than two Courses and the Mizen. At 2 in the Morning, *Aug.* 3. it blew very hard, and the Sea was much raised; so that I furled all my Sails but my Main-sail. Tho' the Wind blew so hard, we had pretty clear Weather till Noon: But then the whole Sky was blackned with thick Clouds, and we had some Rain, which would last a Quarter of an Hour at a Time, and then it would blow very fierce while the Squalls of Rain were over our Heads; but as soon as they were gone the Wind was by much abated, the Stress of the Storm being over. We sounded several Times, but had no Ground till 8 a Clock *Aug.* the 4th in the Evening; and then had 60 Fathom-water, Coral-ground. At 10 we had 56 Fathom fine Sand. At 12 we had 55 Fathom, fine Sand, of a pale blueish Colour. It was now pretty moderate Weather; yet I made no Sail till Morning; but then, the Wind veering about to the S. W. I made Sail and stood to the North: And at 11 a Clock the next Day, *Aug.* 5. we saw Land again, at about 10 Leagues distance. This Noon we were in Lat. 25 deg. 30 min. and in the Afternoon our Cook died, an old Man, who had been sick a great while, being infirm before we came out of *England.*

The 6th of *August* in the Morning we saw an Opening in the Land, and we ran into it, and anchored in 7 and a half Fathom-water, 2 Miles from the Shore, clean Sand. It was somewhat difficult getting in here, by Reason of many Shoals we met with: But I sent my Boat sounding before me. The Mouth of this Sound, which I call'd

Shark's Bay, lies in about 25 deg. S. Lat. and our Reckoning made its Longitude from the C. of *Good Hope* to be about 87 Degrees; which is less by 195 Leagues than is usually laid down in our common Draughts, if our Reckoning was right, and our Glasses did not deceive us. As soon as I came to anchor in this Bay (of which I have given a Plan, Table IV. N°. 6.) I sent my Boat ashore to seek for fresh Water: But in the Evening my Men returned, having found none. The next Morning I went ashore, my self, carrying Pick-axes and Shovels with me, to dig for Water: and Axes to cut Wood. We tried in several Places for Water, but finding none after several Trials, nor in several Miles Compass, we left any farther Search for it, and spending the rest of the Day in cutting Wood, we went aboard at Night.

The Land is of an indifferent Heighth, so that it may be seen 9 or 10 Leagues off. It appears at a Distance very even; but as you come nigher you find there are many gentle Risings, tho' none steep nor high. 'Tis all a steep Shore against the open Sea: But in this Bay or Sound we were now in, the Land is low by the Sea-side, rising gradually in within the Land. The Mould is Sand by the Sea-side, producing a large Sort of Sampier, which bears a white Flower. Farther in, the Mould is reddish, a Sort of Sand producing some Grass, Plants, and Shrubs. The Grass grows in great Tufts, as big as a Bushel, here and there a Tuft: Being intermix'd with much Heath, much of the kind we have growing on our Commons in *England*. Of Trees or Shrubs here are divers Sorts; but none above 10 Foot high: There Bodies about 3 Foot about, and 5 or 6 Foot high before you come to the Branches, which are bushy and compos'd of small Twigs there spreading abroad, tho' thick set, and full of Leaves; which were mostly long and narrow. The

Colour of the Leaves was on one Side whitish, and on the other green; and the Bark of the Trees was generally of the same Colour with the Leaves, of a pale green. Some of these Trees were sweet-scented, and reddish within the Bark, like the Sassafras, but redder. Most of the Trees and Shrubs had at this Time either Blossoms or Berries on them. The Blossoms of the different Sort of Trees were of several Colours, as red, white, yellow, &c. but mostly blue: And these generally smelt very sweet and fragrant, as did some also of the rest. There were also beside some Plants, Herbs, and tall Flowers, some very small Flowers, growing on the Ground, that were sweet and beautiful, and for the most part unlike any I had seen elsewhere.

There were but few Land-Fowls; we saw none but Eagles, of the larger Sorts of Birds; but 5 or 6 Sorts of Small Birds. The biggest Sort of these were not bigger than Larks; some no bigger than Wrens, all singing with great Variety of fine shrill Notes; and we saw some of their Nests with young Ones in them. The Water-Fowls are Ducks, (which had young Ones now, this being the Beginning of the Spring in these Parts;) Curlews, Galdens, Crab-catchers, Cormorants, Gulls, Pelicans; and some Water-Fowl, such as I have not seen any where besides. I have given the Pictures of 4 several Birds on this Coast. [See *Birds:* Fig. 2, 3, 4, 5.]

The Land-Animals that we saw here were only a Sort of Raccoons, different from those of the *West-Indies*, chiefly as to their Legs; for these have very short Fore-Legs; but go jumping upon them as the others do, (and like them are very good Meat:) And a Sort of Guano's, of the same Shape and Size with other Guano's, describ'd [Vol. I. p. 48.] but differing from them in 3 remarkable Particulars: For these had a larger and uglier Head, and had no Tail: And at the Rump, instead of the

Tail there, they had a Stump of a Tail, which appear'd like another Head; but not really such, being without Mouth or Eyes: Yet this Creature seem'd by this Means to have a Head at each End; and, which may be reckon'd a fourth Difference, the Legs also seem'd all 4 of them to be Fore-legs, being all alike in Shape and Length, and seeming by the Joints and Bending to be made as if they were to go indifferently either Head or Tail foremost. They were speckled black and yellow like Toads, and had Scales or Knobs on their Backs like those of Crocodiles, plated on to the Skin, or stuck into it, as part of the Skin. They are very slow in Motion; and when a Man comes nigh them they will stand still and hiss, not endeavouring to get away. Their Livers are also spotted black and yellow: And the Body when opened hath a very unsavory Smell. I did never see such ugly Creatures any where but here. The Guano's I have observ'd to be very good Meat: And I have often eaten of them with Pleasure; but tho' I have eaten of Snakes, Crocodiles and Allegators, and many Creatures that look frightfully enough, and there are but few I should have been afraid to eat of, if prest by Hunger, yet I think my Stomach would scarce have serv'd to venture upon these *N. Holland* Guano's, both the Looks and the Smell of them being so offensive.

The Sea-fish that we saw here (for here was no River, Land or Pond of fresh Water to be seen) are chiefly Sharks. There are Abundance of them in this particular Sound, that I therefore give it the Name of *Shark*'s *Bay*. Here are also Skates, Thornbacks, and other Fish of the Ray-kind; (one Sort especially like the Sea-Devil) and Gar-fish, Boneta's, &c. Of Shell-fish we got here Muscles, Periwinkles, Limpits, Oysters, both of the Pearl-kind and also Eating-Oysters, as well the common Sort as

long Oysters; beside Cockles, &c. The Shore was lined
thick with many Sorts of very strange and beautiful
Shells, for Variety of Colour and Shape, most finely
spotted with Red, Black, or Yellow, &c. such as I have
not seen any where but at this Place. I brought away a
great many of them; but lost all except a very few, and
those not of the best.

There are also some green Turtle weighing about
200 *lb*. Of these we caught 2, which the Water Ebbing
had left behind a Ledge of Rock, which they could not
creep over. These served all my Company 2 Days; and
they were indifferent sweet Meat. Of the Sharks we
caught a great many, which our Men eat very savourily.
Among them we caught one which was 11 Foot long.
The Space between its 2 Eyes was 20 Inches, and 18
Inches from one Corner of his mouth to the other. Its
Maw was like a Leather Sack, very thick, and so tough
that a sharp Knife should scarce cut it: In which we
found the Head and Bones of a *Hippopotomus*; the hairy Lips
of which were still sound and not putrified, and the Jaw
was also firm, out of which we pluckt a great many
Teeth, 2 of them 8 Inches long, and as big as a Man's
Thumb, small at one End, and a little crooked; the rest
not above half so long. The Maw was full of Jelly, which
stank extremely: However I saved for a while the Teeth
and the Shark's Jaw: The Flesh of it was divided among
my Men; and they took Care that no Waste should be
made of it.

'Twas the 7th of *Aug*. when we came into *Shark*'s-Bay;
in which we anchor'd at 3 several Places, and stay'd at
the first of them (on the West-side of the Bay) till the 11th.
During which Time we searched about, as I said, for
fresh Water, digging Wells, but to no Purpose. However,
we cut good Store of Fire-wood at this first anchoring-

place; and my Company were all here very well re-
freshed with Raccoons, Turtle, Shark, and other Fish,
and some Fowls; so that we were now all much brisker
than when we came in hither. Yet still I was for standing
farther into the Bay, partly because I had a Mind to
increase my Stock of fresh Water, which was began to be
low; and partly for the sake of discovering this Part of the
Coast. I was invited to go further, by seeing from this
Anchoring-place all open before me; which therefore I
designed to search before I left the Bay. So on the 11th
about Noon, I steer'd farther in, with an easy Sail, because we had but shallow Water: We kept therefore good
looking out for Fear of Shoals; sometimes shortning,
sometimes deepning the Water. About 2 in the Afternoon we saw the Land a-Head that makes the S. of the
Bay, and before Night we had again Sholdings from that
Shore: And therefore shortned Sail and stood off and on
all Night, under 2 Topsails, continually sounding, having
never more than 10 Fathom, and seldom less than 7.
The Water deepned and sholdned so very gently, that in
heaving the Lead 5 or 6 Times we should scarce have a
Foot difference. When we came into 7 Fathom either way,
we presently went about. From this S. part of the Bay, we
could not see the Land from whence we came in the
Afternoon: And this Land we found to be an Island of 3
or 4 Leagues long, as is seen in the Plan, [Table IV. N°.
6.] but it appearing barren, I did not strive to go nearer
it; and the rather because the Winds would not permit us
to do it without much Trouble, and at the Openings the
Water was generally shoal. I therefore made no farther
Attempts in this S. W. and S. part of the Bay, but steered
away to the Eastward, to see if there was any Land that
Way, for as yet we had seen none there. On the 12th in
the Morning we pass'd by the N. Point of that Land and

were confirm'd in the Persuasion of its being an Island, by seeing an Opening to the East of it, as we had done on the W. Having fair Weather, a small Gale and smooth Water, we stood further on in the Bay, to see what Land was on the E. of it. Our Soundings at first were 7 Fathom, which held so a great while, but at length it decreas'd to 6. Then we saw the Land right a-head, that in the Plan makes the E. of the Bay. We could not come near it with the Ship, having but Shoal-water; and it being dangerous lying there, and the Land extraordinary low, very unlikely to have fresh Water (though it had a few Trees on it, seemingly Mangroves) and much of it probably covered at High-water, I stood out again that Afternoon, deepning the Water, and before Night anchored in 8 Fathom, clean white Sand, about the Middle of the Bay. The next Day we got up our Anchor; and that Afternoon came to an Anchor once more near 2 Islands, and a Shoal of Coral Rocks that face the Bay. Here I scrubb'd my Ship; and finding it very improbable I should get any thing further here, I made the best of my way out to Sea again, sounding all the way: but finding by the Shallowness of the Water that there was no going out to Sea to the East of the two Islands that face the Bay, nor between them, I return'd to the West Entrance, going out by the same way I came in at, only on the East instead of the West-side of the small Shoal to be seen in the Plan; In which Channel we had 10, 12, and 13 Fathom-water, still deepning upon us till we were out at Sea. The Day before we came out I sent a Boat ashore to the most Northerly of the 2 Islands, which is the least of them, catching many small Fish in the mean while with Hook and Line. The Boat's Crew returning, told me, that the Isle produces nothing but a Sort of green, short, hard, prickly Grass, affording neither Wood

nor fresh Water; and that a Sea broke between the 2 Islands,
a Sign that the Water was shallow. They saw a large Turtle,
and many Skates and Thornbacks, but caught none.

It was *August* the 14th when I sail'd out of this Bay or
Sound, the Mouth of which lies, as I said, in 25 deg. 5.
min. designing to coast along to the N. E. till I might
commodiously put in at some other part of *N. Holland.*
In passing out we saw 3 Water-Serpents swimming
about in the Sea, of a yellow Colour, spotted with dark
brown Spots. They were each about 4 Foot long, and
about the Bigness of a Man's Wrist, and were the first I
saw on this Coast, which abounds with several Sorts of
them. We had the Winds at our first coming out at N.
and the Land lying North-Easterly. We plied off and on,
getting forward but little till the next Day: when the
Wind coming at S. S. W. and S. we began to coast it
along the Shore to the Northward, keeping at 6 or 7
Leagues off Shore; and sounding often, we had between
40 and 46 Fathom-water, brown Sand, with some white
Shells. This 15th of *August* we were in Lat. 24 deg. 41
min. On the 16th Day at Noon we were in 23 deg. 22.
min. The Wind coming at E. by N. we could not keep
the Shore aboard, but were forc'd to go farther off, and
lost Sight of the Land. Then sounding we had no Ground
with 80 Fathom-line; however the Wind shortly after
came about again to the Southward, and then we jogg'd
on again to the Northward, and saw many small Dolphins
and Whales, and Abundance of Scuttle-shells swimming
on the Sea; and some Water-snakes every Day. The 17th
we saw the Land again, and took a Sight of it. [See Tab.
IV. N°. 7.]

The 18th in the Afternoon, being 3 or 4 Leagues off
Shore, I saw a Shoal-point, stretching from the Land
into the Sea, a League or more. The Sea broke high on

it; by which I saw plainly there was a Shoal there. I stood farther off, and coasted along Shore, to about 7 or 8 Leagues distance: And at 12 a Clock at Night we sounded, and had but 20 Fathom, hard Sand. By this I found I was upon another Shoal, and so presently steered off W. half an Hour, and had then 40 Fathom. At One in the Morning of the 18th Day we had 85 Fathom: By two we could find no Ground; and then I ventur'd to steer along Shore again, due N. which is two Points wide of the Coast (that lies N. N. E.) for fear of another Shoal. I would not be too far off from the Land, being desirous to search into it where-ever I should find an Opening or any Convenience of searching about for Water, &c. When we were off the Shoal-point I mention'd where we had but 20 Fathom-water, we had in the Night Abundance of Whales about the Ship, some a-head, others a-stern, and some on each side blowing and making a very dismal Noise; but when we came out again into deeper Water they left us. Indeed the Noise that they made by blowing and dashing of the Sea with their Tails, making it all of a Breach and Foam, was very dreadful to us, like the Breach of the Waves in very Shoal-water, or among Rocks. The Shoal these Whales were upon had Depth of Water sufficient, no less than 20 Fathom, as I said; and it lies in Lat. 22. deg. 22 min. The Shore was generally bold all along; we had met with no Shoal at Sea since the *Abrohlo*-shoal, when we first fell on the *N. Holland* Coast in the Lat. of 28. till Yesterday in the Afternoon, and this Night. This Morning also when we expected by the Draught we had with us to have been 11 Leagues off Shore, we were but 4; so that either our Draughts were faulty, which yet hitherto and afterwards we found true enough as to the lying of the Coast, or else here was a Tide unknown to us that de-

ceived us; tho' we had found very little of any Tide on
this Coast hitherto. As to our Winds in the Coasting
thus far, as we had been within the Verge of the general
Trade (tho' interrupted by the Storm I mention'd)
from the Lat. of 28, when we first fell in with the Coast:
And by that Time we were in the Lat. of 25. we had
usually the regular Trade-wind (which is here S. S. E.)
when we were at any Distance from Shore: But we had
often Sea and Land-Breezes, especially when near Shore,
and when in *Shark's-bay*; and had a particular N. West
Wind, or Storm, that set us in thither. On this 18th of
August we coasted with a brisk Gale of the true Trade-
wind at S. S. E. very fair and clear Weather; but haling
off in the Evening to Sea, were next Morning out of
Sight of Land; and the Land now trending away N.
Easterly, and we being to the Norward of it, and the
Wind also shrinking from the S. S. E. to the E. S. E.
(that is, from the true Trade-Wind to the Sea-breeze,
as the Land now lay) we could not get in with the Land
again yet a-while, so as to see it, tho' we trim'd sharp
and kept close on a Wind. We were this 19th day in Lat.
21 deg. 42 min. The 20th we were in Lat. 19 deg. 37
min. and kept close on a Wind to get Sight of the Land
again, but could not yet see it. We had very fair Weather;
and tho' we were so far from the Land as to be out of
Sight of it, yet we had the Sea and Land-Breezes. In the
Night we had the Land-Breeze at S. S. E. a small
gentle Gale; which in the Morning about Sun-rising
would shift about gradually (and withal increasing in
Strength) till about Noon we should have it at E. S. E.
which is the true Sea-breeze here. Then it would blow a
brisk Gale, so that we could scarce carry our Top-sails
double rift: And it would continue thus till 3 in the
Afternoon, when it would decrease again. The Weather

was fair all the while, not a Cloud to be seen; but very hazy, especially nigh the Horizon. We sounded several Times this 20th Day, and at first had no Ground; but had afterwards from 52 to 45 Fathom, coarse brown Sand, mixt with small brown and white Stones, with Dints besides in the Tallow.

The 21st Day also we had small Land-breezes in the Night, and Sea-breezes in the Day: And as we saw some Sea-snakes every Day, so this Day we saw a great many, of two different Sorts or Shapes. One Sort was yellow, and about the Bigness of a Man's Wrist, about 4 Foot long, having a flat Tail about 4 Fingers broad. The other Sort was much smaller and shorter, round and spotted black and yellow. This Day we sounded several Times, and had 45 Fathom Sand. We did not make the Land till Noon, and then saw it first from our Topmast-head. It bore S. E. by E. about 9 Leagues distance; and it appeared like a Cape or Head of Land. The Sea-breeze this Day was not so strong as the Day before, and it veered out more; so that we had a fair Wind to run in with to the Shore, and at Sunset anchored in 20 Fathom, clean Sand, about 5 Leagues from the bluff Point; which was not a Cape (as it appear'd at a great Distance) but the Eastermost End of an Island, about 5 or 6 Leagues in length, and 1 in breadth. There were 3 or 4 Rocky Islands about a League from us between us and the bluff Point; and we saw many other Islands both to the East and West of it, as far as we could see either way from our Topmast-head: And all within them to the S. there was nothing but Islands of a pretty Heighth, that may be seen 8 or 9 Leagues off. By what we saw of them they must have been a Range of Islands of about 20 Leagues in length, stretching from E. N. E. to W. S. W. and for ought I know, as far as to those of *Shark's-Bay*; and to a considerable Breadth also, (for we could see 9 or 10 Leagues in among them) towards the Continent or main Land of *N. Holland*, if there be any such Thing hereabouts: And by the great Tides I met with a while afterwards, more to the N. East, I had a strong Suspicion that here might be a kind of *Archipelago* of Islands, and a Passage possibly to the S. of *N. Holland* and *N. Guinea* into the great *S. Sea* Eastward; which I had Thoughts also of attempting in my Return from *N. Guinea* (had Circumstances permitted) and told my Officers so: But I would not attempt it at this Time, because we wanted Water, and could not depend upon finding it there. This Place is in the Lat. of 20 deg. 21 min. but in the Draught that I had of this Coast, which was *Tasman*'s, it was laid down in 19 deg. 50 min. and the Shore is laid down as all along joining in one Body or Continent, with some Openings appearing like Rivers; and not like Islands, as really they are. See several Sights of it, Table IV. N°. 8, 9, 10. This Place lies more Northerly by 40 min. than is laid down in Mr. *Tasman*'s Draught: And beside its being made a firm, continued Land, only with some Openings like the Mouths of Rivers, I found the Soundings also different from what the prick'd Line of his Course shews them, and generally shallower than he makes them; which inclines me to think that he came not so near the Shore as his Line shews, and so had deeper Soundings, and could not so well distinguish the Islands. His Meridian or Difference of Longitude from *Shark's-Bay* agrees well enough with my Account, which is 232 Leagues, tho' we differ in Lat. And to confirm my Conjecture that the Line of his Course is made too near the Shore, at least not far to the East of this Place, the Water is there so shallow that he could not come there so nigh.

But to proceed; in the Night we had a small Land-breeze, and in the Morning I weighed Anchor, designing to run in among the Islands, for they had large Channels between them, of a League wide at least, and some 2 or 3 Leagues wide. I sent in my Boat before to sound, and if they found Shoal-water to return again; but if they found Water enough, to go ashore on one of the Islands, and stay till the Ship came in: where they might in the mean Time search for Water. So we followed after with the Ship, sounding as we went in, and had 20 Fathom, till within 2 Leagues of the Bluff-head, and then we had shoal Water, and very uncertain Soundings: Yet we ran in still with an easy Sail, sounding and looking out well, for this was dangerous Work. When we came abreast of the Bluff-head, and about 2 Mile from it, we had but 7 Fathom: Then we edg'd away from it, but had no more Water; and running in a little farther, we had but 4 Fathoms; so we anchored immediately; and yet when we had veered out a third of a Cable we had 7 Fathom Water again; so uncertain was the Water. My Boat came immediately aboard, and told me that the Island was very rocky and dry, and they had little Hopes of finding Water there. I sent them to sound, and bad them, if they found a Channel of 8 or 10 Fathom Water, to keep on, and we would follow with the Ship. We were now about 4 Leagues within the outer small rocky Islands, but still could see nothing but Islands within us; some 5 or 6 Leagues long, others not above a Mile round. The large Islands were pretty high; but all appeared dry, and mostly rocky and barren. The Rocks look'd of a rusty yellow Colour, and therefore I despair'd of getting Water on any of them; but was in some Hopes of finding a Channel to run in beyond all these Islands, could I have spent Time here, and either get to the Main of *New*

Holland, or find out some other Islands that might afford us Water and other Refreshments; Besides, that among so many Islands, we might have found some Sort of rich Mineral, or Ambergreece, it being a good Latitude for both these. But we had not sailed above a League farther before our Water grew shoaler again, and then we anchored in 6 Fathom hard Sand.

We were now on the inner Side of the Island, on whose out-side is the Bluff-point. We rode a League from the Island, and I presently went ashore, and carried Shovels to dig for Water, but found none. There grow here 2 or 3 Sorts of Shrubs, one just like Rosemary; and therefore I called this *Rosemary* Island. It grew in great Plenty here, but had no Smell. Some of the other Shrubs had blue and yellow Flowers; and we found 2 Sorts of Grain like Beans: The one grew on Bushes; the other on a Sort of a creeping Vine that runs along on the Ground, having very thick broad Leaves, and the Blossom like a Bean Blossom, but much larger, and of a deep red Colour, looking very beautiful. We saw here some Cormorants, Gulls, Crabcatchers, &c. a few small Land-Birds, and a Sort of white Parrots, which flew a great many together. We found some Shell-fish, *viz.* Limpits, Perriwinkles, and Abundance of small Oysters growing on the Rocks, which were very sweet. In the Sea we saw some green Turtle, a pretty many Sharks, and Abundance of Water-Snakes of several Sorts and Sizes. The Stones were all of rusty Colour, and ponderous.

We saw a Smoak on an Island 3 or 4 Leagues off; and here also the Bushes had been burned, but we found no other Sign of Inhabitants: 'Twas probable that on the Island where the Smoak was there were Inhabitants, and fresh Water for them. In the Evening I went aboard, and consulted with my Officers whether it was best to send thither, or to search among any other of these Islands with my Boat; or else go from hence, and coast along Shore with the Ship, till we could find some better Place than this was to ride in, where we had shoal Water, and lay expos'd to Winds and Tides. They all agreed to go from hence; so I gave Orders to weigh in the Morning as soon as it should be light, and to get out with the Land-breeze.

Accordingly, *August* the 23rd, at 5 in the Morning we ran out, having a pretty fresh Land-breeze at S. S. E. By 8 a Clock we were got out, and very seasonably; for before 9 the Sea-breeze came on us very strong, and increasing, we took in our Top-sails and stood off under 2 Courses and a Mizen, this being as much Sail as we could carry. The Sky was clear, there being not one Cloud to be seen; but the Horizon appeared very hazy, and the Sun at setting the Night before, and this Morning at rising, appeared very red. The Wind continued very strong till 12, then it began to abate: I have seldom met with a stronger Breeze. These strong Sea-breezes lasted thus in their Turns 3 or 4 Days. They sprung up with the Sun-rise; by 9 a Clock they were very strong, and so continued till Noon, when they began to abate; and by Sunset there was little Wind, or a Calm till the Land-breezes came; which we should certainly have in the Morning about 1 or 2 a Clock. The Land-breezes were between the S. S. W. and S. S. E. The Sea-breezes between the E. N. E. and N. N. E. In the Night while Calm, we fish'd with Hook and Line, and caught good Store of Fish, *viz.* Snappers, Breams, Old-Wives and Dog-fish. When these last came we seldom caught any others; for if they did not drive away the other Fish, yet they would be sure to keep them from taking our Hooks, for they would first have them themselves, biting very greedily.

H

We caught also a Monk-fish, of which I brought Home the Picture. See *Fish, Fig.* I.

On the 25th of *August*, we still coasted along Shore, that we might the better see any Opening; kept sounding, and had about 20 Fathom clean Sand. The 26th Day, being about 4 Leagues off Shore, the Water began gradually to sholden from 20 to 14 Fathom. I was edging in a little towards the Land, thinking to have anchored; but presently after the Water decreas'd almost at once, till we had but 5 Fathom. I durst therefore adventure no farther, but steer'd out the same way that we came in; and in a short Time had 10 Fathom (being then about 4 Leagues and a half from the Shore) and even Soundings. I steer'd away E. N. E. coasting along as the Land lies. This Day the Sea-breezes began to be very moderate again, and we made the best of our way along Shore, only in the Night edging off a little for Fear of Sholes. Ever since we left *Shark's-Bay* we had fair clear Weather, and so for a great while still.

The 27th Day, we had 20 Fathom Water all Night, yet we could not see Land till 1 in the Afternoon from our Topmast-head. By 3 we could just discern Land from our Quarter-deck; we had then 16 Fathom. The Wind was at N. and we steer'd E. by N. which is but one Point in on the Land; yet we decreas'd our Water very fast; for at 4 we had but 9 Fathom; the next Cast but 7, which frighted us; and we then tackt instantly and stood off: But in a short Time the Wind coming at N. W. and W. N. W. we tackt again, and steer'd N. N. E. and then deepned our Water again, and had all Night from 15 to 20 Fathom.

The 28th Day we had between 20 and 40 Fathom. We saw no Land this Day, but saw a great many Snakes and some Whales. We saw also some *Boobies*, and

Noddy-birds; and in the Night caught one of these last. It was of another Shape and Colour than any I had seen before. It had a small long Bill, as all of them have, flat Feet like Ducks Feet; its Tail forked like a *Swallow*, but longer and broader, and the Fork deeper than that of the *Swallow*, with very long Wings; the Top or Crown of the Head of this *Noddy* was Coal-black, having also small black Streaks round about and close to the Eyes; and round these Streaks on each Side, a pretty broad white Circle. The Breast, Belly, and under-part of the Wings of this *Noddy* were white; and the Back and upper-part of its Wings of a faint black or smoak Colour. See a Picture of this, and of the common one, *Birds, Fig.* 5, 6. *Noddies* are seen in most Places between the *Tropicks*, as well in the *East-Indies*, and on the Coast of *Brazil*, as in the *West-Indies*. They rest ashore a Nights, and therefore we never see them far at Sea, not above 20 or 30 Leagues, unless driven off in a Storm. When they come about a Ship they commonly perch in the Night, and will sit still till they are taken by the Sea-men. They build on Cliffs against the Sea, or Rocks, as I have said [Vol. I. p. 45.].

The 30th day, being in Lat. 18 deg. 21 min. we made the Land again, and saw many great Smokes near the Shore; and having fair Weather and moderate Breezes, I steer'd in towards it. At 4 in the Afternoon I anchor'd in 8 Fathom Water, clear Sand, about 3 Leagues and a half from the Shore. I presently sent my Boat to sound nearer in, and they found 10 Fathom about a Mile farther in; and from thence still farther in the Water decreased gradually to 9, 8, 7, and at 2 Mile distance to 6 Fathom. This Evening we saw an Eclipse of the Moon, but it was abating before the Moon appear'd to us; for the Horizon was very hazy, so that we could not see the Moon till she had been half an Hour above the Horizon: And at 2 hours, 22 min. after Sun-set, by the Reckoning of our Glasses, the Eclipse was quite gone, which was not of many Digits. The Moon's Center was then 33 deg. 40 min. high.

The 31st of *August* betimes in the Morning I went ashore with 10 or 11 Men to search for Water. We went armed with Muskets and Cutlasses for our defence, expecting to see people there; and carried also Shovels and Pickaxes to dig Wells. When we came near the Shore we saw 3 tall black naked Men on the sandy Bay a-head of us: But as we row'd in, they went away. When we were landed, I sent the Boat with two Men in her to lie a little from the Shore at an Anchor, to prevent being seiz'd; while the rest of us went after the 3 black Men, who were now got on the top of a small Hill about a quarter of a Mile from us, with 8 or 9 Men more in their Company. They seeing us coming, ran away. When we came on the top of the Hill where they first stood, we saw a plain Savannah, about half a Mile from us, farther in from the Sea. There were several Things like Hay-cocks, standing in the Savannah; which at a distance we thought were Houses, looking just like the *Hottentot*'s Houses at the *Cape of G. Hope:* but we found them to be so many Rocks. We searched about these for Water, but could find none, nor any Houses; nor People, for they were all gone, Then we turned again to the Place where we landed, and there we dug for Water.

While we were at work there came 9 or 10 of the Natives to a small Hill a little way from us, and stood there menacing and threatning of us, and making a great Noise. At last one of them came towards us, and the rest followed at a distance. I went out to meet him, and came within 50 Yards of him, making to him all the

Signs of Peace and Friendship I could; but then he ran away, neither would they any of them stay for us to come nigh them; for we tried two or three Times. At last I took two Men with me, and went in the Afternoon along by the Sea-side, purposely to catch one of them, if I could, of whom I might learn where they got their fresh Water. There were 10 or 12 of the Natives a little way off, who seeing us three going away from the rest of our Men, followed us at a distance. I thought they would follow us: But there being for a while a Sand-bank between us and them, that they could not then see us, we made a halt, and hid our selves in a bending of the Sand-bank. They knew we must be thereabouts, and being 3 or 4 times our Number, thought to seize us. So they dispers'd themselves, some going to the Seashore, and others beating about the Sand-hills. We knew by what Rencounter we had had with them in the Morning that we could easily out-run them; So a nimble young Man that was with me, seeing some of them near, ran towards them; and they for some time, ran away before him. But he soon over-taking them, they faced about and fought him. He had a Cutlass, and they had wooden Lances; with which, being many of them, they were too hard for him. When he first ran towards them I chas'd two more that were by the Shore; But fearing how it might be with my young Man, I turn'd back quickly, and went up to the top of a Sandhill, whence I saw him near me, closely engag'd with them. Upon their seeing me, one of them threw a Lance at me, that narrowly miss'd me. I discharg'd my Gun to scare them, but avoided shooting any of them; till finding the young Man in great danger from them, and my self in some; and that tho' the Gun had a little frighted them at first, yet they had soon learnt to despise it, tossing up their Hands, and crying *Pooh, Pooh, Pooh*; and coming on afresh with a great Noise, I thought it high time to charge again, and shoot one of them, which I did. The rest, seeing him fall, made a stand again; and my young Man took the Opportunity to disengage himself, and come off to me; my other Man also was with me, who had done nothing all this while, having come out unarm'd; and I return'd back with my Men, designing to attempt the Natives no farther, being very sorry for what had happened already. They took up their wounded Companion; and my young Man, who had been struck through the Cheek by one of their Lances, was afraid it had been poison'd: But I did not think that likely. His Wound was very painful to him, being made with a blunt Weapon: But he soon recover'd of it.

Among the *N. Hollanders*, whom we were thus engag'd with, there was one who by his Appearance and Carriage, as well in the Morning as this Afternoon, seem'd to be the Chief of them, and a kind of Prince or Captain among them. He was a young brisk Man, not very tall, nor so personable as some of the rest, tho' more active and couragious: He was painted (which none of the rest were at all) with a Circle of white Paste or Pigment (a sort of Lime, as we thought) about his Eyes, and a white streak down his Nose from his Forehead to the tip of it. And his Breast and some part of his Arms were also made white with the same Paint; not for Beauty or Ornament, one would think, but as some wild *Indian* Warriors are said to do, he seem'd thereby to design the looking more Terrible; this his Painting adding very much to his natural Deformity; for they all of them have the most unpleasant Looks and the worst Features of any People that ever I saw, tho' I have seen great variety of Savages. These *New-Hollanders* were probably the same

sort of People as those I met with on this Coast in my
Voyage round the World; [See Vol. I. p. 311 etc.] for the
Place I then touched at was not above 40 or 50 Leagues
to the N. E. of this: And these were much the same
blinking Creatures (here being also abundance of
the same kind of Flesh-flies teizing them) and with the
same black Skins, and Hair frizled, tall and thin, &c.
as those were: But we had not the Opportunity to see
whether these, as the former, wanted two of their Fore-
Teeth.

We saw a great many places where they had made
Fires; and where there were commonly 3 or 4 Boughs
stuck up to Windward of them; for the Wind (which is the
Sea-breeze) in the day-time blows always one way with
them; and the Land-breeze is but small. By their Fire-
places we should always find great heaps of Fish-shells, of
several sorts; and 'tis probable that these poor Creatures
here lived chiefly on the Shell-fish, as those I before
describ'd did on small Fish, which they caught in Wires
or Holes in the Sand at Low-water. These gather'd
their Shell-fish on the Rocks at Low-water; but had no
Wires (that we saw) whereby to get any other sorts of
Fish: As among the former I saw not any heaps of
Shells as here, though I know they also gather'd some
Shell-fish. The Lances also of those were such as these
had; however they being upon an Island, with their
Women and Children, and all in our Power, they did not
there use them against us, as here on the Continent,
where we saw none but some of the Men under Head,
who come out purposely to observe us. We saw no
Houses at either Place; and I believe they have none,
since the former People on the Island had none, tho' they
had all their Families with them.

Upon returning to my Men I saw that tho' they had

dug 8 or 9 Foot deep, yet found no Water. So I returned aboard that Evening, and the next day being *September* 1st, I sent my Boatswain ashore to dig deeper, and sent the Sain with him to catch Fish. While I staid aboard I observed the flowing of the Tide, which runs very swift here, so that our Nun-buoy would not bear above the Water to be seen. It flows here (as on that part of *N. Holland* I described formerly) about 5 Fathom: And here the Flood runs S. E. by S. till the last Quarter; then it sets right in towards the Shore (which lies here S. S. W. and N. N. E.) and the Ebb runs N. W. by N. When the Tides slackned we fish'd with Hook and Line, as we had already done in several Places on this Coast; on which in this Voyage hitherto, we had found but little Tides: But by the Heighth, and Strength, and Course of them hereabouts, it should seem that if there be such a Passage or Streight going through Eastward to the Great *South-Sea*, as I said one might suspect, one would expect to find the Mouth of it somewhere between this Place and *Rosemary* Island, which was the part of *New Holland* I came last from.

Next Morning my Men came aboard and brought a Rundlet of brackish Water which they got out of another Well that they dug in a Place a mile off, and about half as far from the Shore; but this Water was not fit to drink. However we all concluded that it would serve to boil our Oatmeal, for Burgoo, whereby we might save the Remains of our other Water for drinking, till we should get more; and accordingly the next Day we brought aboard 4 Hogsheads of it: But while we were at work about the Well we were sadly pester'd with the Flies, which were more troublesome to us than the Sun, tho' it shone clear and strong upon us all the while, very hot. All this while we saw no more of the Natives, but saw some of the Smoaks of some of their Fires at 2 or 3 miles distance.

The Land hereabouts was much like the part of *New Holland* that I formerly described [Vol. I. p. 311.] 'tis low, but seemingly barricado'd with a long Chain of Sand-hills to the Sea, that let's nothing be seen of what is farther within Land. At high Water the Tides rising so high as they do, the Coast shews very low; but when 'tis low Water it seems to be of an indifferent heighth. At low Water-mark the Shore is all Rocky, so that then there is no Landing with a Boat: but at high Water a Boat may come in over those Rocks to the Sandy Bay, which runs all along on this Coast. The Land by the Sea for about 5 or 600 yards is a dry Sandy Soil, bearing only Shrubs and Bushes of divers sorts. Some of these had them at this time of the Year, yellow Flowers or Blossoms, some blue, and some white; most of them of a very fragrant Smell. Some had Fruit like Peascods; in each of which there were just ten small Peas; I opened many of them, and found no more nor less. There are also here some of that sort of Bean which I saw at *Rosemary*-Island: And another sort of small, red, hard Pulse, growing in Cods also, with little black Eyes like Beans. I know not their Names, but have seen them used often in the *East-Indies* for weighing Gold; and they make the same use of them at *Guinea*, as I have heard, where the Women also make Bracelets with them to wear about their Arms. These grow on Bushes; but here are also a Fruit like Beans growing on a creeping sort of Shrub-like Vine. There was great plenty of all these sorts of Cod-fruit growing on the Sand-hills by the Sea-side, some of them green, some ripe, and some fallen on the Ground: But I could not perceive that any of them had been gathered by the Natives;

and might not probably be wholesome Food.

The Land farther in, that is lower than what borders on the Sea, was so much as we saw of it, very plain and even; partly Savannahs, and partly Woodland. The Savannahs bear a sort of thin coarse Grass. The Mould is also a coarser Sand than that by the Sea-side, and in some places 'tis Clay. Here are a great many Rocks in the large Savannah we were in, which are 5 or 6 Foot high, and round at top like a Hay-cock, very remarkable; some red, and some white. The Woodland lies farther in still; where there were divers sorts of small Trees, scarce any three Foot in circumference; their Bodies 12 or 14 Foot high, with a Head of small Knibs or Boughs. By the sides of the Creeks, especially nigh the Sea, there grow a few small black Mangrove-Trees.

There are but few Land-Animals. I saw some Lizards; and my Men saw two or three Beasts like hungry Wolves, lean like so many Skeletons, being nothing but Skin and Bones: 'Tis probable that it was the Foot of one of those Beasts that I mention'd as seen by us in *N. Holland*, [Vol. I. p. 312.] We saw a Rackoon or two, and one small speckled Snake.

The Land-fowls that we saw here were Crows (just such as ours in *England*) small Hawks, and Kites; a few of each sort: But here are plenty of small Turtle-Doves, that are plump, fat and very good Meat. Here are 2 or 3 sorts of smaller Birds, some as big as Larks, some less; but not many of either sort. The Sea-Fowl are Pelicans, Boobies, Noddies, Curlews, Sea-pies, &c. and but few of these neither.

The Sea is plentifully stock'd with the largest Whales that I ever saw; but not to compare with the vast ones of the *Northern* Seas. We saw also a great many Green Turtle, but caught none; here being no place to set a Turtle-Net

F. 3.

A Noddy. of N. Holland.

F. 5.

The head & greatest part
of ÿ neck of this bird is
red, & therein differs from
the Avosetta of Italy.

A Comon Noddy.

F. 6.

F. 4

The Bill & Leggs of this Bird are of a Bright Red.

in; here being no Channel for them, and the Tides running so strong. We saw some Sharks, and Parracoots; and with Hooks and Lines we caught some Rock-fish and Old-Wives. Of Shell-fish, here were Oysters both of the common kind for Eating, and of the Pearl kind: And also Wilks, Conchs, Muscles, Limpits, Perriwinkles, &c. and I gather'd a few strange Shells; chiefly a sort not large, and thick-set all about with Rays or Spikes growing in Rows.

And thus having ranged about, a considerable time, upon this Coast, without finding any good fresh Water, or any convenient Place to clean the Ship, as I had hop'd for: And it being moreover the heighth of the dry Season, and my Men growing Scorbutick for want of Refresh-ments, so that I had little incouragement to search further; I resolved to leave this Coast, and accordingly in the beginning of *September* set sail towards *Timor*.

An Account of Several Plants

Collected in

Brazil, New Holland, Timor, and *New Guinea,* referring to the Figures Engraven on the Copper Plates.

TAB 1. Fig. 1. *Cotton-flower* from *Baya* in *Brazil.* The Flower consists of a great many Filaments, almost as small as Hairs, betwixt three and four Inches long, of a Murrey-colour; on the Top of them stand small ash-colour'd *Apices.* The Pedicule of the Flower is inclos'd at the Bottom with 5 narrow stiff Leaves, about 6 Inches long. There is one of this *Genus* in Mr. *Ray*'s Supplement, which agrees exactly with this in every Respect, only that is twice larger at the least. It was sent from *Surinam* by the Name of *Momoo.*

Tab. 1. Fig. 2. *Jasminum Brasilianum luteum, mali limoniæ folio nervoso, petalis crassis.*

Tab. 1. Fig. 3. *Crista Pavonis Brasiliana Bardanæ foliis.* The Leaves are very tender and like the top Leaves of *Bardana major,* both as to Shape and Texture: In the Figure they are represented too stiff and too much serrated.

Tab. 1. Fig. 4. *Filix Brasiliana Osmundæ minori serrato folio.* This fern is of that Kind, which bears its Seed-Vessels in Lines on the Edge of the Leaves.

Tab. 2. Fig. 1. *Rapuntium Novæ Hollandiæ, flore magno coccineo.* The *Perianthium* compos'd of five long-pointed Parts, the Form of the Seed-Vessel and the Smallness of the Seeds, together with the irregular Shape of the Flower and Thinness of the Leaves, argue this Plant to be a *Rapuntium.*

Plants found in New Holland.

Tab. 2. Fig. 2. *Fucus foliis capillaceis brevissimis, vesiculis minimis donatis.* This elegant *Fucus* is of the *Erica Marina* or *Sargazo* kind, but has much finer Parts than that. It was collected on this Coast of *New Holland*.

Tab. 2. Fig. 2. *Ricinoides Novæ Hollandiæ anguloso crasso folio.* This Plant is shrubby, has thick woolly Leaves, especially on the under side. Its Fruit is tricoccous, hoary on the out-side with a *Calix* divided into 5 Parts. It comes near *Ricini fructu parvo frucosa Curassavica, folio Phylli, P. B. pr.*

Tab. 2. Fig. 2. *Solanum spinosum Novæ Hollandiæ Phylli foliis subrotundis.* This new *Solanum* bears a blueish Flower like the others of the same Tribe; the Leaves are of a whitish Colour, thick and woolly on both Sides, scarce an Inch long and near as broad. The Thorns are very sharp and thick set, of a deep Orange colour, especially towards the Points.

Tab. 3. Fig. 1. *Scabiosa (forte) Novæ Hollandiæ, statices foliis subtus argenteis.* The Flower stands on a Foot-stalk 4 Inches long, included in a rough Calix of a yellowish Colour. The Leaves are not above an Inch long, very narrow like *Thrift*, green on the upper and hoary on the under side, growing in Tufts. Whether this Plant be a *Scabious, Thrift* or *Helichrysum* is hard to judge from the imperfect Flower of the dry'd Specimen.

Tab. 3. Fig. 2. *Alcea Novæ Hollandiæ foliis augustis utrinque villosis.* The Leaves, Stalk, and under side of the Perianthium of this Plant are all woolly. The Petala are very tender, 5 in Number, scarce so large as the Calix: In the middle stands a *Columella* thick set with thrummy *apiculæ*, which argue this Plant to belong to the Malvaceous Kind.

Tab. 3. Fig. 3. Of what *Genus* this Shrub or Tree is, is uncertain, agreeing with none yet described, as far as

can be judg'd by the State it is in. It has a very beautiful
Flower, of a red Colour, as far as can be guess'd by the
dry *Specimen*, consisting of 10 large *Petala*, hoary on both
Sides, especially underneath; the Middle of the Flower is
thick set with *Stamina*, which are woolly at the Bottom,
the Length of the *Petala*, each of them crown'd with its
Apex. The *Calix* is divided into 5 round pointed Parts.
The Leaves are like those of *Amelanchier Lob.* green at Top
and very woolly underneath, not running to a Point, as
is common in others, but with an Indenture, at the
upper-end.

Tab. 3. Fig. 4. *Dammara ax Nova-Hollandia, Sanamundæ
secundæ Chysii foliis.* This new *Genus* was first sent from
Amboyna by Mr. *Rumphius*, by the Name of *Dammara*, of
which he transmitted 2 Kinds; one with narrow and long
stiff Leaves, the other with shorter and broader. The first
of them is mention'd in Mr. *Petiver*'s *Centuria*, p. 350. by
the Name of *Arbor Hortensis Javanorum foliis visce augu-
stioribus aromaticis floribus, spicatis flamineis lutescentibus;*
Mus. Pet. As also in Mr. *Ray*'s Supplement to his History
of Plants now in the Press. This is of the fame *Genus*
with them, agreeing both in Flower and Fruit, tho' very
much differing in Leaves. The Flowers are stamineous
and seem to be of an herbaceous Colour, growing among
the Leaves, which are short and almost round, very stiff
and ribb'd on the under side, of a dark Green above, and
a Pale Colour underneath, thick set on by Pairs, answering one another crossways, so that they cover the Stalk.
The Fruit is as big as a Pepper-corn, almost round, of a
whitish Colour, dry and tough, with a Hole on the Top,
containing small Seeds. Any one that sees this Plant
without its Seed-Vessels, would take it for an *Erica* or
Sanamunda. The Leaves of this Plant are of a very aroma-
tick Taste.

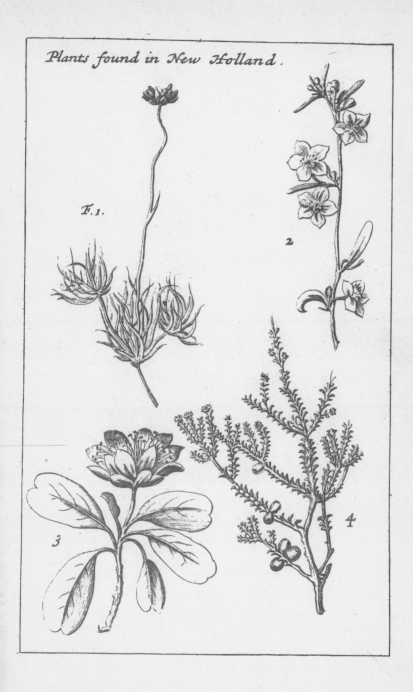

Plants found in New Holland.

F.1.

2

3

4

Tab. 4. Fig. 1. *Equisetum Novæ Hollandiæ frutesceus foliis longissimis.* 'Tis doubtful whether this be an *Equisetum* or not; the Textures of the Leaves agrees best with that *Genus* of any, being articulated one within another at each Joint, which is only proper to this Tribe. The longest of them are about 9 Inches.

Tab. 4. Fig. 2. *Colutea Novæ Hollandiæ floribus amplis coccineis, umbellatim dispositis macula purpurea notatis.* There being no Leaves to this Plant, 'tis hard to say what *Genus* it properly belongs to. The Flowers are very like to the *Colutea Barbæ Jovis folio flore coccineo Breynii*; of the same Scarlet Colour, with a large deep Purple Spot in the *Vexillum*, but much bigger, coming all from the same Point after the Manner of an Umbel. The Rudiment of the Pod is very woolly, and terminates in a Filament near 2 Inches long.

Tab. 4. Fig. 3. *Conyza Novæ Hollandiæ angustis Rorismarini foliis.* This Plant is very much branch'd and seems to be woody. The Flowers stand on very short Pedicules, arising from the *Sinus* of the Leaves, which are exactly like *Rosemary*, only less. It tastes very bitter now dry.

Tab. 4. Fig. 4. *Mohoh Insulæ Timor.* This is a very odd Plant, agreeing with no describ'd *Genus*. The Leaf is almost round, green on the upper side and whitish underneath, with several Fibres running from the Insertion of the Pedicule towards the Circumference 'tis umbilicated as *Cotyledon aquatica* and *Faba Ægyptia.* The Flowers are white, standing on single Foot-stalks, of the Shape of a *Stramonium*, but divided into 4 Points only, as is the *Perianthium.*

Tab. 5. Fig. 1. *Fucus ex Nova Guinea uva marina dictus, foliis variis.* This beautiful *Fucus* is thick set with very small short Tufts of Leaves, which by the Help of a magnifying Glass, seem to be round and articulated, as if they were Seed-Vessels; besides these, there are other broad Leaves, chiefly at the Extremity of the Branches, serrated on the Edges. The *Vesiculæ* are round, of the Bigness express'd in the Figure.

Tab. 5. Fig. 2. *Fucus ex Nova Guinea Fluviatilis Pisanæ J. B. foliis.* These Plants are so apt to vary in their Leaves, according to their different States, that 'tis hard to say this is distinct from the last. It has in several Places (not all express'd in the Figure) some of the small short Leaves, or Seed-Vessels mention'd in the former; which makes me apt to believe it the same, gather'd in a different State; besides the broad Leaves of that and this agree as to their Shape and Indentures.

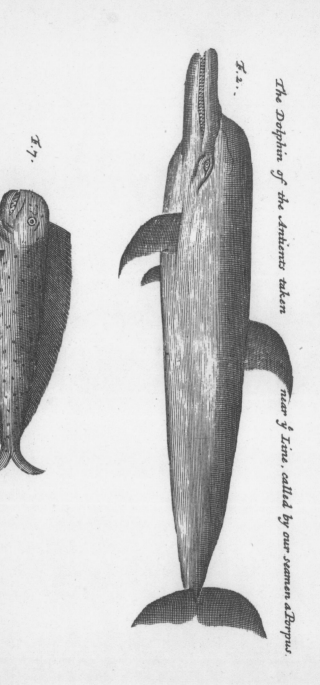

The Dolphin of the Antients taken near y̆ Line, called by our seamen a Porpus.

F. 2.

F. 7.

A Dolphin as it is usually called by our seamen, taken in the open Sea.

A Fish of the Tunng kind taken on y̆ Coast of N. Holland

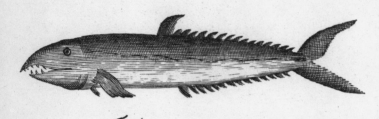

F. 5.

A Fish called by the seamen the Old Wife

F. 4.

An Account of some FISHES *that are figured in* Plate 2 *and* 3.

See Plate 3. Fig. 5.

THIS is a Fish of the Tunny-kind, and agrees well enough with the Figure in Tab. 3. of the Appendix to Mr. *Willughby*'s History of Fishes under the Name of *Gurabuca*; it differs something, in the Fins especially, from *Piso*'s Figure of the *Guarapucu*.

See Plate 3. Figure 4.

This resembles the Figure of the *Guaperva maxima candata* in *Willughby*'s *Ichthyol.* Tab. 9. 23. and the *Guaparva* of *Piso*, but does not answer their Figures in every particular.

See Plate 2. Figure 2.

There are 2 Sorts of *Porpusses:* The one the long-snouted *Porpuss*, as the Seamen call it; and this is the *Dolphin* of the *Greeks*. The other is the Bottle-nose *Porpuss*, which is generally thought to be the *Phæcena* of *Aristotle*.

See Plate 2. Figure 7.

This is the *Guaracapema* of *Piso* and *Marcgrave*, by others called the *Dorado*. 'Tis figured in *Willughby*'s *Ichthyol.* Tab. O. 2. under the Name of *Delphin Belgis*.

A Fish taken on the Coast of New Holland

F.3.

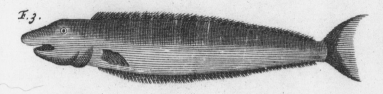

A Cuttle taken near N. Holland.

F.8.

The Monk Fish.

F.1.

A Flying Fish taken:
in ye open Sea

F.9.

F.6.

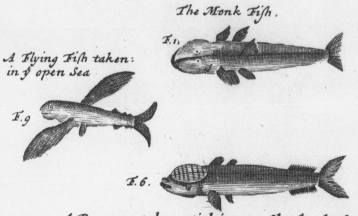

A Remora taken sticking to Sharks backs.

A
CONTINUATION
OF A
VOYAGE
TO
NEW-HOLLAND, &c.
In the YEAR 1699.

Wherein are defcribed,

The Iflands *Timor*, *Rotee* and *Anabao*. A Paffage between the Iflands *Timor* and *Anabao*. *Copang* and *Laphao* Bays. The Iflands *Omba*, *Fetter*, *Bande* and *Bird*. A Defcription of the Coaft of *New-Guinea*. The Iflands *Pulo Sabuda*, *Cockle*, King *William*'s, *Providence*, *Garret Dennis*, *Ant. Cave*'s and St. *John*'s. Alfo a new Paffage between *N. Guinea* and *Nova Britannia*. The Iflands *Ceram*, *Bonao*, *Bouro*, and feveral Iflands before unknown. The Coaft of *Java*, and Streights of *Sunda*. Author's Arrival at *Batavia*, *Cape of Good Hope*, St. *Helens*, *I. Afcenfion*, &c. Their Inhabitants, Cuftoms, Trade, &c. Harbours, Soil, Birds, Fifh, &c. Trees, Plants, Fruits, &c.

Illuftrated with MAPS and DRAUGHTS: Alfo divers Birds, Fifhes, &c. not found in this Part of the World, Ingraven on Eighteen Copper-Plates.

By Captain WILLIAM DAMPIER.

LONDON,

Printed for JAMES *and* JOHN KNAPTON, at the *Crown* in St. *Paul*'s Church-Yard. MDCCXXIX.

PART II

THE CONTENTS

CHAP. I

THE A.'s *Departure from the Coast of* New Holland, *with the Reasons of it. Water Snakes. The A.'s Arrival at the Island* Timor. *Search for fresh Water on the South-side of the Island, in vain, Fault of the Charts. The Island* Rotee. *A Passage between the Islands* Timor *and* Anabao. *Fault of the Charts. A Dutch Fort, called* Concordia. *Their Suspicion of the A. The Island* Anabao *described. The A.'s Parly with the Governour of the Dutch Fort. They, with great Difficulty, obtain leave to water.* Copang *Bay. Coasting along the North-side of* Timor. *They find Water and an Anchoring-place. A Description of a small Island, seven Leagues East from the Watering Bay.* Laphao *Bay. How the* A. *was treated by the* Portugueze *there. Designs of making further Searches upon and about the Island. Port* Sesial. *Return to* Babao *in* Copang *Bay. The A.'s Entertainment at the Fort of* Concordia. *His Stay seven Weeks at* Babao.

CHAP. II

A particular Description of the Island Timor. *Its Coast. The Island* Anabao. *Fault of the Draughts. The Channel between* Timor *and* Anabao. Copang-*bay. Fort* Concordia. *A particular Description of the Bay. The Anchoring-place, called* Babao. *The Malayans here kill all the Europeans they can.* Laphao, *a Portugueze Settlement described. Port* Ciccale. *The Hills, Water, Low-lands, Soil, Woods, Metals, in the Island* Timor. *Its Trees.* Cana fistula-*tree described.*

Wild Fig-trees described. Two new Sorts of Palm-trees described. The Fruits of the Island. The Herbs. Its Land Animals. Fowls. The Ringing Bird. Its Fish. Cockle-merchants and Oysters. Cockles as big as a Man's Head. Its original Natives described. The Portugueze and Dutch Settlements. The Malayan Language generally spoken here. L' Orantuca on the Island Ende. The Seasons, Winds, and Weather at Timor.

CHAP. III

Departure from Timor. The Islands Omba and Fetter. A burning Island. Their missing the Turtle-Isles. Bande-Isles. Bird-Island. They descry the Coast of New-Guinea. They anchor on the Coast of New-Guinea. A Description of the Place, and of a strange Fowl found there. Great Quantities of Mackerel. A white Island. They anchor at an Island called by the Inhabitants Pulo Sabuda. A Description of it and its Inhabitants and Product. The Indians manner of Fishing there. Arrival at Mabo, the North West Cape of New-Guinea. A Description of it. Cockle-Island. Cockles of seventy-eight Pound Weight. Pidgeon-Island. The Wind hereabouts. An empty Cockle-shell weighing two hundred fifty-eight Pound. King William's Island. A Description of it. Plying on the Coast of New-Guinea. Fault of the Draughts. Providence Island. They cross the Line. A Snake pursued by Fish. Squally Island. The Main of New-Guinea.

CHAP. IV

The main Land of New-Guinea. Its Inhabitants. Slingers Bay. Small Islands. Garret Dennis Isle described. Its Inhabitants. Their Proes. Anthony Cave's Island. Its Inhabitants. Trees full of Worms found in the Sea. St. John's

Island. The main Land of New-Guinea. *Its Inhabitants. The Coast described. Cape and Bay St.* George. *Cape* Orford. *Another Bay. The Inhabitants there. A large Account of the Author's Attempts to trade with them. He names the Place Port* Mountague. *The Country thereabouts described, and its Produce. A Burning Island described. A new Passage found.* Nova Britannia. *Sir* George Rook's *Island. Long Island and* Crown *Island, discovered and described. Sir R.* Rich's *Island. A Burning Island. A strange Spout. A Conjecture concerning a new Passage Southward.* King William's *Island. Strange Whirlpools. Distance between Cape* Mabo *and Cape* St. George *computed.*

CHAP. V

The A.'s *Return from the Coast of* New-Guinea. *A deep Channel. Strange Tides. The Island* Ceram *described. Strange Fowls. The Islands* Bonao, Bouro, Misacombi, Pentare, Laubana, *and* Potoro. *The Passage between* Pentare *and* Laubana. *The Island* Timor. Babao *Bay. The Island* Rotee. *More Islands than are commonly laid down in the Draughts. Great Currents. Whales. Coast of* New-Holland. *The* Tryal-Rocks. *The Coast of* Java. Princes Isle. *Streights of* Sunda. Thwart-the-way *Island. Indian Proes, and their Traffick. Passage through the Streight. Arrival at* Batavia.

CHAP. VI

The A. *continues in* Batavia-*Road to refit, and to get Provisions.* English *Ships then in the Road. Departure from* Batavia. *Touch at the* Cape of Good Hope. *And at St.* Helena. *Arrival at the Island of* Ascension. *A Leak Sprung. Which being impossible to be stopped, the Ship is lost, but the Men saved. They find Water upon the Island: And are brought back to* England.

CHAP. I

The A.'s Departure from the Coast of New Holland, *with the Reasons of it. Water-Snakes. The A.'s Arrival at the Island* Timor. *Search for fresh Water on the South-side of the Island, in vain. Fault of the Charts. The Island* Rotee. *A Passage between the Islands* Timor *and* Anabao. *Fault of the Charts. A Dutch Fort, called* Concordia. *Their Suspicion of the A. The Island* Anabao *described. The A.'s Parly with the Governour of the Dutch Fort. They, with great Difficulty, obtain Leave to water.* Copang *Bay. Coasting along the North-side of* Timor. *They find Water and an Anchoring place. A Description of a small Island, seven Leagues East from the Watering Bay.* Laphao *Bay. How the A. was treated by the* Portugueze *there. Designs of making further Searches upon and about the Island. Port* Sesial. *Return to* Babao *in* Copang *Bay. The A.'s Entertainment at the Fort of* Concordia. *His Stay seven Weeks at* Babao.

I HAD spent about 5 Weeks in ranging off and on the Coast of *New-Holland*, a Length of about 300 Leagues: and had put in at 3 several Places, to see what there might be thereabouts worth discovering; and at the same Time to recruit my Stock of fresh Water and Provisions for the further Discoveries I purposed to attempt on the *Terra Australis*. This large and hitherto almost unknown Tract of Land is situated so very advantageously in the richest Climates of the World, the *Torrid* and *Temperate Zones*; having in it especially all the Advantages of the *Torrid Zone*, as being known to reach from the *Equator* it self (within a Degree) to the *Tropick* of *Capricorn*, and beyond it; that in coasting round it, which I design'd by this Voyage, if possible: I could not but hope to meet with some fruitful Lands, Continent or Islands, or both, productive of any of the rich Fruits, Drugs, or Spices, (perhaps Minerals also, &c.) that are in the other Parts of the *Torrid Zone*, under equal Parallels of Latitude; at least a Soil and Air capable of such, upon transplanting them hither, and Cultivation. I meant also to make as diligent a Survey as I could, of the several smaller Islands, Shores, Capes, Bays, Creeks, and Harbours, fit as well for Shelter as Defence, upon fortifying them; and of the Rocks and Shoals, the Soundings, Tides, and Currents, Winds and Weather, Variation, &c. Whatever might be beneficial for Navigation, Trade or Settlement; or be of use to any who should prosecute the same Designs hereafter; to whom it might be serviceable to have so much of their Work done to their Hands; which they might advance and perfect by their own repeated Experiences. As there is no Work of this Kind brought to Perfection at once, I intended especially to observe what Inhabitants I should meet with, and to try to win them over to somewhat of Traffick and useful Intercourse, as there might be Commodities among any of them that might be fit for Trade or Manufacture, or any found in which they might be employed. Though as to the *New Hollanders* hereabouts, by the Experience I had had of their Neighbours formerly, I expected no great Matters from them.

With such Views as these, I set out at first from *England*; and would, according to the Method I proposed formerly [Vol. I.] have gone Westward, through the *Magellanick* Streight, or round *Terra del Fuego* rather, that I might have begun my Discoveries upon the Eastern and least known Side of the *Terra Australis*. But that way 'twas not possible for me to go, by Reason of the Time of Year in which I came out; for I must have been compassing the South of *America* in a very high Latitude, in the Depth of the Winter there. I was therefore necessitated to go Eastward by the *Cape of Good Hope*; and when I should be past it, 'twas requisite I should keep in a pretty high Latitude, to avoid the general Trade-winds that would be against me, and to have the Benefit of the

variable Winds: By all which I was in a Manner unavoidably determin'd to fall in first with those Parts of
New Holland I have hitherto been describing. For should
it be ask'd why at my first making that Shore, I did not
coast it to the Southward, and that way try to get round
to the East of *New Holland* and *New Guinea*; I confess I
was not for spending my Time more than was necessary
in the higher Latitudes; as knowing that the Land there
could not be so well worth the discovering, as the Parts
that lay nearer the Line, and more directly under the
Sun. Besides, at the Time when I should come first on
New Holland, which was early in the Spring, I must,
had I stood Southward, have had for some Time a great
deal of Winter-weather, increasing in Severity, though
not in Time, and in a Place altogether unknown; which
my Men, who were heartless enough to the Voyage at
best, would never have born, after so long a Run as from
Brazil hither.

For these Reasons therefore I chose to coast along to
the Northward, and so to the East, and so thought to come
round by the South of *Terra Australis* in my Return back,
which should be in the Summer-season there: And this
Passage back also I now thought I might possibly be able
to shorten, should it appear, at my getting to the East
Coast of *New Guinea*, that there is a Channel there coming
out into these Seas, as I now suspected near *Rosemary
Island:* Unless the high Tides and great Indraught
thereabout should be occasion'd by the Mouth of some
large River; which hath often low Lands on each Side of
its Outlet, and many Islands and Sholes lying at its Entrance. But I rather thought it a Channel or Streight, than
a River: And I was afterwards confirmed in this Opinion,
when by coasting *New Guinea*, I found that other Parts of
this great Tract of *Terra Australis*, which had hitherto

been represented as the Shore of a Continent, were certainly Islands; and 'tis probably the same with *New Holland:* Though for Reasons I shall afterwards shew, I could not return by the way I propos'd to my self, to fix the Discovery. All that I had now seen from the Latitude of 27 d. South to 25, which is *Shark's Bay*; and again from thence to *Rosemary Islands*, and about the Latitude of 20; seems to be nothing but Ranges of pretty large Islands against the Sea, whatever might be behind them to the Eastward, whether Sea or Land, Continent or Islands.

But to proceed with my Voyage. Though the Land I had seen as yet, was not very inviting, being but barren towards the Sea, and affording me neither fresh Water, nor any great Store of other Refreshments, nor so much as a fit Place for careening; yet I stood out to Sea again, with Thoughts of coasting still along Shore (as near as I could) to the North Eastward, for the further Discovery of it: Perswading my self, that at least the Place I anchor'd at in my *Voyage round the World*, in the Latitude of 16 deg. 15 min. from which I was not now far distant, would not fail to afford me sweet Water upon digging, as it did then; for the brackish Water I had taken in here, though it serv'd tolerably well for boiling, was yet not very wholsome.

With these Intentions I put to Sea on the 5th of *September* 1699, with a gentle Gale, sounding all the way; but was quickly induc'd to alter my Design. For I had not been out above a Day, but I found that the Sholes among which I was engaged all the while on the Coast, and was like to be engag'd in, would make it a very tedious Thing to sail along by the Shore, or to put in where I might have occasion. I therefore edged farther off to Sea, and so deepned the Water from 11 to 32

Fathom. The next Day, being *September* the 6th, we could but just discern the Land, though we had then no more than about 30 Fathom, uncertain Soundings; For even while we were out of Sight of Land, we had once but 7 Fathom, and had also great and uncertain Tides whirling about, that made me afraid to go near a Coast so shallow, where we might be soon a-ground, and yet have but little Wind to bring us off: For should a Ship be near a Shoal, she might be hurl'd upon it unavoidably by a strong Tide, unless there should be a good Wind to work her and keep her off. Thus also on the 7th Day we saw no Land, though our Water decreas'd again to 26 Fathom; for we had deepned it, as I said, to 30.

This Day we saw two Water-snakes, different in Shape from such as we had formerly seen. The one was very small, though long; the other long and as big as a Man's Leg, having a red Head; which I never saw any have, before or since. We had this Day, Lat. 16 d. 9 m. by Observation.

I was by this Time got to the North of the Place I had thought to have put in at, where I dug Wells in my former Voyage; and though I knew by the Experience I had of it then, that there was a deep Entrance in thither from the Eastward; yet by the Shoals I had hitherto found so far stretcht on this Coast, I was afraid I should have the same Trouble to coast all along afterwards beyond that Place: And besides the Danger of running almost continually amongst Shoals on a strange Shore, and where the Tides were strong and high; I began to bethink my self, that a great Part of my Time must have been spent in being about a Shore I was already almost weary off, which I might employ with greater Satisfaction to my Mind, and better Hopes of Success in going forward to *New Guinea*. Add to this the

particular Danger I should have been in upon a Lee-
shore, such as is here describ'd, when the North-West
Monsoon should once come in; the ordinary Season of
which was not now far off, though this Year it staid beyond the common Season; and it comes on storming at
first, with Tornadoes, violent Gusts, &c. Wherefore
quitting the Thoughts of putting in again at *New Holland*,
I resolv'd to steer away for the Island *Timor*; where,
besides getting fresh Water, I might probably expect to be
furnished with Fruits, and other Refreshments to recruit
my Men, who began to droop; some of them being already
to my great Grief, afflicted with the Scurvy, which was
likely to increase upon them and disable them, and was
promoted by the brackish Water they took in last for
boiling their Oatmeal. 'Twas now also towards the latter
End of the dry Season; when I might not probably have
found Water so plentifully upon digging at that Part of
New Holland, as when I was there before in the wet
Season. And then, considering the Time also that I
must necessarily spend in getting in to the Shore, through
such Sholes as I expected to meet with; or in going about to
avoid them; and in digging of Wells when I should come
thither: I might very well hope to get to *Timor*, and find
fresh Water there, as soon as I could expect to get it at
New Holland; and with less Trouble and Danger.

On the 8th of *September* therefore, shaping our Course
for *Timor*, we were in Lat. 15 d. 37 m. We had 26
Fathom, coarse Sand; and we saw one Whale. We
found them lying most commonly near the Shore,
or in Shoal Water. This Day we also saw some small white
Clouds; the first that we had seen since we came out of
Shark's Bay. This was one Sign of the Approach of the
North-North-West Monsoon. Another Sign was the
shifting of the Winds; for from the Time of our coming to

our last Anchoring place, the Sea-Breezes which before were Easterly and very strong, had been whiffling about and changing gradually from the East to the North, and thence to the West, blowing but faintly, and now hanging mostly in some Point of the West. This Day the Winds were at South-West by West, blowing very faint; and the 9th Day we had the Wind at North-West by North, but then pretty fresh; and we saw the Clouds rising more and thicker in the North-West. This Night at 12 we lay by for a small low sandy Island, which I reckoned my self not far from. The next Morning at Sun-rising we saw it from the Top-mast-head, right a-head of us; and at Noon were up within a Mile of it: When, by a good Observation, I found it to lye in 13 d. 55 m. I have mentioned it in my first Vol. pag. 310. but my Account then made it to lye in 13 d. 50 m. We had Abundance of Boobies and *Man of War* Birds flying about us all the Day; especially when we came near the Island; which had also Abundance of them upon it; though it was but a little Spot of Sand, scarce a Mile round.

I did not anchor here, nor send my Boat ashore; there being no appearance of getting any Thing on that Spot of Sand, besides Birds that were good for little: Though had I not been in haste, I would have taken some of them. So I made the best of my way to *Timor*; and on the 11th in the Afternoon we saw 10 small Land-birds, about the Bigness of Larks, that flew away North West. The 13th we saw a great many Sea-snakes. One of these, of which I saw great Numbers and Variety in this Voyage, was large, and all black: I never saw such another for his Colour.

We had now had for some Days small Gales, from the South-South-West to the North-North-West, and the Sky still more cloudy especially in the Mornings and

Evenings. The 14th it look'd very black in the North-West all the Day; and a little before Sun-set we saw, to our great Joy, the Tops of the high Mountains of *Timor*, peeping out of the Clouds, which had before covered them, as they did still the lower Parts.

We were now running directly towards the Middle of the Island, on the South-side: But I was in some doubt whether I should run down along Shore on this South-side towards the East-end; or pass about the West-end, and so range along on the North-side, and go that way towards the East-end: But as the Winds were now Westerly, I thought it best to keep on the South-side, till I should see how the Weather would prove; For, as the Island lies, if the Westerly Winds continued and grew tempestuous, I should be under the Lee of it, and have smooth Water, and so could go along Shore more safely and easily on this South-side: I could sooner also run to the East-end, where there is the best Shelter, as being still more under the Lee of the Island when those Winds blow. Or if, on the other Side, the Winds should come about again to the Eastward, I could but turn back again, (as I did afterwards;) and passing about the West-end, could there prosecute my Search on the North-side of the Island for Water, or Inhabitants, or a good Harbour, or whatever might be useful to me. For both Sides of the Island were hitherto alike to me, being wholly unacquainted here; only as I had seen it at a Distance in my former Voyage. [*See* Vol. I. pag. 309.]

I had heard also, that there were both *Dutch* and *Portugueze* Settlements on this Island; but whereabouts, I knew not: However, I was resolved to search about till I found, either one of these Settlements, or Water in some other place.

It was now almost Night, and I did not care to run

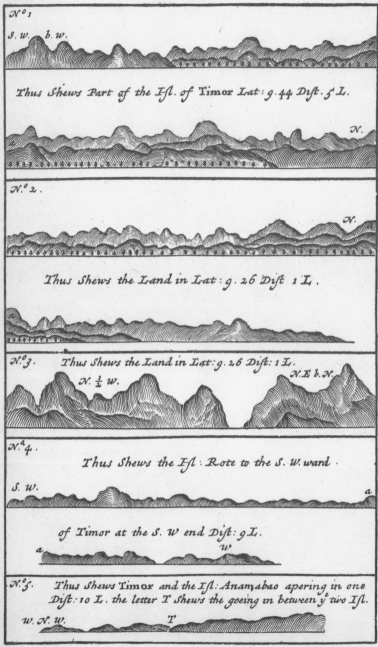

Table V   **Timor**

N.º 1

S. W. b. W.

Thus Shews Part of the Isl. of Timor Lat: 9.44 Dist. 5 L.

N.

N.º 2.

N.

Thus Shews the Land in Lat: 9. 26 Dist 1 L.

N.º 3.   *Thus Shews the Land in Lat: 9. 26 Dist: 1 L.*

N. ½ W.

N. E. b. N.

N.ª 4.

Thus Shews the Isl: Rote to the S. W. ward.

S. W.

a

of Timor at the S. W end Dist: 9 L.

a

W

N.º 5.   *Thus Shews Timor and the Isl: Anamabao apering in one*
Dist: 10 L. the letter T Shews the goeing in between y͙ two Isl.

W. N. W.

T

near the Land in the dark, but clapt on a Wind, and
stood off and on till the next Morning, being *September*
15th, when I steered in for the Island, which now appear'd very plain, being high, double and treble Land,
very remarkable, on whatever Side you view it. *See a*
Sight of it in 2 Parts, Table V. N°. 1. aa. At 3 in the
Afternoon we anchored in 14 Fathom, soft black oasy
Ground, about a Mile from the Shore. *See 2 Sights more*
of the Coast, in Table V. N°. 2, 3. and the Island it self in
the *Particular Map*; which I have here inserted, to shew
the Course of the Voyage from hence to the Eastward;
as the *General Map*, set before the Title of this Volume,
shews the Course of the whole Voyage. But in making the
Particular Map, I chose to begin only with *Timor*, that
I might not, by extending it too far, be forced to contract
the Scale too much among the Islands, *&c.* of the *New*
Guinea Coast; which I chiefly designed it for.

The Land by the Sea, on this South-side, is low and
sandy, and full of tall Streight-bodied Trees like Pines,
for about 200 Yards inwards from the Shore. Beyond
that, further in towards the Mountains, for a Breadth of
about 3 Miles more or less, there is a Tract of swampy
Mangrovy Land, which runs all along between the sandy
Land of the Shore on one Side of it, and the Feet of the
Mountains on the other. And this low Mangrovy Land
is overflown every Tide of Flood, by the Water that
flows into it through several Mouths or Openings in the
outer sandy Skirt against the Sea. We came to an Anchor
right against one of these Openings; and presently I
went in my Boat to search for fresh Water, or get Speech
of the Natives; for we saw Smoaks, Houses, and Plantations against the Sides of the Mountains, not far from
us. It was ebbing Water before we got ashore, though the
Water was still high enough to float us in without any

K

great Trouble. After we were within the Mouth, we found a large Salt-Water Lake, which we hoped might bring us up through the Mangroves to the fast Land: But before we went further, I went ashore on the sandy Land by the Sea-side, and look'd about me; but saw there no Sign of fresh Water. Within the sandy Bank, the Water forms a large Lake: Going therefore into the Boat again, we rowed up the Lake towards the firm Land, where no doubt there was fresh Water, could we come at it. We found many Branches of the Lake entring within the Mangrove Land, but not beyond it. Of these we left some on the Right-hand, and some on the Left, still keeping in the biggest Channel; which still grew smaller, and at last so narrow, that we could go no farther, ending among the Swamps and Mangroves. We were then within a Mile of some Houses of the *Indian* Inhabitants, and the firm Land by the Sides of the Hills: But the Mangroves thus stopping our way, we return'd as we came: But it was almost dark before we reach'd the Mouth of the Creek. 'Twas with much ado that we got out of it again; for it was now low Water, and there went a rough short Sea on the Bar; which, however, we past over without any Damage, and went aboard.

The next Morning at five we weighed, and stood along Shore to the Eastward, making use of the Sea and Land-Breezes. We found the Sea-Breezes here from the S. S. E. to the S. S. W. the Land-Breezes from the N. to the N. E. We coasted along about 20 Leagues, and found it all a streight, bold, even Shore, without Points, Creeks or Inlets for a Ship: And there is no anchoring till within a Mile or a Mile and an half of the Shore. We saw scarce any Opening fit for our Boats; and the fast Land was still barricado'd with Mangroves; So that here was no hope to get Water; nor was it likely that there should be hereabouts any *European* Settlement, since there was no Sign of a Harbour.

The Land appear'd pleasant enough to the Eye: For the Sides and Tops of the Mountains were cloath'd with Woods mix'd with Savannahs; and there was a Plantation of the *Indian* Natives, where we saw the Coco-Nuts growing, and could have been glad to have come at some of them. In the Draught I had with me, a Shoal was laid down hereabouts; but I saw nothing of it, going, or coming; and so have taken no Notice of it in my Map.

Weary of running thus fruitlessly along the South-side of the Island to the Eastward, I resolv'd to return the way I came; and compassing the West-end of the Island, make a Search along the North-side of it. The rather, because the North-North-West Monsoon, which I had design'd to be shelter'd from by coming the way I did, did not seem to be near at Hand, as the ordinary Season of them required; but on the contrary I found the Winds returning again to the South-Eastward; and the Weather was fair, and seem'd likely to hold so; and consequently the North-North-West Monsoon was not like to come in yet. I considered therefore that by going to the North-side of the Island, I should there have the smooth Water, as being the Lee-side as the Winds now were; and hoped to have better riding at Anchor or Landing on that Side, than I could expect here, where the Shore was so lined with Mangroves.

Accordingly, the 18th about Noon I altered my Course, and steered back again towards the South-West-end of the Island. This Day we struck a Dolphin; and the next Day saw two more, but struck none: We also saw a Whale.

In the Evening we saw the Island *Rotee*, and another Island to the South of it, not seen in my Map; both

lying near the South-West-end of *Timor*. On both these
Islands we saw Smoaks by Day, and Fires by Night, as we
had seen on *Timor* ever since we fell in with it. I was told
afterwards by the *Portugueze*, that they had Sugar-works
on the Island *Rotee*; but I knew nothing of that now; and
the Coast appearing generally dry and barren, only
here and there a Spot of Trees, I did not attempt anchoring there, but stood over again to the *Timor* Coast.

September the 21st, in the Morning, being near *Timor*, I
saw a pretty large Opening, which immediately I entred
with my Ship, sounding as I went in: But had no Ground
till I came within the East Point of the Mouth of the
Opening, where I anchored in 9 Fathom, a League from
the Shore. The Distance from the East-side to the West-
side of this Opening, was about 5 Leagues. But whereas I
thought this was only an Inlet or large Sound that ran a
great way into the Island *Timor*, I found afterwards that
it was a Passage between the West End of *Timor* and
another small Island called *Anamabào* or *Anabao:* Into
which Mistake I was led by my Sea-Chart, which represented both Sides of the Opening as Parts of the same
Coast, and called all of it *Timor: See all this rectified, and a
View of the whole Passage, as I found it, in a small Map I
have made of it. Table VI. N°. 1.*

I designed to sail into this Opening till I should come
to firm Land; for the Shore was all set thick with Mangroves here by the Sea, on each Side; which were very
green, as were also other Trees more within Land. We
had now but little Wind; therefore I sent my Boat away,
to sound, and to let me know by Signs what Depth of
Water they met with, if under 8 Fathom; but if more, I
order'd them to go on, and make no Signs. At 11 that
Morning, having a pretty fresh Gale, I weighed, and
made sail after my Boat; but edg'd over more to the West

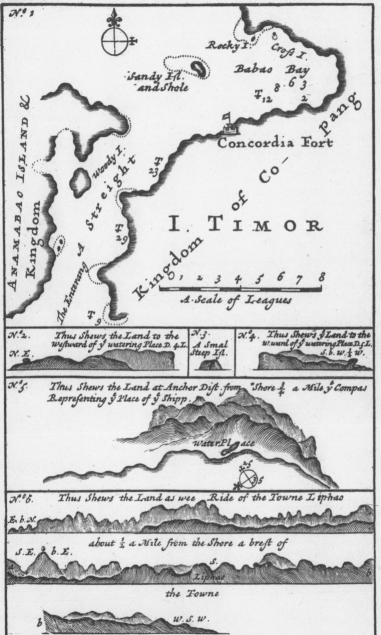

Shore, because I saw many smaller Openings there, and was in Hopes to find a good Harbour where I might secure the Ship; for then I could with more Safety send my Boats to seek for fresh Water. I had not sailed far before the Wind came to the South-East and blew so strong, that I could not with Safety venture nearer that Side, it being a Lee-shore. Besides, my Boat was on the East-side of the *Timor* Coast; for the other was, as I found afterwards, the *Anabao* Shore; and the great Opening I was now in, was the Streight between that Island and *Timor*; towards which I now tack'd and stood over. Taking up my Boat therefore, I ran under the *Timor* Side, and at 3 a Clock anchored in 29 Fathom, half a Mile from the Shore. That Part of the South-West Point of *Timor*, where we anchored in the Morning, bore now South by West, distance 3 Leagues: And another Point of the Island bore North-North-East, distance 2 Leagues.

Not long after, we saw a Sloop coming about the Point last mention'd, with *Dutch* Colours; which I found, upon sending my Boat aboard, belonged to a *Dutch* Fort, (the only one thay have in *Timor*) about 5 Leagues from hence, call'd *Concordia*. The Governour of the Fort was in the Sloop, and about 40 Soldiers with him. He appear'd to be somewhat surprised at our coming this way; which it seems is a Passage scarce known to any but themselves; as he told the Men I sent to him in my Boat. Neither did he seem willing that we should come near their Fort for Water. He said also, that he did not know of any Water on all that Part of the Island, but only at the Fort; and that the Natives would kill us, if they met us ashore. By the small Arms my Men carried with them in the Boat, they took us to be Pirates, and would not easily believe the Account my Men gave them of what we were, and whence we came. They said that about 2

Years before this, there had been a stout Ship of *French* Pirates here; and that after having been suffered to Water, and to refresh themselves, and been kindly used, they had on a sudden gone among the *Indians*, Subjects of the Fort, and plunder'd them and burnt their Houses. And the *Portugueze* here told us afterwards, that those Pirates, whom they also had entertain'd, had burnt their Houses, and had taken the *Dutch* Fort, (though the *Dutch* car'd not to own so much,) and had driven the Governour and Factory among the wild *Indians* their Enemies. The *Dutch* told my Men further, that they could not but think we had of several Nations (as is usual with Pirate Vessels) in our Ship, and particularly some *Dutch* Men, though all the Discourse was in *French*; (for I had not one who could speak *Dutch:*) Or else, since the common Draughts make no Passage between *Timor* and *Anabao*, but lay down both as one Island; they said they suspected we had plundered some *Dutch* Ship of their particular Draughts, which they are forbid to part with.

With these Jealousies the Sloop returned towards their Fort, and my Boat came back with this News to me: But I was not discouraged at this News; not doubting but I should perswade them better, when I should come to talk with them. So the next Morning I weighed, and stood towards the Fort. The Winds were somewhat against us, so that we could not go very fast, being obliged to tack 2 or 3 Times: And coming near the farther End of the Passage between *Timor* and *Anabao*, we saw many Houses on each Side not far from the Sea, and several Boats lying by the Shore. The Land on both Sides was pretty high, appearing very dry and of a reddish Colour, but highest on the *Timor* Side. The Trees on either Side were but small, the Woods thin, and in many Places the Trees were dry and withered.

The Island *Anamabao* or *Anabao*, is not very big, not exceeding 10 Leagues in length, and 4 in Breadth; yet it has 2 Kingdoms in it, *viz.* that of *Anamabao* on the East-side towards *Timor*, and the North-East-end; and that of *Anabao*, which contains the South-West-end and the West-side of the Island; but I know not which of them is biggest. The Natives of both are of the *Indian* kind, of a swarthy Copper-colour, with black lank Hair. Those of *Anamabao* are in League with the *Dutch*, as these after-wards told me, and with the Natives of the Kingdom of *Copang* in *Timor*, over-against them, in which the *Dutch* Fort *Concordia* stands: But they are said to be inveterate Enemies to their Neighbours of *Anabao*. Those of *Anabao*, besides managing their small Plantations of Roots and a few Coco-nuts, do fish, strike Turtle, and hunt Buffalo's; killing them with Swords, Darts, or Lances. But I know not how they get their Iron; I suppose, by Traffick with the *Dutch* or *Portugueze*, who send now and then a Sloop and trade thither, but well-arm'd; for the Natives would kill them, could they surprize them. They go always armed themselves; And when they go a fishing or a hunt-ing, they spend 4 or 5 Days or more in ranging about, before they return to their Habitation. We often saw them, after this, at these Employments; but they would not come near us. The Fish or Flesh that they take, besides what serves for present spending, they dry on a Barbacue or wooden Grate, standing pretty high over the Fire, and so carry it home when they return. We came sometimes afterwards to the Places where they had Meat thus a drying, but did not touch any of it.

But to proceed; I did not think to stop any where till I came near the Fort; which yet I did not see: But coming to the End of this Passage, I found that if I went any farther I should be open again to the Sea. I therefore stood in close to the Shore, on the East-side, and anchored in 4 Fathom Water, sandy Ground; a Point of Land still hindring me from seeing the Fort. But I sent my Boat to look about for it; and in a short Time she returned, and my Men told me they saw the Fort, but did not go near it; and that it was not above 4 or 5 Miles from hence. It being now late, I would not send my Boat thither till the next Morning: Mean while about 2 or 300 *Indians*, Neighbours of the Fort, and sent probably from thence, came to the sandy Bay just against the Ship; where they staid all Night, and made good Fires. They were armed with Lances, Swords and Targets, and made a great Noise all the Night: We thought it was to scare us from landing, should we attempt it: But we took little Notice of them.

The next Morning, being *September* the 23d, I sent my Clerk ashore in my Pinnace to the Governour, to satisfy him that we were *English* Men: and in the *King*'s ship, and to ask Water of him; sending a young Man with him, who spake *French*. My Clerk was with the Governour pretty early; and in Answer to his Queries about me, and my Business in these Parts, told him that I had the King of *England*'s Commission, and desired to speak with him. He beckned to my Clerk to come ashore; but assoon as he saw some small Arms in the Stern-Sheets of the Boat, he commanded him into the Boat again, and would have him be gone. My Clerk sollicited him that he would allow him to speak with him; and at last the Governour consented that he should come ashore; and sent his Lieutenant and 3 Merchants, with a Guard of about a hundred of the Native *Indians* to receive him. My Clerk said that we were in much want of Water, and hop'd they wou'd allow us to come to their Watering-place, and fill. But the Governour replied, that he had Orders not to supply any Ships but their own *East-India Campany*; neither must they allow any *Europeans* to come the Way that we came; and wondred how we durst come near their Fort. My Clerk answered him, that had we been Enemies, we must have come ashore among them for Water: But, said the Governour, you are come to inspect into our Trade and Strength; and I will have you therefore be gone with all Speed. My Clerk answered him, that I had no such Design, but, without coming nearer them, would be contented if the Governour would send Water on Board where we lay, about 2 Leagues from the Fort; and that I would make any reasonable Satisfaction for it. The Governour said that we should have what Water we wanted, provided we came no nearer with the Ship: And ordered, that assoon as we pleased, we should send our Boat full of empty Casks, and come to an Anchor with it off the Fort, till he sent Slaves to bring the Casks ashore, and fill them; for that none of our Men must come ashore. The same Afternoon I sent up my Boat as he had directed, with an Officer, and a present of some Beer for the Governour; which he would not accept of; but sent me off about a Ton of Water.

On the 24th in the Morning I sent the same Officer again in my Boat; and about Noon the Boat returned again with the two principal Merchants of the Factory, and the Lieutenant of the Fort; for whose Security they had kept my Officer and one of my Boat's-crew as Hostages, confining them to the Governour's Garden all the Time: For they were very shy of trusting any of them to go into their Fort, as my Officer said: Yet afterwards they were not shy of our Company; and I found that my Officer maliciously endeavour'd to make them shy of me. In the Even I gave the *Dutch* Officers that came aboard, the best Entertainment I could; and bestowing some

Presents on them, sent them back very well pleased; and my Officer and the other Man were returned to me. Next Morning I sent my Boat ashore again with the same Officer; who brought me word from the Governour, that we must pay 4 *Spanish* Dollars, for every Boat's-load of Water: But in this he spake falsly, as I understood afterwards from the Governour himself, and all his Officers, who protested to me that no such Price was demanded, but left me to give the Slaves what I pleased for their Labour: The Governour being already better satisfied about me, then when my Clerk spoke to him, or than that Officer I sent last would have caused him to be: For the Governour being a civil, genteel and sensible Man, was offended at the Officer for his being so industrious to misrepresent me. I received from the Governour a little Lamb, very fat; and I sent him 2 of the *Guinea*-hens that I brought from *St. Jago*, of which there were none here.

I had now 11 Buts of Water on Board, having taken in 7 here, which I would have paid for, but that at present I was afraid to send my Boat ashore again; For my Officer told me, among other of his Inventions, that there were more Guns mounted in the Fort, than when we first came; and that he did not see the Gentlemen that were aboard the Day before; intimating as if they were shy of us; and that the Governour was very rough with him; and I not knowing to the contrary at present, consulted with my other Officers what was best to be done; for by this the Governour should seem to design to quarrel with us. All my other Officers thought it natural to infer so much, and that it was not safe to send the Boat ashore any more, lest it should be seiz'd on; but that it was best to go away, and seek more Water where we could find it. For having now (as I said) 11 Buts aboard; and the Land being promising this way, I did not doubt finding

Water in a short Time. But my Officer who occasion'd these Fears in us by his own Forgeries, was himself for going no further; having a Mind, as far as I could perceive, to make every Thing in the Voyage, to which he shew'd himself averse, seem as cross and discouraging to my Men as possible, that he might hasten our Return; being very negligent and backward in most Businesses I had occasion to employ him in; doing nothing well or willingly, though I did all I could to win him to it. He was also industrious to stir up the Sea-men to Mutiny; telling them, among other Things, that any *Dutch* Ship might lawfully take us in these Seas; but I knew better, and avoided every Thing that could give just Offence.

The rest of my Officers therefore being resolved to go from hence, and having bought some Fish of some *Anamabeans*, who, seeing our Ship, came purposely to sell some, passing to and fro every Day; I sail'd away on the 26th about 5 in the Afternoon. We pass'd along between a small low sandy Island (over against the Fort), full of Bays and pretty high Trees; sounding as we went along; and had from 25 to 35 Fathom, oasy Ground. *See the little Map of this Passage, Table VI. N°. 1.*

The 27th in the Morning we anchored in the Middle of the Bay, called *Copang* Bay, in 12 Fathom, soft Oaze, about 4 Leagues above the *Dutch* Fort. Their Sloop was riding by the Fort, and in the Night fired a Gun; but for what Reason I know not; and the Governour said afterwards, 'twas the Skipper's own doing, without his Order. Presently after we had anchored, I went in the Pinnace to search about the Bay for Water, but found none. Then, returning a-board, I weighed, and ran down to the North-Entrance of the Bay, and at 7 in the Evening anchored again, in 37 Fathom, soft Oaze, close by the sandy Island, and about 4 Leagues from the *Dutch* Fort. The 28th I sent both my Boats ashore on the sandy Island, to cut Wood; and by Noon they both came back laden. In the Afternoon I sent my Pinnace ashore on the North Coast or Point of *Copang* Bay, which is call'd *Babao*. Late in the Night they returned, and told me that they saw great Tracks of Buffalo's there, but none of the Buffalo's themselves; neither did they find any fresh Water. They also saw some green Turtle in the Sea, and one Alligator.

The 29th I went out of *Copang* Bay, designing to Coast it along Shore on the North-side of *Timor* to the Eastward; as well to seek for Water, as also to acquaint my self with the Island, and to search for the *Portugueze* Settlements; which we were informed were about forty Leagues to the Eastward of this Place.

We coasted along Shore with Land and Sea-Breezes. The Land by the Shore was of a moderate height, with high and very remarkable Hills farther within the Country; their Sides all spotted with Woods and Savannahs. But these on the Mountains Sides appeared of a rusty Colour not so pleasant and flourishing as those that we saw on the South-side of the Island; for the Trees seemed to be small and withering; and the Grass in the Savannahs also look'd dry, as if it wanted Moisture. But in the Valleys, and by the Sea-side, the Trees look'd here also more green. Yet we saw no good Anchoring-place, or Opening, that gave us any Incouragement to put in; till the 30th Day in the Afternoon.

We were then running along Shore, at about 4 Leagues distance, with a moderate Sea-breeze; when we opened a pretty deep Bay, which appeared to be a good Road to anchor in. There were two large Valleys, and one smaller one, which descending from the Mountains came all into one Valley by the Sea-side against this Bay, which was full of tall green Trees. I presently stood in with the Ship, till within two Leagues of the Shore; and then sent in my Pinnace commanded by my chief Mate, whose great Care, Fidelity, and Diligence, I was well assured of; ordering him to seek for fresh Water; and if he found any, to sound the Bay, and bring me Word what anchoring there was; and to make haste aboard.

As soon as they were gone, I stood off a little, and lay by. The Day was now far spent; and therefore it was late before they got ashore with the Boat; so that they did not come aboard again that Night. Which I was much concern'd at; because in the Evening, when the Sea-Breeze was done and the Weather calm, I perceived the Ship to drive back again to the Westward. I was not yet acquainted with the Tides here; for I had hitherto met with no strong Tides about the Island, and scarce any running in a Stream, to set me along Shore either way. But after this Time, I had pretty much of them; and found at present the Flood set to the Eastward, and the Ebb to the Westward. The Ebb (with which I was now carried) sets very strong, and runs 8 or 9 Hours. The Flood runs but weak, and at most lasts not above 4 hours; and this too is perceived only near the Shore; where checking the Ebb, it swells the Seas, and makes the Water rise in the Bays and Rivers 8 or 9 Foot. I was afterwards credibly informed by some *Portugueze*, that the Current runs always to the Westward in the Mid-Channel between this Island and those that face it in a Range to the North of it, *viz. Misicomba* (or *Omba*) *Pintare, Laubana, Ende,* &c.

We were driven 4 Leagues back again, and took particular Notice of a Point of Land that looked like *Flamborough-head,* when we were either to the East or

West of it; and near the Shore it appeared like an Island. Four or five Leagues to the East of this Point, is another very remarkable bluff Point, which is on the West-side of the Bay that my Boat was in. *See two Sights of this Land, Table VI. N°. II. III.* We could not stem the Tide, till about 3 a Clock in the Afternoon; when the Tide running with us, we soon got abreast of the Bay, and then saw a small Island to the Eastward of us. *See a Sight of it, Table VI. N°. IV.* About 6 we anchored in the Bottom of the Bay, in 25 Fathom, soft Oaze, half a Mile from the Shore.

I made many false Fires in the Night, and now and then fired a Gun, that my Boat might find me; but to no Purpose. In the Morning I found my self driven again by the Tide of Ebb 3 or 4 Leagues to the Westward of the Place where I left my Boat. I had several Men looking out for her; but could not get Sight of her: Besides, I continued still driving to the Westward; for we had but little Wind, and that against us. But by 10 a Clock in the Morning we had the Comfort of seeing the Boat; and at 11 she came aboard, bringing 2 Barrecoes of very good Water.

The Mate told me there was good Anchoring close by the Watering-place; but that there ran a very strong Tide, which near the Shore made several Races; so that they found much Danger in getting ashore, and were afraid to come off again in the Night, because of the Riplings the Tide made.

We had now the Sea-breeze, and steered away for this Bay; but could hardly stemm the Tide, till about 3 in the Afternoon; when the Tide being turned with us, we went along briskly, and about 6 anchored in the Bay, in 25 Fathom, soft Oaze, half a Mile from the Shore.

The next Morning I went ashore to fill Water, and before Night sent aboard 8 Tons. We fill'd it out of a large

Pond within 50 Paces of the Sea. It look'd pale, but was very good, and boiled Pease well. I saw the Tract of an *Alligator* here. Not far from the Pond, we found the Rudder of a *Malayan* Proe, 3 great Jars in a small Shed set up against a Tree, and a Barbacue whereon there had been Fish and Flesh of Buffaloes drest, the Bones lying but a little from it.

In 3 Days we fill'd about twenty six Tun of Water, and then had on Board about 30 Ton in all. The 2 following Days we spent in Fishing with the Saine, and the first Morning caught as many as served all my Ship's Company: But afterwards we had not so good Success. The rest of my Men, which could be spared from the Ship, I sent out; Some with the Carpenter's Mate, to cut Timber for my Boats, &c. These went always guarded with 3 or 4 armed Men to secure them: I shewed them what Wood was fitting to cut for our Use, especially the Calabash and Maho; I shewed them also the manner of stripping the Maho-bark, and of making therewith Thread, Twine, Ropes, &c. Others were sent out a Fowling; who brought Home Pidgeons, Parrots, Cackatoos, &c. I was always with one Party or other, my self; especially with the Carpenters, to hasten them to get what they could, that we might be gone from hence.

Our Water being full, I sail'd from hence *October the* 6th about 4 in the Afternoon, designing to coast along Shore to the Eastward, till I came to the *Portugueze* Settlements. By the next Morning we were driven 3 or 4 Leagues to the West of the Bay; but in the Afternoon, having a faint Sea-breeze, we got again abreast of it. It was the 11th Day at Noon before we got as far as the small Island before-mentioned, which lies about 7 Leagues to the East of the Watering Bay: For what we gained in the Afternoon by the Benefit of the Sea-breezes we lost again in the Evenings and Mornings, while it was calm, in the Interval of the Breezes. But this Day the Sea-breeze blowing fresher than ordinary, we past by the Island and run before Night about 7 Leagues to the East of it.

This Island is not half a Mile long, and not above 100 Yards in breadth, and look'd just like a Barn, when we were by it: It is pretty high, and may be seen from a Ship's Topmast-head about 10 Leagues. The Top, and Part of the Sides, are covered with Trees, and it is about 3 Leagues from *Timor*; 'tis about Mid-way between the Watering-place and the *Portugueze* first and main Settlement by the Shore.

In the Night we were again driven back toward the Island, 3 Leagues: But the 12th Day, having a pretty brisk Sea-breeze, we coasted along Shore; and seeing a great many Houses by the Sea, I stood in with my Ship till I was within 2 Miles of them, and then sent in my Boat, and lay by till it returned. I sent an Officer to command the Boat; and a *Portugueze* Seaman that I brought from *Brazil*, to speak with the Men that we saw on the Bay; there being a great many of them, both Foot and Horse. I could not tell what Officer there might be amongst them; but I ordered my Officer to tell the Chief of them that we were *English*, and came hither for Refreshment. As soon as the Boat came ashore, and the Inhabitants were informed who we were, they were very glad, and sent me Word that I was welcome, and should have any thing that the Island afforded; and that I must run a little farther about a small Point, where I should see more Houses; and that the Men would stand on the Bay, right against the Place where I must anchor. With this News the Boat immediately returned; adding withal, that the Governour lived about 7 Miles up in the Country; and that the chief Person here was a Lieutenant, who desired me, as soon as the Ship was at Anchor, to send ashore one of my Officers to go to the Governour, and certify him of our Arrival. I presently made Sail towards the Anchoring-place, and at 5 a Clock anchored in *Laphao* Bay, in 20 Fathom, soft Oaze, over against the Town. A description of which, and of the *Portugueze* Settlement there, shall be given in the following Chapter.

Assoon as I came to Anchor, I sent my Boat ashore with my second Mate, to go to the Governour. The Lieutenant that lived here, had provided Horses and Guides for him, and sent 4 Soldiers with him for his Guard, and, while he was absent, treated my Men with Arack at his own House, where he and some others of the Townsmen shew'd them many broad thin Pieces of Gold; telling them that they had Plenty of that Metal, and would willingly traffick with them for any Sort of *European* Commodities. About 11 a Clock my Mate returned on Board, and told me he had been in the Country, and was kindly received by the Gentleman he went to wait upon; who said we were welcome, and should have any thing the Island afforded; and that he was not himself the Governour, but only a Deputy. He asked why we did not salute their Fort when we anchored; My Mate answer'd, that we saw no Colours flying, and therefore did not know there was any Fort till he came ashore and saw the Guns; and if we had known that there was a Fort, yet that we could not have given any Salute till we knew that they would answer it with the like Number of Guns. The Deputy said, it was very well; and that he had but little Powder; and therefore would gladly buy some of us, if we had any to spare; which my Mate told him, we had not.

The 13th the Deputy sent me aboard a Present of 2 young Buffaloes, 6 Goats, 4 Kids, 140 Coco-nuts, 300 ripe Mangoes, and 6 ripe Jacks. This was all very ac-

L

ceptable; and all the Time we lay here, we had fresh
Provision, and Plenty of Fruits; so that those of my Men
that were sick of the Scurvy, soon recover'd and grew
lusty. I staid here till the 22d, went ashore several Times,
and once purposely to see the Deputy; who came out of
the Country also on purpose to see and talk with me. And
then indeed there were Guns fired for Salutes, both aboard
my Ship and at the Fort. Our Interview was in a small
Church, which was fill'd with the better Sort of People;
the poorer Sort thronging on the Outside, and looking
in upon us: For the Church had no Wall but at the East-
end; the Sides and the West-end being open, saving only
that it had Boards about 3 or 4 Foot high from the
Ground. I saw but 2 white Men among them all;
One was a *Padre* that came along with the Lieutenant;
the other was an Inhabitant of the Town. The rest were
all Copper-colour'd, with black lank Hair. I staid there
about 2 Hours, and we spoke to each other by an
Interpreter. I asked particularly about the Seasons of
the Year, and when they expected the North-North-
West Monsoon. The Deputy told me, that they expected
the Wind to shift every Moment; and that some Years
the North-North-West Monsoon set in in *September*, but
never failed to come in *October*; and for that Reason
desir'd me to make what haste I could from hence; for
'twas impossible to ride here when those Winds came. I
asked him if there was no Harbour hereabouts, where I
might be secured from the Fury of these Winds at their
first coming. He told me, that the best Harbour in the
Island was at a Place called *Babao*, on the North-side of
Copang Bay; that there were no Inhabitants there, but
Plenty of Buffaloes in the Woods, and Abundance of
Fish in the Sea; that there was also fresh Water: That
there was another Place, call'd *Port Sesiall*, about 20

Leagues to the Eastward of *Laphao*; that there was a River of fresh Water there, and Plenty of Fish, but no Inhabitants: Yet that, if I would go thither, he would send People with Hogs, Goats and Buffaloes, to truck with me for such Commodities as I had to dispose of.

I was afterwards told, that on the East-end of the Island *Ende* there was also a very good Harbour, and a *Portugueze* Town; that there was great Plenty of Refreshments for my Men, and Dammer for my Ship; that the Governour or Chief of that Place, was call'd Captain *More*; that he was a very courteous Gentleman, and would be very glad to entertain an *English* Ship there; and if I designed to go thither, I might have Pilots here that would be willing to carry me, if I could get the Lieutenant's Consent. That it was dangerous going thither without a Pilot, by Reason of the violent Tides that run between the Islands *Ende* and *Solor*. I was told also, that at the Island *Solor* there were a great many Dutchmen banisht from other Places for certain Crimes. I was willing enough to go thither, as well to secure my Ship in a good Harbour, where I might careen her, (there being Dammer also, which I could not get here, to make use of instead of Pitch, which I now wanted,) and where I might still be refreshing my Men and supporting them, in order to my further Discoveries; as also to inform my self more particularly concerning these Places as yet so little known to us. Accordingly I accepted the Offer of a Pilot and two Gentlemen of the Town, to go with me to *Larentucka* on the Island *Ende:* And they were to come on Board my Ship the Night before I sailed. But I was hindred of this Design by some of my Officers, who had here also been very busie in doing me all the Injury they could underhand.

But to proceed. While I staid here, I went ashore every

Day, and my Men took there Turns to go ashore and traffick for what they had Occasion for; and were now all very well again: And to keep themselves in Heart, every Man bought some Rice, more or less, to recruit them after our former Fatigues. Besides, I order'd the Purser to buy some for them, to serve them instead of Pease, which were now almost spent. I fill'd up my Water-Casks again here, and cut more Wood; and sent a Present to the Lieutenant, *Alexis Mendosa*, designing to be gone; for while I lay here, we had some Tornadoes and Rain, and the Sky in the North-West looked very black Mornings and Evenings, with Lightning all Night from that Quarter; which made me very uneasy and desirous to depart hence; because this Road lay expos'd to the North-North-West and North Winds, which were now daily expected, and which are commonly so violent, that 'tis impossible for any Ship to ride them out: Yet, on the other Hand, it was absolutely necessary for me to spend about 2 Months Time longer in some Place hereabouts, before I could prosecute my Voyage farther to the Eastward; for Reasons which I shall give hereafter in its proper Place in the ensuing Discourse. When therefore I sent the Present to the Governour, I desired to have a Pilot to *Larentucka* on the Island *Ende*; where I desir'd to spend the Time I had to spare. He now sent me Word that he could not well do it, but would send me a Letter to *Port Sesiall* for the Natives, who would come to me there and supply me with what Provision they had.

I staid 3 Days, in hopes yet to get a Pilot for *Larentucka*, or at least the Letter from the Governour to *Port Sesiall*. But seeing neither, I sail'd from hence the 22d of *October*, coasting to the Eastward, designing for *Sesiall*; and before Night, was about 10 Leagues to the East of *Laphao*. I kept about 3 Leagues off Shore, and my Boat ranged along close by the Shore, looking into every Bay and Cove; and at Night returned on Board. The next Morning, being 3 or 4 Leagues farther to the Eastward, I sent my Boat ashore again to find *Sesiall*. At Noon they returned, and told me they had been at *Sesiall*, as they guess'd; that there were two *Portugueze* Barks in the Port, who threatned to fire at them, but did not; telling them this was *Porto del Roy de Portugal*. They saw also another Bark, which ran and anchor'd close by the Shore; and the Men ran all away for fear: But our Men calling to them in *Portugueze*, they at last came to them, and told them that *Sesiall* was the Place which they came from, where the 2 Barks lay: Had not these Men told them, they could not have known it to be a Port, it being only a little bad Cove, lying open to the North; having 2 Ledges of Rocks at its Entrance, one on each Side; and a Channel between, which was so narrow, that it would not be safe for us to go in. However I stood in with the Ship, to be better satisfied; and when I came near it, found it answer my Men's Description. I lay by a-while, to consider what I had best do; for my Design was to lye in a Place where I might get fresh Provisions if I could: For though my Men were again pretty well recruited; and those that had been sick of the Scurvy, were well again; yet I design'd, if possible, to refresh them as much and as long as I could, before I went farther. Besides, my Ship wanted cleaning; and I was resolved to clean her, if possible.

At last after much Consideration, I thought it safer to go away again for *Babao*; and accordingly stood to the Westward. We were now about 60 Leagues to the East of *Babao*. The Coast is bold all the way, having no Sholes, and but one Island which I saw and describ'd coming to the Eastward. The Land in the Country is very moun-

tainous; but there are some large Valleys towards the
East-end. Both the Mountains and Valleys on this Side,
are barren; some wholly so; and none of them appear
so pleasant as the Place where I watered. It was the 23d
Day in the Evening when I stood back again for *Babao*.
We had but small Sea and Land-breezes. On the 27th
we came into *Copang* Bay; and the next Day having
sounded *Babao* Road, I ran in and came to an Anchor
there, in 20 Fathom, soft Oaze, 3 Mile from the Shore.
One Reason, as I said before, of my coming hither, was to
ride secure, and to clean my Ship's Bottom; as also to
endeavour by Fishing and Hunting of Buffaloes, to refresh my Men and save my salt Provision. It was like to
be some Time before I could clean my Ship, because I
wanted a great many Necessaries, especially a Vessel to
careen by. I had a Long-Boat in a Frame, that I brought
out of *England*, by which I might have made a Shift to do
it; but my Carpenter was uncapable to set her up. Besides, by that Time the Ship's-sides were calk'd, my
Pitch was almost spent; which was all owing to the
Carpenter's wilful Waste and Ignorance; so that I had
nothing to lay on upon the Ship's Bottom. But instead of
this, I intended to make Lime here, which with Oyl
would have made a good Coat for her. Indeed had it
been adviseable, I would have gone in between *Cross*
Island and *Timor*, and have hal'd my Ship ashore; for
there was a very convenient Place to do it in; but my
Ship being sharp, I did not dare to do it: Besides, I must
have taken every thing out of her; and I had neither
Boats to get my Things ashore, nor Hands to look after
them when they were there; for my Men would have been
all employed; and though here are no *Indians* living near,
yet they come hither in Companies when Ships are here,
on Purpose to do any Mischief they can to them; and

'twas not above 2 Years since a *Portugueze* Ship riding here, and sending her Boat for Water to one of the Galleys, the Men were all killed by the *Indians*. But to secure my Men, I never suffer'd them to go ashore unarmed; and while some were at Work, others stood to guard them.

We lay in this Place from *October* the 28th, till *December* the 12th. In which Time we made very good Lime with Shells, of which here are plenty. We cut Palmeto-leaves to burn the Ship's-sides; and giving her as good a Heel as we could, we burned her Sides, and paid them with Lime and Water for want of Oyl to mix with it. This stuck on about 2 Months, where 'twas well burned. We did not want fresh Provisions all the Time we lay here, either of Fish or Flesh. For there were fair sandy Bays on the Point of *Babao*, where in 2 or 3 Hours in a Morning we used with our Sain to drag ashore as much Fish as we could eat all the Day; and for a Change of Diet, when we were weary of Fish, I sent 10 or 11 armed Men a hunting for Buffaloes; who never came empty home. They went ashore in the Evening or early in the Morning, and before Noon always returned with their Burdens of *Buffalo*, enough to suffice us 2 Days; by which Time we began to long for Fish again.

On the 11th of *November*, the Governour of *Concordia* sent one of his Officers to us, to know who we were. For I had not sent thither, since I came to Anchor last here. When the Officer came aboard, he ask'd me why we fired so many Guns the 4th and 5th Days; (which we had done in Honour of King *William*, and in Memory of the Deliverance from the Powder-Plot:) I told him the occasion of it; and he replied that they were in some Fear at the Fort that we had been *Portugueze*, and that we were coming with Soldiers to take their Fort; He asked

me also why I did not stay and fill my Water at their
Fort, before I went away from thence? I told him the
Reason of it, and withal offered him Money; bidding
him take what he thought reasonable: He took none, and
said he was sorry there had been such a Misunderstanding between us; and knew that the Governour would
be much concerned at it. After a short Stay, he went
ashore; and the next Morning came aboard again, and
told me the Governour desired me to come ashore to
the Fort and dine with him; and, if I doubted any thing,
he would stay aboard till I returned. I told him I had no
Reason to mistrust any thing against me, and would go
ashore with him; so I took my Clerk and my Gunner, and
went ashore in my Pinnace: The Gunner spoke very good
French, and therefore I took him to be my Interpreter,
because the Governour speaks *French:* He was an honest
Man, and I found him always diligent and obedient. It
was pretty late in the Afternoon before we came ashore;
so that we had but little Time with the Governour. He
seem'd to be much dissatisfied at the Report my Officer
had made to me; (of which I have before given an Account;) and said it was false, neither would he now
take any Money of me; but told me I was welcome; as
indeed I found by what he provided. For there was
plenty of very good Victuals, and well drest; and the
Linnen was white and clean; and all the Dishes and
Plates, of Silver or fine China. I did not meet any where
with a better Entertainment, while I was abroad; nor
with so much Decency and Order. Our Liquor was Wine,
Beer, Toddy, or Water, which we liked best after Dinner.
He shew'd me some Drawers full of Shells, which were
the strangest and most curious that I had ever seen. He
told me, before I went away, that he could not supply
me with any Naval Stores; but if I wanted any fresh

Provision, he would supply me with what I had occasion for. I thank'd him, and told him I would send my Boat for some Goats and Hogs, though afterwards on second Thoughts I did not do it: For 'twas a great way from the Place where we lay, to the Fort; and I could not tell what Mischief might befall any of my Men, when there, from the Natives; especially if incouraged by the *Dutch*, who are Enemies to all *Europeans* but such as are under their own Government. Therefore I chose rather to fish and hunt for Provisions, than to be beholden to the *Dutch*, and pay dearly for it too.

We found here, as I said before, Plenty of Game; so that all the Time we lay at this Place, we spent none or very little of our Salt-provisions; having Fish or fresh Buffaloe every Day. We lay here 7 Weeks; and although the North-North-West Monsoon was every Day expected when I was at *Laphao*, yet it was not come, so that if I had prosecuted my Voyage to the Eastward without staying here, it had been but to little Advantage. For if I had gone out, and beaten against the Wind a whole Month, I should not have got far; it may be 40, 50, or 60 Leagues; which was but 24 Hours run for us with a large Wind; besides the Trouble and Discontent, which might have arisen among my Men in beating to Windward to so little Purpose, there being nothing to be got at Sea; but here we lived and did eat plentifully every Day without Trouble. The greatest Inconveniency of this Place, was want of Water; this being the latter Part of the dry Season, because the Monsoon was very late this Year. About 4 Days before we came away, we had Tornadoes, with Thunder, Lightning and Rain, and much Wind; but of no long Continuance; at which Time we filled some Water. We saw very black Clouds, and heard it thunder every Day for near a Month before, in the Mountains; and saw it rain, but none came near us: And even where we hunted, we saw great Trees torn up by the Roots, and great Havock made among the Woods by the Wind; yet none touched us.

CHAP. II

A particular Description of the Island Timor. *Its Coast. The Island* Anabao. *Fault of the Draughts. The Channel between* Timor *and* Anabao. Copang-*bay.* Fort Concordia. *A particular description of the Bay. The Anchoring-place, called* Babao. *The Malayans here kill all the Europeans they can.* Laphao, *a Portugueze Settlement, described.* Port Ciccale. *The Hills, Water, Low-lands, Soil, Woods, Metals, in the Island* Timor. *Its Trees.* Cana-fistula-*tree described. Wild Fig-trees described. Two new sorts of Palm-trees described. The Fruits of the Island. The Herbs. Its Land-Animals. Fowls. The Ringing Bird. Its Fish. Cockle-merchants and Oysters. Cockles as big as a Man's Head. Its original Natives described. The Portugueze and Dutch Settlements. The Malayan Language generally spoken here.* L' Orantuca *on the Island* Ende. *The Seasons, Winds, and Weather at* Timor.

THE Island *Timor,* as I have said in my Voyage round the World, is about seventy Leagues long, and fourteen or sixteen broad. It lies nearly North-East and South-West. The Middle of it lies in about 9 *d.* South Lat. It has no Navigable Rivers, nor many Harbours; but abundance of Bays, for Ships to ride in at some Seasons of the Year. The Shore is very bold, free from Rocks, Shoals or Islands; excepting a few which are visible, and therefore easily avoided. On the South-side there is a Shole laid down in our Draughts, about thirty Leagues from the South-West-end; I was fifteen or twenty Leagues further to the East than that distance, but saw nothing of the Shole; neither could I find any Harbour. It is a pretty even Shore, with Sandy Bays and low Land for about three or four Miles up; and then 'tis mountainous. There is no Anchoring but with half a League or a League at farthest from the Shore; and the low Land that bounds the Sea, hath nothing but red Mangroves, even from the Foot of the Mountains till you come within a hundred and fifty or two hundred paces of the Sea;

and then you have Sandbanks, cloath'd with a sort of Pine; so that there is no getting Water on this side, because of the Mangroves.

At the South-West end of *Timor*, is a pretty high Island, called *Anabao*. It is about ten or twelve Leagues long, and about four broad; near which the *Dutch* are settled. It lies so near *Timor*, that 'tis laid down in our Draughts as part of that Island; yet we found a narrow deep Channel fit for any Ships to pass between them. This Channel is about ten Leagues long, and in some places not above a League wide. It runs North-East and South-West, so deep that there is no Anchoring but very nigh the Shore. There is but little Tide; the Flood setting North, and the Ebb to the Southward. At the North-East-end of this Channel, are two Points of Land, not above a League asunder; one on the South-side upon *Timor*, called *Copang;* the other on the North-side, upon the Island *Anabao*. From this last point, the Land trends away Northerly two or three Leagues, opens to the Sea, and then bends in again to the Westward.

Being past these Points, you open a Bay of about eight Leagues long, and four wide. This Bay trends in on the South-side North-East by East from the South-point before mentioned; making many small Points or little Coves. About a League to the East of the said South-point, the *Dutch* have a small Stone Fort, situated on a firm Rock close by the Sea: This Fort they call *Concordia*. On the East-side of the Fort, there is a small River of fresh Water, which has a broad boarded Bridge over it, near to the Entry into the Fort. Beyond this River is a small sandy Bay, where the Boats and Barks land and convey their Traffick in or out of the Fort. About an hundred Yards from the Sea-side, and as many from the Fort, and forty Yards from the Bridge on the East-side, the Company have a fine Garden, surrounded with a good Stone-Wall; In it is plenty of all sorts of Sallads, Cabbages, Roots for the Kitchen; in some parts of it are Fruit-trees, as Jaca's, Pumplenose, Oranges, sweet Lemons, &c. and by the Walls are Coco-nut and Toddy-trees in great plenty. Besides these, they have Musk and Water-Melons, Pine-Apples, Pomecitrons, Pome-gran-ates, and others sorts of Fruits. Between this Garden and the River, there is a Penn for black Cattle, whereof they have plenty. Beyond the Companies Ground, the Natives have their Houses, in number about fifty or sixty. There are forty or fifty Soldiers belonging to this Fort, but I know not how many Guns they have ; For I had only opportunity to see one Bastion, which had in it four Guns. Within the Walls there is a neat little Church or Chapel.

Beyond *Concordia* the Land runs about seven Leagues to the bottom of the Bay; then it is not above a League and half from side to side, and the Land trends away Northerly to the North-Shore, then turns about again to the Westward, making the South-side of the Bay. About three Leagues and a half from the bottom of the Bay on this side, there is a small Island about a Musket-shot from the Shore; and a Riff of Rocks that runs from it to the Eastward about a mile. On the West-side of the Island is a Channel of three Fathom at low Water, of which depth it is also within, where Ships may haul in and carreen. West from this Island the Land rounds away in a Bite or Elbow, and at last ends in a low point of Land, which shoots forth a Ledge of Rocks a mile into the Sea, which is dry at Low-Water. Just against the low Point of Land, and to the West of the Ledge of Rocks, is another pretty high and rocky, yet woody Island, about half a mile from the low Point; which Island hath a Ledge of corally Rocks running from it all along to the other small Island, only leaving one Channel between them. Many of these Rocks are to be seen at Low-Water, and there seldom is Water enough for a Boat to go over them till quarter Flood or more. Within this Ledge there is two or three Fathom Water, and without it no less than ten or twelve Fathom close to the Rocks. A League without this last Rocky Island, is another small low sandy Island, about four Miles from the low Point, three Leagues from the *Dutch*-Fort *Concordia*, and three Leagues and a half from the South-West-point of the Bay. Ships that come in this way, must pass between this low Isle and the low Point, keeping near the Isle.

In this Bay there is any depth of Water from thirty to three Fathom, very good oazy holding Ground. This affords the best Shelter against all Winds of any place about the Island *Timor*. But from *March* to *October*, while either the Southerly Winds or only Land and Sea-breezes hold, the *Concordia* Side is best to ride in; but when the more violent Northerly Winds come, then the best riding is between the two rocky Islands in nineteen or twenty Fathom. If you bring the Westermost Island to bear South-West by West about a League distance, and the low Point West by South; then the Body of the sandy Island will bear South-West half West, distance two Leagues; and the Ledges of Rocks shooting from each, make such a Bar, that no Sea can come in. Then you have the Land from West by South to East-North-East, to defend you on that Side: And other Winds do not here blow violently. But if they did, yet you are so Land-lock'd, that there can be no Sea to hurt you. This Anchoring place is call'd *Babao*, about five Leagues from *Concordia*. The greatest Inconveniency in it, is the multitude of Worms. Here is fresh Water enough to be

had in the wet Season; every little Gull discharging
fresh Water into the Sea. In the dry Season you must
search for it in standing Ponds or Gulls, where the wild
Buffaloes, Hogs, &c. resort every Morning and Evening
to drink; where you may lye and shoot them, taking care
that you go strong enough and well-armed against the
Natives upon all occasions. For though there are no Inhabitants near this place; yet the *Malayans* come in great
Companies when Ships are here; and if they meet with
any *Europeans*, they kill them, of what Nation soever they
be, not excepting the *Portugueze* themselves. 'Tis but two
Years since a *Portugueze* Ship riding here, had all the
Boats crew cut off as they were watering; as I was inform'd by the *Dutch*. Here likewise is plenty of Fish of
several sorts, which may be catch'd with a Sain; also
Tortoise and Oysters.

From the North-East-point of this Bay, on the North-
side of the Island, the Land trends away North-North-
East for four or five Leagues; afterward North-East or
more Easterly; And when you are fourteen or fifteen
Leagues to the Eastward of *Babao*, you come up with a
Point that makes like *Flamborough-Head*, if you are
pretty nigh the Land; but if at a distance from it on
either side, it appears like an Island. This point is very
remarkable, there being none other like it in all this
Island. When you are abreast of this Point, you will see
another Point about four Leagues to the Eastward; and
when you are abreast of this latter Point, you will see a
small Island bearing East or East by North (according to
your distance from the Land,) just rising out of the Water:
When you see it plain, you will be abreast of a pretty deep
sandy Bay, which hath a point in the Middle, that
comes sloaping from the Mountains, with a curious
Valley on each side: The sandy Bay runs from one Valley

to the other. You may sail into this Bay, and anchor a little to the Eastward of the Point in twenty Fathom Water, half a Mile from the Shore, soft Oaze. Then you will be about two Leagues from the West-point of the Bay, and about eight Leagues from the small Island before mentioned, which you can see pretty plain bearing East-North-East a little Northwardly. Some other Marks are set down in the foregoing Chapter. In this sandy Bay you will find fresh Water in two or three places. At Spring-tides you will see many Riplings, like Sholes; but they are only Eddies caused by the two Points of the Bay.

We saw Smoaks all Day up in the Mountains, and Fires by Night, at certain places, where we supposed the the Natives lived, but saw none of them.

The Tides ran between the two Points of the Bay, very strong and uncertain: Yet it did not rise and fall above nine Foot upon a Spring-tide: But it made great Riplings and a roaring Noise; whirling about like Whirlpools. We had constantly eddy Tides under the Shore, made by the Points on each side of the Bay.

When you go hence to the Eastward, you may pass betwen the small Island, and *Timor*; and when you are five or six Leagues to the Eastward of the small Island, you will see a large Valley to the Eastward of you; then running a little further, you may see Houses on the Bay: You may luff in, but anchor not till you go about the next Point. Then you will see more Houses, where you may run into twenty or thirty Fathom, and anchor right against the Houses, nearest the West-end of them. This place is called *Laphao*. It is a *Portugueze* Settlement, about sixteen Leagues from the Watering-bay.

There are in it about forty or fifty Houses, and one Church. The Houses are mean and low, the Walls generally made of Mud or watled, and their Sides made

up with Boards: They are all thatch'd with Palm or
Palmeto-Leaves. The Church also is very small: The
East-end of it is boarded up to the Top; but the Sides and
the West-end are only boarded three or four foot high;
the rest is all open: There is a small Altar in it, with two
Steps to go up to it, and an Image or two; but all very
mean. 'Tis also thatch'd with Palm or Palmeto-Leaves.
Each House has a Yard belonging to it, fenced about
with wild Canes nine or ten Foot high. There is a Well
in each Yard, and a little Bucket with a String to it to
draw Water withal. There is a Trunk of a Tree made
hollow, placed in each Well, to keep the Earth from
falling in. Round the Yards there are many Fruit-trees
planted; as Coco-nuts, Tamarins and Toddy-trees.

They have a small Hovel by the Sea-side, where there
are six small old Iron Guns standing on a decayed Plat-
form, in rotten Carriages. Their Vents are so big, that
when they are fired, the strength of the Powder flying
out there, they give but a small Report, like that of a
Musket. This is their Court of Guard; and here were a
few armed-men watching all the time we lay here.

The Inhabitants of the Town, are chiefly a sort of
Indians, of a Copper-colour, with black lank Hair:
They speak *Portugueze*, and are of the *Romish* Religion;
but they take the Liberty to eat Flesh when they please.
They value themselves on the account of their Religion
and descent from the *Portugueze*; and would be very
angry, if a Man should say they are not *Portugueze:* Yet
I saw but three White Men here, two of which were
Padres. There are also a few *Chinese* living here. It is a
place of pretty good Trade and Strength, the best on this
Island, *Porta-Nova* excepted. They have three or four
small Barks belonging to the place; with which they
trade chiefly about the Island with the Natives, for Wax,

Gold, and Sandall-wood. Sometimes they go to *Batavia*, and fetch *European* Commodities, Rice, &c.

The *Chinese* trade hither from *Macao*; and I was informed that about twenty Sail of small Vessels come from thence hither every Year. They bring coarse Rice, adulterated Gold, Tea, Iron, and Iron-tools, Porcellane, Silks, &c. They take in exchange pure Gold, as 'tis gathered in the Mountains, Bees-wax, Sandall-wood, Slaves, &c. Sometimes also here comes a Ship from *Goa*. Ships that trade here, begin to come hither the latter-end of *March*; and none stay here longer than the latter-end of *August*. For should they be here while the North-North-West Monsoon blows, no Cables nor Anchors would hold them; but they would be driven ashore and dash'd in pieces presently. But from *March* till *September*, while the South-South-East Monsoon blows, Ships ride here very secure; For then, though the Wind often blows hard, yet 'tis off Shore; so that there is very smooth Water, and no fear of being driven ashore; And yet even then they moor with three Cables; two towards the Land, Eastward and Westward; and the third right off to Seaward.

As this is the second place of Traffick, so 'tis in Strength the second place the *Portugueze* have here, though not capable of resisting a hundred Men: For the Pirates that were at the *Dutch* Fort, came hither also; and after they had fill'd their Water, and cut Fire-wood, and refresh'd themselves, they plunder'd the Houses, set them on fire, and went away. Yet I was told, that the *Portugueze* can draw together five or six hundred Men in twenty four Hours time, all armed with Hand-Guns, Swords and Pistols; but Powder and Bullets are scarce and dear. The chief Person they have on the Island, is named *Antonio Henriquez*; They call him usually by the Title of Captain

More or *Maior*. They say he is a white Man, and that he was sent hither by the Vice-Roy of *Goa*. I did not see him; for he lives, as I was informed, a great way from hence, at a place call'd *Porta Nova*, which is at the East-end of the Island, and by report is a good Harbour; but they say, that this Captain *More* goes frequently to Wars in Company with the *Indians* that are his Neighbours and Friends, against other *Indians* that are their Enemies. The next Man to him is *Alexis Mendosa*; he is a Lieutenant, and lives six or seven Miles from hence, and rules this part of the Country. He is a little Man of the *Indian*-Race, Copper-coloured, with black lank Hair. He speaks both the *Indian* and *Portugueze* Languages; is a Roman Catholick, and seems to be a civil brisk Man. There is another Lieutenant at *Laphao*; who is also an *Indian*; speaks both his own and the *Portugueze* Language very well; is old and infirm, but was very courteous to me.

They boast very much of their Strength here, and say they are able at any time to drive the *Dutch* away from the Island, had they Permission from the King of *Portugal* so to do. But though they boast thus of their Strength, yet really they are very weak; for they have but a few small Arms, and but little Powder: They have no Fort, nor Magazine of Arms; nor does the Vice-Roy of *Goa* send them any now: For though they pretend to be under the King of *Portugal*, they are a sort of lawless People, and are under no Government. It was not long since the Vice-Roy of *Goa* sent a Ship hither, and a Land-Officer to remain here: But Captain *More* put him in Irons, and sent him aboard the Ship again; telling the Commander, that he had no occasion for any Officers; and that he could make better Officers here, than any that could be sent him from *Goa*: And I know not whether there has been any other Ship sent from *Goa* since: So that they have no Supplies from thence: Yet they need not want Arms and Ammunition, seeing they trade to *Batavia*. However, they have Swords and Lances as other *Indians* have; and tho' they are ambitious to be called *Portugueze*, and value themselves on their Religion, yet most of the Men and all the Women that live here, are *Indians*; and there are very few right *Portugueze* in any part of the Island. However, of those that call themselves *Portugueze*, I was told there are some thousands; and I think their Strength consists more in their Numbers than in good Arms or Discipline.

The Land from hence trends away East by North about 14 Leagues, making many Points and sandy Bays, where Vessels may Anchor.

Fourteen Leagues East from *Laphao*, there is a small Harbour called *Ciccale* by the *Portugueze*, and commended by them for an excellent Port; but it is very small, has a narrow Entrance, and lies open to Northerly Winds: Though indeed there are two Ledges of Rocks, one shooting out from the West Point, and the other from the East Point, which break off the Sea; for the Rocks are dry at low Water. This Place is about 60 Leagues from the South-west-end of the Island.

The whole of this Island *Timor*, is a very uneven rough Country, full of Hills and small Valleys. In the Middle of it there runs a Chain of high Mountains, almost from one end to the other. It is indifferently well watered (even in the dry times) with small Brooks and Springs, but no great Rivers; the Island being but narrow, and such a Chain of Mountains in the middle, that no Water can run far; but, as the Springs break out on one side or other of the Hills, they make their nearest Course to the Sea. In the wet Season, the Valleys and low Lands by the Sea are overflown with Water; and then the small

Drills that run into the Sea, are great Rivers; and the Gulleys, which are dry for 3 or 4 Months before, now discharge an impetuous Torrent. The low Land by the Sea-side, is for the most part friable, loose, sandy Soil; yet indifferently fertile and cloathed with Woods. The Mountains are checquered with Woods, and some Spots of Savannahs: Some of the Hills are wholly covered with tall, flourishing Trees; others but thinly; and these few Trees that are on them, look very small, rusty and withered; and the Spots of Savannahs among them, appear rocky and barren. Many of the Mountains are rich in Gold, Copper or both: The Rains wash the Gold out of Mountains, which the Natives pick up in the adjacent Brooks, as the *Spaniards* do in *America:* How they get the Copper, I know not.

The Trees that grow naturally here, are of divers Sorts; many of them wholly unknown to me; but such as I have seen in *America* or other places, and grow here likewise, are these, *viz.* Mangrove, white, red and black; Maho, Calabash, several Sorts of the Palm-kind: The Cotton-trees are not large, but tougher than those in *America:* Here are also Locust-trees of 2 or 3 Sorts, bearing Fruit, but not like those I have formerly seen; these bear a large white Blossom, and yield much Fruit, but it is not sweet.

Cana-fistula-trees, are very common here; the Tree is about the Bigness of our ordinary Apple-Trees; their Branches not thick, nor full of Leaves, These and the before-mentioned, blossom in *October* and *November*; the Blossoms are much like our Apple-Tree Blossoms, and about that Bigness: At first they are red; but before they fall off, when spread abroad, they are white; so that these Trees in their Season appear extraordinarily pleasant, and yield a very fragrant Smell. When the

Fruit is ripe, it is round, and about the Bigness of a Man's Thumb; of a dark brown Colour, inclining to red, and about 2 Foot or 2 Foot and half long. We found many of them under the Trees, but they had no Pulp in them. The Partitions in the Middle, are much at the same Distance with those brought to *England*, of the same Substance, and such small flat Seed in them: But whether they be the true *Cana-fistula* or no, I cannot tell, because I found no black Pulp in them.

The *Calabashes* here are very prickly: The Trees grow tall and tapering; whereas in the *West-Indies* they are low and spread much abroad.

Here are also wild *Tamarind*-trees, not so large as the true; though much resembling them both in the Bark and Leaf.

Wild Fig-trees here are many, but not so large as those in *America*. The Fruit grows, not on the Branches singly, like those in *America*, but in Strings and Clusters, 40 or 50 in a Cluster, about the Body and great Branches of the Tree, from the very Root up to the Top. These Figs are about the Bigness of a Crab-Apple, of a greenish Colour, and full of small white Seeds; they smell pretty well, but have no Juice or Taste; they are ripe in *November*.

Here likewise grows *Sandal*-wood, and many more Sorts of Trees fit for any Uses. The tallest among them, resemble our Pines; they are streight and clear-bodied, but not very thick; the Inside is reddish near the Heart, and hard and ponderous.

Of the Palm-kind there are 3 or 4 Sorts; two of which Kinds I have not seen any where but here. Both Sorts are very large, and tall. The first Sort had Trunks of about 7 or eight Foot in Circumference, and about 80 or 90 Foot high. These had Branches at the Top like Coco-nut-Trees, and their Fruit like Coco-nuts, but smaller: The

Plants found in New Holland & Timor.

F.1

2.

3.

4.

Nut was of an oval Form, and about the Bigness of a Duck's Egg: The Shell black and very hard. 'Twas almost full of Kernel, having only a small empty Space in the Middle, but no Water as Coco-nuts have. The Kernel is too hard to be eaten. The Fruit somewhat resembles that in *Brazil* formerly mentioned. The Husk or Outside of the Fruit, was very yellow, soft and pulpy, when ripe; and full of small Fibres; and when it fell down from the Tree, would mash and smell unsavoury.

The other Sort was as big and tall as the former; the Body growing streight up without Limbs, as all Trees of the Palm-kind do: But instead of a great many long green Branches growing from the Head of the Tree, these had short Branches about the Bigness of a Man's Arm, and about a Foot long; each of which spread it self into a great many small tough Twigs, that hung full of Fruit like so many Ropes of Onions. The Fruit was as big as a large Plumb; and every Tree had several Bushels of Fruit. The Branches that bore this Fruit, sprouted out at about 50 or 60 Foot heighth from the Ground. The Trunk of the Tree was all of one Bigness, from the Ground to that Heighth; but from thence it went tapering smaller and smaller to the Top, where it was no bigger that a Man's Leg, ending in a Stump: And there was no Green about the Tree, but the Fruit; so that it appeared like a dead Trunk.

Besides Fruit-Trees, here were many Sorts of tall streight-bodied Timber-Trees; one Sort of which, was like Pine. These grow plentifully all round the Island by the Sea-side, but not far within Land. 'Tis hard Wood, of a reddish Colour, and very ponderous.

The Fruits of this Island, are *Guavoes, Mangoes, Jaca's, Coco-nuts, Plantains, Bonanoes, Pine-Apples, Citrons, Pomegranates, Oranges, Lemons, Limes, Musk-Melons, Water-*

Melons, Pumpkins, &c. Many of these have been brought hither by the *Dutch* and *Portugueze*; and most of them are ripe in *September* and *October*. There were many other excellent Fruits, but not now in Season; as I was inform'd both by *Dutch* and *Portugueze*.

Here I met with an Herb, which in the *West-Indies* we call *Calalaloo*. It grows wild here. I eat of it several Times, and found it as pleasant and wholesome as Spinage. Here are also Pursly, Sampier, &c. *Indian* Corn thrives very well here, and is the common Food of the Islanders; though the *Portugueze* and their Friends sow some Rice, but not half enough for their Subsistence.

The Land-Animals are Buffaloes, Beeves, Horses, Hogs, Goats, Sheep, Monkeys, Guanoes, Lizards, Snakes, Scorpions, Centumpees, &c. Beside the tame Hogs and Buffaloes, there are many wild all over the Country, which any may freely kill. As for the Beeves, Horses, Goats and Sheep, it is probable they were brought in by the *Portugueze* or *Dutch*; especially the Beeves; for I saw none but at the *Dutch* Fort *Concordia*.

We also saw Monkeys, and some Snakes. One Sort yellow, and as big as a Man's Arm, and about 4 Foot long: Another Sort no bigger than the Stem of a Tobacco-pipe, about 5 Foot long, green all over his Body, and with a flat red Head as big as a Man's Thumb.

The Fowls are wild Cocks and Hens, Eagles, Hawks, Crows, 2 Sorts of Pidgeons, Turtle-doves, 3 or 4 Sorts of Parrots, Parrakites, Cockatoes, Black-birds; besides a Multitude of smaller Birds of divers Colours, whose charming Musick makes the Woods very pleasant. One Sort of these pretty little Birds my Men call'd the Ringing-bird; because it had 6 Notes, and always repeated all his Notes twice one after another; beginning high and shrill, and ending low. This Bird was about the

Bigness of a Lark, having a small sharp black Bill and blue Wings; the Head and Breast were of a pale red, and there was a blue Streak about its Neck. Here are also Sea or Water-Fowls, as Men of War-Birds, Boobies, Fishing-hawks, Herons, Goldens, Crab-catchers, &c. The tame Fowl are Cocks, Hens, Ducks, Geese; the 2 last Sorts I only saw at the *Dutch* Fort; of the other Sort there are not many but among the *Portugueze:* The Woods abound with Bees, which make much Honey and Wax.

The Sea is very well stock'd with Fish of divers Sorts, *viz.* Mullets, Bass, Breames, Snooks, Mackarel, Parra-coots, Gar-fish, Ten-pounders, Scuttle-fish, String-rays, Whip-rays, Rasperages, Cockle-merchants, or Oyster-crackers, Cavallies, Conger-Eels, Rock-fish, Dog-fish, &c. The Rays are so plentiful, that I never drew the Sain but I catch'd some of them; which we salted and dryed. I caught one whose Tail was 13 Foot long. The *Cockle-Merchants* are shaped like Cavallies, and about their Bigness. They feed on Shell-fish, having 2 very hard, thick, flat Bones in their Throat, with which they break in Pieces the Shells of the Fish they swallow. We always find a great many Shells in their Maws, crushed in Pieces. The Shell-fish, are Oysters of 3 Sorts, *viz.* Long-Oysters, Common Oysters, growing upon Rocks in great Abundance, and very flat; and another Sort of large Oysters, fat and crooked; the Shell of this, not easily to be distinguished from a Stone. Three or four of these roasted, will suffice a Man for one Meal. Cockles, as big as a Man's Head; of which 2 or 3 are enough for a Meal; they are very fat and sweet. Craw-fish, Shrimps, &c. Here are also many green Turtle, some Alligators and Grandpisces, &c.

The Original Natives of this Island, are *Indians,* they are of a middle Stature, streight-bodied, slender-limb'd,

long-visag'd; their Hair black and lank; their Skins very
swarthy. They are very dextrous and nimble, but withal
lazy in the highest Degree. They are said to be dull in
every Thing but Treachery and Barbarity. Their Houses
are but low and mean, their Cloathing only a small
Cloath about their Middle; but some of them for
Ornament have Frontlets of Mother of Pearl, or thin
Pieces of Silver or Gold, made of an oval Form, of the
Breadth of a Crown-piece, curiously notched round the
Edges; Five of these placed one by another a little above
the Eye-brows, making a sufficient Guard and Ornament
for their Fore-head. They are so thin, and placed on their
Fore-heads so artificially, that they seem riveted thereon:
And indeed the Pearl-Oyster-shells make a more splendid
Show, than either Silver or Gold. Others of them have
Palmeto-caps made in divers Forms.

As to their Marriages, they take as many Wives as they
can maintain; and sometimes they sell their Children to
purchase more Wives. I enquir'd about their Religion,
and was told they had none. Their common Subsistence
is by *Indian* Corn, which every Man plants for himself.
They take but little Pains to clear their Land; for in the
dry Time they set Fire to the withered Grass and
Shrubs, and that burns them out a Plantation for the
next wet Season. What other Grain they have, beside
Indian Corn, I know not. Their Plantations are very
mean; for they delight most in hunting; and here
are wild Buffaloes and Hogs enough, though very shy,
because of their so frequent hunting.

They have a few Boats and some Fishermen. Their
Arms are Lances, thick round short Truncheons and
Targets; with these they hunt and kill their Game, and
their Enemies too; for this Island is now divided into
many Kingdoms, and all of different Languages; though

in their Customs and Manner of living, as well as Shape and Colour, they seem to be of one Stock.

The chiefest Kingdoms are *Cupang*, *Amabie*, *Lortribie*, *Pobumbie*, *Namquimal*; the Island also of *Anamabao* or *Anabao*, is a Kingdom. Each of these hath a Sultan who is supreme in his Province and Kingdom, and hath under him several *Raja's* and other inferiour Officers. The Sultans for the most Part are Enemies to each other; which Enmities are fomented and kept up by the *Dutch*, whose Fort and Factory is in the Kingdom of *Cupang*; and therefore the Bay near which they are settled, is commonly called *Cupang*-Bay. They have only as much Ground as they can keep within Reach of their Guns; yet this whole Kingdom is at Peace with them; and they freely trade together; as also with the Islanders on *Anabao*, who are in Amity as well with the Natives of *Cupang*, as with the *Dutch* residing there; but they are implacable Enemies to those of *Amabie*, who are their next Neighbours, and in Amity with the *Portugueze:* as are also the Kingdoms of *Pobumbie*, *Namquimal* and *Lortribie*. It is very probable, that these 2 *European* Settlements on this Island, are the greatest Occasion of their continued Wars. The *Portugueze* vaunt highly of their Strength here, and that they are able at Pleasure to rout the *Dutch*, if they had Authority so to do from the King of *Portugal*; and they have written to the Vice-roy of *Goa* about it: And though their Request is not yet granted, yet (as they say) they live in Expectation of it. These have no Forts, but depend on their Alliance with the Natives: And indeed they are already so mixt, that it is hard to distinguish whether they are *Portugueze* or *Indians*. Their Language is *Portugueze*; and the Religion they have, is *Romish*. They seem in Words to acknowledge the King of *Portugal* for their Sovereign; yet they will not accept of any Officers sent by him. The speak indifferently the *Malayan* and their own native Languages, as well as *Portugueze*; and the chiefest Officers that I saw, were of this Sort; neither did I see above 3 or 4 white Men among them; and of these, 2 were Priests. Of this mixt Breed there are some thousands; of whom some have small Arms of their own, and know how to use them. The chiefest Person (as I before said) is called Captain *More* or *Maior:* He is a white Man, sent hither by the Vice-Roy of *Goa*, and seems to have great Command here. I did not see him; for he seldom comes down. His Residence is at a Place called *Porta Nova*; which the People at *Laphao* told me was a great way off; but I could not get any more particular Account. Some told me that he is most commonly in the Mountains, with an Army of *Indians*, to guard the Passes between them and the *Cupangayans*, especially in the dry Times. The next Man to him is *Alexis Mendosa:* He is a right *Indian*, speaks very good *Portugueze*, and is of the *Romish* Religion. He lives 5 or 6 Miles from the Sea, and is called the Lieutenant. (This is he whom I call'd Governour, when at *Laphao*.) He commands next to Captain *More*, and hath under him another at this Fort (at the Seaside) if it may be so called. He also is called Lieutenant, and is an *Indian Portugueze*.

Besides this Mungrel-Breed of *Indians* and *Portugueze*, here are also some *China*-Men, Merchants from *Maccao:* They bring hither coarse Rice, Gold, Tea, Iron-work, Porcelane, and Silk both wrought and raw: They get in Exchange pure Gold as it is here gather'd, Bees-wax, Sandall-Wood, Coire, &c. It is said there are about 20 small *China* Vessels come hither every Year from *Maccao*; and commonly one Vessel a Year from *Goa*, which brings *European* Commodities and Callicoes, Muslins, &c. Here are likewise some small Barks belonging to this

Place, that trade to *Batavia*, and bring from thence both *European* and *Indian* Goods and Rice. The Vessels generally come here in *March*, and stay till *September*.

The *Dutch*, as I before said, are setled in the Kingdom of *Cupang*, where they have a small neat Stone Fort. It seems to be pretty strong; yet, as I was informed, had been taken by a *French* Pirate about 2 Years ago: The *Dutch* were used very barbarously, and ever since are very jealous of any Strangers that come this Way; which I my self experienced. These depend more on their own Strength than on the Natives their Friends; having good Guns, Powder, and Shot enough on all Occasions, and Soldiers sufficient to manage the Business here, all well disciplin'd and in good Order; which is a Thing the *Portugueze* their Neighbours are altogether destitute of, they having no *European* Soldiers, few Arms, less Ammunition, and their Fort consisting of no more than 6 bad Guns planted against the Sea, whose Touch-holes (as was before observed) are so enlarg'd by Time, that a great Part of the Strength of the Powder flies away there; and having Soldiers in pay, the Natives on all Occasions are hired; and their Government now is so loose, that they will admit of no more Officers from *Portugal* or *Goa*. They have also little or no Supply of Arms or Ammunition from thence, but buy it as often as they can, of the *Dutch*, *Chinese*, &c. So that upon the whole it seems improbable that they should ever attempt to drive out the *Dutch*, for fear of loosing themselves, notwithstanding their boasted Prowess and Alliance with the Natives: And indeed, as far as I could hear, they have Business enough to keep their own present Territories from the Incursions of the *Cupangayans*; who are Friends to the *Dutch*, and whom doubtless the *Dutch* have ways enough to preserve in their Friendship; besides that they have an inveterate

Malice to their Neighbours, insomuch that they kill all they meet, and bring away their Heads in Triumph. The great Men of *Cupang* stick the Heads of those they have killed, on Poles; and set them on the Tops of their Houses; and these they esteem above all their other Riches. The inferiour Sort bring the Heads of those they kill, into Houses made for that Purpose; of which there was one at the *Indian* Village near the Fort *Concordia*, almost full of Heads, as I was told. I know not what Encouragement they have for their Inhumanity.

The *Dutch* have always 2 Sloops belonging to their Fort; in these they go about the Island, and trade with the Natives; and, as far as I could learn, they trade indifferently with them all. For though the Inland People are at war with each other, yet those by the Sea-side seem to be little concerned; and, generally speaking the *Malayan* Language, are very sociable and easily induced to trade with those that speak that Language; which the *Dutch* here always learn; Besides, being well acquainted with the Treachery of these People, they go well arm'd among them, and are very vigilant never to give them an Opportunity to hurt them; and it is very probable that they supply them with such Goods, as the *Portugueze* cannot.

The *Malayan* Language, as I have before said, is generally spoken amongst all the Islands hereabouts. The greater the Trade is, the more this Language is spoken: In some it is become their only Language; in others it is but little spoken, and that by the Sea-side only. With this Language the *Mahometan* Religion did spread it self, and was got hither before any *European* Christians came: But now, though the Language is still used, the *Mahometan* Religion falls, where-ever the *Portugueze* or *Dutch* are settled; unless they be very weak, as at *Solor* and *Ende*, where the chief Language is *Malayan*, and the Religion Mahometanism; though the *Dutch* are settled at *Solor*, and the *Portugueze* at the East-end of the Island *Ende*, at a Place called *Lorantuca*; which, as I was informed, is a large Town, hath a pretty strong Fort and safe Harbour. The chief Man there (as at *Timor*) is called Captain *More*, and is as absolute as the other. These 2 principal Men are Enemies to each other; and by their Letters and Messages to *Goa*, inveigh bitterly against each other; and are ready to do all the ill Offices they can; yet neither of them much regards the Vice-Roy of *Goa*, as I was inform'd.

L' Orantuca is said to be more populous then any Town on *Timor*; the Island *Ende* affording greater Plenty of all manner of Fruit, and being much better supplied with all Necessaries, than *Laphao*; especially with Sheep, Goats, Hogs, Poultry, &c. but it is very dangerous getting into this Harbour, because of the violent Tides, between the Islands *Ende* and *Solor*. In the middle Channel between *Timor* and the Range of Islands to the Northward of it, whereof *Ende* and *Solor* are 2, there runs a constant Current all the Year to the Westward; though near either Shore there are Tides indeed; but the Tide of Flood, which sets West, running 8 or 9 Hours, and the Ebb not exceeding 3 or 4 Hours, the Tide in some Places riseth 9 or 10 Foot on a Spring.

The Seasons of the Year here at *Timor*, are much the same as in other Places in South Latitude. The fair Weather begins in *April* or *May*, and continues to *October*, then the Tornadoes begin to come, but no violent bad Weather till the Middle of *December*. Then there are violent West or North-West Winds, with Rain, till towards the Middle of *February*. In *May* the Southerly Winds set in, and blow very strong on the North-side of the Island, but fair. There is great Difference of Winds on the 2 Sides of the Island: For the Southerly Winds are but very faint on the South-side, and very hard on the North-side; and the bad Weather on the South-side comes in very violent in *October*, which on the North-side comes not till *December*. You have very good Sea and Land-breezes, when the Weather is fair; and may run indifferently to the East or West, as your Business lies. We found from *September* to *December* the Winds veering all round the Compass gradually in 24 Hours Time; but such a constant Western Current, that it's much harder getting to the East than West at or near Spring Tides: Which I have more than once made Tryal off. For weighing from *Babao* at 6 a Clock in the Morning on the 12th Instant, we kept plying under the Shore till the 20th, meeting with such a Western Current, that we gain'd very little. We had Land and Sea-breezes; but so faint, that we could hardly stem the Current; and when it was calm between the Breezes, we drove a-Stern faster than ever we sailed a-Head.

CHAP. III

Departure from Timor. *The Islands* Omba *and* Fetter. *A burning Island.
Their Missing the* Turtle-Isles. Bande-*Isles.* Bird-*Island. They descry
the Coast of* New-Guinea. *They anchor on the Coast of* New-Guinea. *A
description of the Place, and of a strange Fowl found there. Great quantities
of Mackerel. A white Island. They anchor at an Island called by the
Inhabitants* Pulo Sabuda. *A description of it, and its Inhabitants, and
Product. The Indians manner of Fishing there. Arrival at* Mabo, *the
North-West Cape of* New-Guinea. *A Description of it.* Cockle-*Island.
Cockles of seventy-eight pound Weight.* Pidgeon-*Island. The Winds here-
abouts. An empty Cockle-shell weighing two hundred fifty-eight Pound.*
King William's *Island. A Description of it. Plying on the Coast of*
New-Guinea. *Fault of the Draughts.* Providence *Island. They cross the
Line. A Snake pursued by Fish. Squally Island. The Main of* New-Guinea.

ON the 12th of *December* 1699, we sailed from *Babao*,
coasting along the Island *Timor* to the Eastward,
towards *New Guinea*. It was the 20th before we got as far
as *Laphao*, which is but forty Leagues. We saw black
Clouds in the North-West, and expected the Wind from
that Quarter above a Month sooner.

That Afternoon we saw the opening between the
Islands *Omba* and *Fetter*, but feared to pass through in the
Night. At two a Clock in the Morning, it fell calm; and
continued so till Noon, in which time we drove with the
Current back again South-West six or seven Leagues.

On the 22d, steering to the Eastward to get through
between *Omba* and *Fetter*, we met a very strong Tide
against us, so that we, although we had a very fresh Gale,
yet made way very slowly; yet before Night, got through.
By a good Observation we found that the South-East-
point of *Omba* lies in Latitude 8 d. 25 m. In my Draughts
it's laid down in 8 deg. 10 min. My true Course from
Babao, is East, 25 deg. North, distance one hundred
eighty three miles. We sounded several times when near

N

Omba, but had no ground. On the North-East point of
Omba we saw four or five Men, and a little further three
pretty Houses on a low Point, but did not go ashore.

At five this Afternoon, we had a Tornado, which
yielded much Rain, Thunder and Lightning; yet we had
but little Wind. The 24th in the Morning we catched a
large Shark, which gave all the Ships Company a
plentiful Meal.

The 27th we saw the burning Island, it lies in Latitude
6 deg. 36 min. South; it is high, and but small. It runs
from the Sea a little sloaping towards the Top; which is
divided in the Middle into two Peaks, between which
issued out much Smoak: I have not seen more from any
Vulcano. I saw no Trees; but the North-side appeared
green, and the rest look'd very barren.

Having past the burning Island, I shap'd my Course for
two Islands called *Turtle Isles,* which lye North-East by
East a little Easterly, and distant about fifty Leagues
from the burning Isle. I fearing the Wind might veer to
the Eastward of the North, steered 20 Leagues North-
East, then North-East by East. On the 28th we saw two
small low Islands, called *Luca-parros,* to the North of us.
At Noon I accounted my self 20 Leagues short of the
Turtle Isles.

The next Morning, being in the Latitude of the *Turtle
Islands,* we look'd out sharp for them, but saw no appearance of any Island, till 11 a Clock; when we saw an
Island at a great distance. At first we supposed it might
be one of the *Turtle Isles:* But it was not laid down true,
neither in Latitude nor Longitude from the *burning Isle,*
nor from the *Luca-parros,* which last I took to be a great
help to guide me, they being laid down very well from
the *Burning Isle,* and that likewise in true Latitude and
distance from *Omba:* So that I could not tell what to

Tab.VII · **Timor** *and other Islands between it and* N. **Guinea**

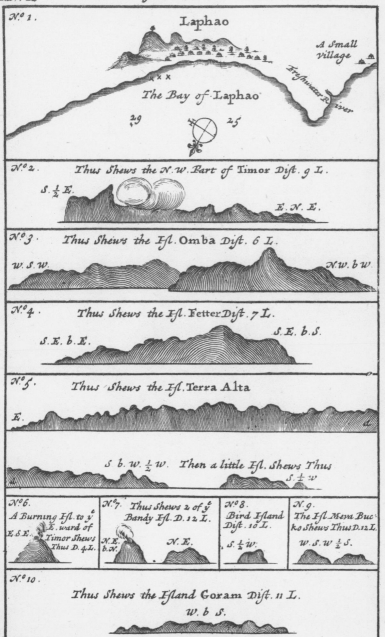

N.° 1.

Laphao

A small village

The Bay of Laphao

Freshwater River

29 25

N.° 2. *Thus Shews the N.W. Part of Timor Dist. 9 L.*

S. ½ E.

E. N. E.

N.° 3. *Thus Shews the Isl. Omba Dist. 6 L.*

W. S. W.

N. W. b W.

N.° 4. *Thus Shews the Isl. Fetter Dist. 7 L.*

S. E. b. E.

S. E. b. S.

N.° 5. *Thus Shews the Isl. Terra Alta*

E.

S. b. W. ½ W. Then a little Isl. Shews Thus

S. ½ W.

N.° 6.
A Burning Isl. to ye E. ward of Timor Shews Thus D. 4 L.
E. S. E.

N.° 7. *Thus Shews 2 of ye Bandy Isl. D. 12 L.*
N. E. b. N.
N. E.

N.° 8.
Bird Island Dist. 10 L.
S. ½ W.

N. 9.
The Isl. Meva Bucko Shews Thus D. 12 L.
W. S. W. ½ S.

N.° 10.

Thus Shews the Island Goram Dist. 11 L.

W. b S.

think of the Island now in sight; we having had fair
Weather, so that we could not pass by the *Turtle Isles*
without seeing them; and This in sight was much too far
off for them. We found Variation 1 deg. 2 min. East. In
the Afternoon I steered North-East by East for the Islands
that we saw. At 2 a Clock I went and look'd over the
Fore-yard, and saw 2 Islands at much greater distance than
the *Turtle Islands* are laid down in my Draughts; one of
them was a very high peak'd Mountain, cleft at Top, and
much like the *burning Island* that we past by, but bigger
and higher; the other was a pretty long high flat Island.
Now I was certain that these were not the *Turtle Islands*,
and that they could be no other than the *Bande-Isles*; yet
we steered in, to make them plainer. At 3 a Clock we discovered another small flat Island to the North-West of the
others, and saw a great deal of Smoak rise from the Top
of the high Island; At 4 we saw other small Islands, by
which I was now assured that these were the *Bande-Isles*
there. At 5 I altered my Course and steered East, and at
8 East-South-East; because I would not be seen by the
Inhabitants of those Islands in the Morning. We had
little Wind all Night: and in the Morning as soon as 'twas
Light, we saw another high peak'd Island: At 8 it bore
South-South-East half East, distance 8 Leagues. And
this I knew to be *Bird-Isle*. 'Tis laid down in our Draughts
in Latitude 5 deg. 9 min. South, which is too far Southerly
by 27 Miles according to our Observation; And the
like Error in laying down the *Turtle-Islands*, might be the
Occasion of our missing them.

At night I shortned Sail, for fear of coming too nigh
some Islands, that stretch away bending like a half Moon
from *Ceram* towards *Timor*, and which in my Course I
must of necessity pass through. The next Morning betimes, I saw them; and found them to be at a farther dis-

tance from *Bird*-Island, than I expected. In the Afternoon
it fell quite calm; and when we had a little Wind, it was
so unconstant, flying from one Point to another, that I
could not without difficulty get through the Islands where
I designed: Besides, I found a Current setting to the
Southward; so that it was betwixt 5 and 6 in the Evening,
before I past through the Islands; and then just
weathered little *Waiela*, whereas I thought to have been
2 or 3 Leagues more Northerly. We saw the day before,
betwixt 2 and 3, a Spout but a small distance from us. It
fell down out of a black Cloud, that yielded great store of
Rain, Thunder and Lightning: This Cloud hovered to
the Southward of us for the space of three Hours, and
then drew to the Westward a great pace; at which time
it was that we saw the Spout, which hung fast to the
Cloud till it broke; and then the Cloud whirl'd about to
the South-East, then to East-North-East; where meeting
with an Island, it spent it self and so dispersed; and immediately we had a little of the Tail of it, having had none
before. Afterward we saw a Smoak on the Island *Kosiway*,
which continued till Night.

On *New-years-day* we first described the Land of *New-
Guinea*, which appear'd to be high Land; And the next
day we saw several high Islands on the Coast of *New-
Guinea*, and ran in with the main Land. The Shore here
lies along East-South-East and West-North-West. It is
high even Land, very well cloathed with tall flourishing
Trees, which appear'd very green and gave us a very
pleasant Prospect. We ran to the Westward of four mountainous Islands; and in the Night had a small Tornado,
which brought with it some Rain and a fair Wind. We
had fair Weather for a long time; only when near any
Land, we had some Tornadoes; but off, at Sea, commonly clear Weather; though if in sight of Land,

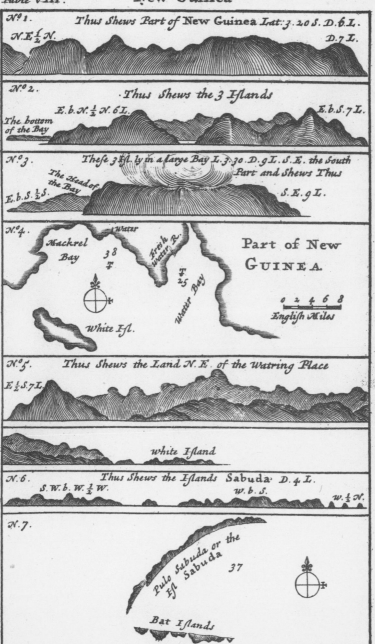

Table VIII.   New Guinea

Nº 1.   Thus Shews Part of New Guinea Lat: 3. 20 S. D. 6 L.
N. E. ½ N.   D. 7 L.

Nº 2.   Thus Shews the 3 Islands
         E. b. N. ½ N. 6 L.   E. b. S. 7 L.
The bottom
of the Bay

Nº 3.   These 3 Isl. ly in a large Bay L. 3. 30. D. 9 L. S. E. the South
                                    Part and Shews Thus
         The Head of
         the Bay
E. b. S. ½ S.   S. E. 9 L.

Nº 4.   Water
         Mackrel   Fresh Water R.   Part of New
         Bay   38   GUINEA.
                  T
                          T
                          25
                                                         0 2 4 6 8
                                                         English Miles
              White Isl.   Water Bay

Nº 5.   Thus Shews the Land N. E. of the Watring Place
E. ½ S. 7 L.

                           white Island

Nº 6.   Thus Shews the Islands Sabuda D. 4 L.
    S. W. b. W. ½ W.   w. b. S.   w. ½ N.

Nº 7.

              Pulo Sabuda or the
                   Isl Sabuda   37

              Bat Islands

we usually saw many black Clouds hovering about it.

On the 5th and 6th of *January*, we plied to get in with the Land; designing to anchor, fill Water, and spend a little time in searching the Country, till after the change of the Moon; For I found a strong Current setting against us. We anchor'd in 38 Fathom Water, good oazie Ground. We had an Island of a League long without us, about 3 Miles distant; and we rode from the Main about a Mile. The Eastermost Point of Land seen, bore East by South half South, distance 3 Leagues: And the Westermost, West-South-West half South, distance 2 Leagues. So soon as we anchor'd, we sent the Pinnace to look for Water, and try if they could catch any Fish. Afterwards we sent the Yawle another way to see for Water. Before Night the Pinnace brought on board several sorts of Fruits, that they found in the Woods, such as I never saw before. One of my Men killed a stately Land-Fowl, as big as the largest Dunghil-Cock. It was of a Sky-colour; only in the middle of the Wings was a white Spot, about which were some reddish Spots: On the Crown it had a large Bunch of long Feathers, which appear'd very pretty. His Bill was like a Pidgeons; he had strong Legs and Feet, like Dunghil-Fowls; only the Claws were reddish. His Crop was full of small Berries. It lays an Egg as big as a large Hen's Egg; for our Men climb'd the Tree where it nested, and brought off one Egg. They found Water; and reported that the Trees were large, tall and very thick; and that they saw no sign of People. At night the Yawle came aboard, and brought a wooden Fissgigg, very ingeniously made; the Matter of it was a small Cane; They found it by a small Barbecue, where they also saw a shatter'd Canoa.

The next Morning I sent the Boatswain ashore a fishing, and at one Haul he catcht 352 Mackarels, and

about 20 other Fishes; which I caused to be equally
divided among all my Company. I sent also the Gunner
and chief Mate, to search about if they could find convenient anchoring nearer a Watering-place: By night they
brought word that they had found a fine Stream of good
Water, where the Boat could come close to, and it was very
easie to be fill'd; and that the Ship might anchor as near to
it as I pleas'd: So I went thither. The next Morning therefore we anchor'd in 25 Fathom Water, soft oazie Ground,
about a Mile from the River: We got on board 3 Tun of
Water that Night; and caught 2 or 3 Pike-fish, in shape
much like a Parracota, but with a longer Snout, something resembling a Garr, yet not so long. The next day I
sent the Boat again for Water, and before night all my
Casks were full.

Having fill'd here about 15 Tuns of Water, seeing we
could catch but little Fish, and had no other Refreshments, I intended to sail next day; but finding that we
wanted Wood, I sent to cut some; and going ashore to
hasten it, at some distance from the place where our
Men were, I found a small Cove, where I saw two
Barbecues, which appear'd not to be above 2 Months
standing: The Sparrs were cut with some sharp Instrument; so that, if done by the Natives, it seems that they
have Iron. On the 10th, a little after 12 a-Clock, we
weighed and stood over to the North-side of the Bay;
and at 1 a-Clock stood out with the Wind at North and
North-North-West. At 4 we past out by a White Island,
which I so named from its many white Cliffs, having no
name in our Draughts. It is about a League long, pretty
high, and very woody: 'Tis about 5 Miles from the Main,
only at the West-end it reaches within 3 Miles of it. At
some distance off at Sea, the West-point appears like a
Cape-land; The North-side trends away North-North-

Plants found in y Sea neer   New Guinea.

F. 1.

2.

West, and the East-side East-South-East. This Island lies in Latitude 3 degrees 4 min. South; and the Meridian Distance from *Babao*, 500 and 12 Miles East. After we were out to Sea, we plied to get to the Northward; but met with such a strong Current against us, that we got but little. For if the Wind favour'd us in the night, that we got 3 or 4 Leagues; we lost it again, and were driven as far astern next Morning; so that we plyed here several Days.

The 14th, being past a point of Land that we had been 3 Days getting about, we found little or no Current; so that having the Wind at North-West by West and West-North-West, we stood to the Northward, and had several Soundings: At 3 a-Clock, 38 Fathom; the nearest part of *New-Guinea* being about 3 Leagues distance: At 4, 37; at 5, 36; at 6, 36; at 8, 33 Fathom; Then the Cape was about 4 Leagues distant; so that as we ran off, we found our Water shallower. We had then some Islands to the Westward of us, at about four Leagues distance.

A little after noon we saw Smokes on the Islands to the West of us; and having a fine Gale of Wind, I steered away for them: At 7 a-Clock in the Evening we anchored in 35 Fathom, about two Leagues from an Island, good soft oazie Ground. We lay still all night, and saw Fires ashore. In the Morning we weighed again, and ran farther in, thinking to have shallower Water; but we ran within a Mile, of the Shore, and came to in 38 Fathom, good soft holding Ground. While we were under Sail, 2 Canoes came off within call of us: They spoke to us, but we did not understand their Language, nor Signs. We wav'd to them to come aboard, and I call'd to them in the *Malayan* Language to do the same; but they would not; yet they came so nigh us, that we could shew them such Things as we had to truck with them; Yet neither would this entice them to come aboard; but they made Signs for us to come ashore, and away they went. Then I went after them in my Pinnace, carrying with me Knives, Beads, Glasses, Hatchets, &c. When we came near the Shore, I called to them in the *Malayan* Language: I saw but 2 Men at first, the rest lying in Ambush behind the Bushes; but assoon as I threw ashore some Knives and other Toys, they came out, flung down their Weapons, and came into the Water by the Boat's Side, making Signs of Friendship by pouring Water on their Heads with one Hand, which they dipt into the Sea. The next Day in the Afternoon several other Canoas came aboard, and brought many Roots and Fruits, which we purchas'd.

This Island has no Name in our Draughts, but the Natives call it *Pulo Sabuda*. It is about 3 Leagues long, and 2 Miles wide, more or less. It is of a good Heighth, so as to be seen 11 or 12 Leagues. It is very Rocky; yet above the Rocks, there is good yellow and black Mould; not deep, yet producing plenty of good tall Trees, and bearing any Fruits or Roots which the Inhabitants plant. I do not know all its Produce; but what we saw, were Plantains, Coco-Nuts, Pine-Apples, Oranges, Papaes, Potatoes, and other large Roots. Here are also another sort of wild Jaca's, about the bigness of a Mans two Fists, full of Stones or Kernels, which eat pleasant enough when roasted. The Libby Tree grows here in the Swampy Valleys, of which they make Sago Cakes: I did not see them make any, but was told by the Inhabitants that it was made of the Pith of the Tree, in the same Manner I have described in my Voyage round the World. They shew'd me the Tree whereof it was made, and I bought about 40 of the Cakes. I bought also 3 or 4 Nutmegs in their Shell, which did not seem to have been long gathered; but whether they be the Growth of this Island

This Fish is of a pale red all parts of it except y Eye take on y Coast of New Guinea

Strange & large Batts on I. Pulo Sabuda in New Guinea

This Birds Eye is of a Bright red

or not, the Natives would not tell whence they had them, and seem'd to prize them very much. What Beasts the Island affords, I know not: But here are both Sea and Land-Fowl. Of the first, Boobies and Men of War-Birds are the chief; some Goldens, and small Milk-white Crab-catchers. The Land-fowls are Pidgeons, about the Bigness of Mountain-Pidgeons in *Jamaica*; and Crows about the Bigness of those in England, and much like them; but the inner Part of their Feathers are white, and the Outside black; so that they appear all black, unless you extend the Feathers. Here are large Sky-colour'd Birds, such as we lately kill'd on *New Guinea*; and many other small Birds, unknown to us. Here are likewise Abundance of Bats, as big as young Coneys; their Necks, Head, Ears and Noses, like Foxes; their Hair rough; that about their Necks, is of a whitish yellow, that on their Heads and Shoulders black; their Wings are 4 Foot over, from Tip to Tip: They smell like Foxes. The Fish are Bass, Rock-fish, and a Sort of Fish like Mullets, Old-wives, Whip-rays, and some other Sorts that I know not, but no great Plenty of any; for 'tis deep Water till within less than a Mile of the Shore; then there is a Bank of Coral Rocks, within which you have Shoal Water, white clean Sand: So there is no good Fishing with the Sain.

This Island lies in Latitude 2 deg. 43 min. South, and Meridian distance from Port *Babao* on the Island *Timor*, 486 Miles. Besides this Island, here are 9 or 10 other small Islands, as they are laid down in the Draughts.

The Inhabitants of this Island are a Sort of very tawny *Indians*, with long black Hair; who in their Manners differ but little from the *Mindanayans*, and others of these Eastern Islands. These seem to be the chief; for besides them we saw also shock curlpated *New-Guinea Negroes*; many of which are Slaves to the others, but I think not all. They are very poor, wear no Cloaths, but have a Clout about their Middle, made of the Rinds of the Tops of Palmeto Trees; but the Women had a Sort of Callicoe-Cloaths. Their chief Ornaments are Blue and Yellow-Beads, worn about their Wrists. The Men arm themselves with Bows and Arrows, Lances, broad Swords like those of *Mindanao*; their Lances are pointed with Bone. They strike Fish very ingeniously with wooden Fiss-gigs, and have a very ingenious way of making the Fish rise: For they have a Piece of Wood curiously carv'd and painted much like a Dolphin (and perhaps other Figures;) these they let down into the Water by a Line with a small Weight to sink it; when they think it low enough, they haul the Line into their Boats very fast, and the Fish rise up after this Figure; and they stand ready to strike them when they are near the Surface of the Water. But their chief Livelihood is from their Plantations. Yet they have large Boats, and go over to *New-Guinea*, where they get Slaves, fine Parrots, &c. which they carry to *Goram* and exchange for Callicoes. One Boat came from thence a little before I arriv'd here; of whom I bought some Parrots; and would have bought a Slave, but they would not barter for any Thing but Callicoes, which I had not. Their Houses on this Side were very small, and seem'd only to be for Necessity; but on the other Side of the Island we saw good large Houses. Their Proes are narrow with Outlagers on each Side, like other *Malayans*. I cannot tell of what Religion these are; but I think they are not *Mahometans*, by their drinking Brandy out of the same Cup with us without any Scruple. At this Island we continued till the 20th Instant, having laid in Store of such Roots and Fruits as the Island afforded.

Table IX   New Guinea

No 1.

W.N.W. 7 L.   N. W. b. W. 6 L.   N.W. ½ N. 8 L.

N. 7 L.

No 2.

W.S.W. 3 L. A Small Sandy Isl. This loe land is part of N. Guinea Lat. 2. ⅗. S.

N.N.E. 6 L.

N.E. b. N. 6 L.   Shole Isl.   E.N.E. 3 L.

No 3.

S. b. W. 9 L. These Isl. is y same as a bove and makes thus. at these bearings. and lays to y E. ward of y Isl. Meſſel W.S.W. 9 L.

No 4.

S.W. b. S.   S. b. W. 8 L.

No 5.

S. S. W. 8 L.

a

W. S. W. 6 L.   W. b. N. 7 L.

This head is y N. moſt head of Meſſel Isl. and maketh

a thus   at these bearings, and a bondance of small Isl. round it. he rises thus as y sland a way

No 6   to y N. w. ward of it.

The N. head of Meſſel

S. S. W. 5 L.   W. b. S. 4 L.   W. N. W   N.W. b. W. 6 L.   a

When youw have y N. moſt head of Meſſel W.S.W. 5 L. that lays of these Isl. at these bearings. and at y same time y land of N. Guinea or Cape Mabo sheweth as a loe and a ning of Islands a bout 13 L. at this side.

a   N. W. b. N. ½ N.

No 7.

C. Mabo   N. 18 L.

N. N. W. ½ W. 5 L.   a

Isl. N.N.E. 3 L.

N.E. b. N. 12 L.

a

On the 20th, at half Hour after 6 in the Morning, I weigh'd, and standing out we saw a large Boat full of Men lying at the North-point of the Island. As we passed by, they rowed towards their Habitations, where we supposed they had withdrawn themselves for fear of us (tho' we gave them no Cause of Terrour,) or for some Differences among themselves.

We stood to the Northward till 7 in the Evening; then saw a Ripling; and the Water being discoloured, we sounded, and had but 22 Fathom. I went about and stood to the Westward till 2 next Morning, then tack'd again, and had these several Soundings: At 8 in the Evening, 22; at 10, 25; at 11, 27; at 12, 28 Fathom; at 2 in the Morning 26; at 4, 24; at 6, 23; at 8, 28; at 12, 22.

We passed by many small Islands, and among many dangerous Shoals, without any remarkable Occurrence, till the 4th of *February*, when we got within 3 Leagues of the North-West Cape of *New-Guinea*, called by the *Dutch* Cape *Mabo*. Off this Cape there lies a small woody Island, and many Islands of different Sizes to the North and North-East of it. This Part of *New Guinea* is high Land, adorn'd with tall Trees that appeared very green and flourishing. The Cape it self is not very high, but ends in a low sharp Point; and on either Side there appears another such Point at equal Distances, which makes it resemble a Diamond. This only appears when you are abreast of the middle Point; and then you have no Ground within 3 Leagues of the Shore.

In the Afternoon we past by the Cape, and stood over for the Islands. Before it was dark, we were got within a League of the Westermost; but had no Ground with 50 Fathom of Line. However fearing to stand nearer in the dark, we tack'd and stood to the East, and plyed all Night. The next Morning we were got 5 or 6 Leagues

to the Eastward of that Island; and having the Wind
Easterly, we stood in to the Northward among the
Islands; sounded, and had no Ground. Then I sent in my
Boat to sound, and they had Ground with 50 Fathom near
a Mile from the Shore. We tack'd before the Boat came
aboard again, for fear of a Shoal that was about a Mile
to the East of that Island the Boat went to; from whence
also a Shoal-point stretched out it self till it met the other:
They brought with them such a Cockle, as I have mentioned in my Voyage round the World, found near
Celebes; and they saw many more, some bigger than that
which they brought aboard, as they said; and for this
Reason I named it *Cockle*-Island. I sent them to sound
again, ordering them to fire a Musquet if they found good
anchoring; we were then standing to the Southward, with
a fine Breeze. Assoon as they fired, I tack'd and stood in:
They told me they had 50 Fathom when they fired. I
tack'd again, and made all the Sail I could to get out,
being near some Rocky Islands and Shoals to Leeward
of us. The Breeze increased, and I thought we were out of
Danger; but having a Shoal just by us, and the Wind
falling again, I ordered the Boat to tow us, and by their
Help we got clear from it. We had a strong Tide setting
to the Westward.

At 1 a-Clock, being past the Shoal, and finding
the Tide setting to the Westward, I anchor'd in 35
Fathom, coarse Sand, with small Coral and Shells.
Being nearest to *Cockle-Island*, I immediately sent both
the Boats thither; one to cut Wood, and the other to fish.
At 4 in the Afternoon, having a small Breeze at South-
South-West, I made a Sign for my Boats to come aboard.
They brought some Wood, and a few small Cockles, none
of them exceeding 10 Pound weight; whereas the Shell
of the great one weighed 78 Pound; but it was now high

Water, and therefore they could get no bigger. They also brought on Board some Pidgeons, of which we found Plenty on all the Islands where we touch'd in these Seas. Also in many Places we saw many large Batts, but kill'd none, except those I mention'd at *Pulo Sabuda*. As our Boats came aboard, we weigh'd and made Sail, steering East-South-East, as long as the Wind held; In the Morning we found we had got 4 or 5 Leagues to the East of the Place where we weighed. We stood to and fro till 11; and finding that we lost Ground, anchor'd in 42 Fathom, coarse gravelly Sand, with some Coral. This Morning we thought we saw a Sail.

In the Afternoon I went ashore on a small woody Island, about 2 Leagues from us. Here I found the greatest Number of Pidgeons that ever I saw either in the *East* or *West-Indies*, and small Cockles in the Sea round the Island, in such Quantities that we might have laden the Boat in an Hour's Time: These were not above 10 or 12 Pound Weight. We cut some Wood, and brought off Cockles enough for all the Ship's Company; but having no small Shot, we could kill no Pidgeons. I return'd about 4 a-Clock; and then my Gunner and both Mates went thither, and in less than 3 quarters of an Hour they kill'd and brought off 10 Pidgeons. Here is a Tide: The Flood sets West and the Ebb East; but the latter is very faint, and but of small Continuance. And so we found it ever since we came from *Timor*. The Winds we found Easterly, between North-East and East-South-East; so that if these continue, it is impossible to beat farther to the Eastward on this Coast against Wind and Current. These Easterly Winds encreased from the Time we were in the Latitude of about 2 deg. South; and as we drew nigher the Line, they hung more Easterly. And now being to the North of the Continent of *New*

Guinea, where the Coast lies East and West, I find the Trade-wind here at East; which yet in higher Latitudes is usually at North-North-West and North-West; and so I did expect them here, it being to the South of the Line.

The 7th in the Morning I sent my Boat ashore on *Pidgeon-Island*, and staid still Noon. In the Afternoon my Men returned, brought 22 Pidgeons, and many Cockles, some very large, some small: They also brought one empty Shell, that weigh'd 258 Pound.

At 4 a-Clock we weigh'd, having a small Westerly Wind, and a Tide with us; at 7 in the Evening we anchor'd in 42 Fathom, near *King William's Island*, where I went ashore the next Morning, drank his Majesty's Health, and honour'd it with his Name. It is about 2 Leagues and a half in length, very high, and extraordinarily well cloathed with Woods. The Trees are of divers Sorts, most unknown to us, but all very green and flourishing; many of them had Flowers, some white, some purple, others yellow; all which smelt very fragrantly. The Trees are generally tall and streight-bodied, and may be fit for any Uses. I saw one of a clean Body, without Knot or Limb, 60 or 70 Foot high by Estimation. It was 3 of my Fathoms about, and kept its Bigness without any sensible Decrease even to the Top. The Mould of the Island is black, but not deep; it being very rocky. On the Sides and Top of the Island, are many Palmeto-Trees, whose Heads we could discern over all the other Trees, but their Bodies we could not see.

About 1 in the Afternoon we weighed and stood to the Eastward, between the Main and *King William's Island*; leaving the Island on our Larboard side, and sounding till we were past the Island; and then we had no Ground. Here we found the Flood setting East by

North, and the Ebb West by South. There were Shoals and small Islands between us and the Main, which caused the Tide to set very inconstantly, and make many Whirlings in the Water; yet we did not find the Tide to set strong any way, nor the Water to rise much.

On the 9th, being to the Eastward of *King William's Island*, we plied all Day between the Main and other Islands, having Easterly Winds and fair Weather till 7 the next Morning. Then we had very hard Rain till 8, and saw many Shoals of Fish. We lay becalm'd off a pretty deep Bay on *New-Guinea*, about 12 or 14 Leagues wide, and 7 or 8 Leagues deep, having low Land near its Bottom, but high Land without. The Eastermost Part of *New-Guinea* seen, bore East by South, distant 12 Leagues: Cape *Mabo* West-South-West half South, distant 7 Leagues.

At 1 in the Afternoon it began to rain, and continu'd till 6 in the Evening; so that having but little Wind and most Calms, we lay still off the foremention'd Bay, having *King William's Island* still in Sight, though distant by Judgment 15 or 16 Leagues West. We saw many Shoals of small Fish, some Sharks, and 7 or 8 Dolphins; but catcht none. In the Afternoon, being about 4 Leagues from the Shore, we saw an Opening in the Land, which seem'd to afford good Harbour: In the Evening we saw a large Fire there; and I intended to go in (if Winds and Weather would permit) to get some Acquaintance with the Natives.

Since the 4th Instant that we passed Cape *Mabo*, to the 12th, we had small Easterly Winds and Calms, so that we anchor'd several Times; where I made my Men cut Wood, that we might have a good Stock when a Westerly Wind should present; and so we ply'd to the Eastward, as Winds and Currents would permit; having

not got in all above 30 Leagues to the Eastward of Cape
Mabo. But on the 12th, at 4 in the Afternoon, a small
Gale sprung up at North-East by North, with Rain: At
5 it shuffled about to North-West, from thence to the
South-West, and continued between those 2 Points a
pretty brisk Gale; so that we made Sail and steered
away North-East, till the 13th in the Morning, to get
about the *Cape of Good Hope*. When 'twas Day, we steer'd
North-East half East, then North-East by East till 7
a-Clock; and being then 7 or 8 Leagues off Shore, we
steer'd away East; the Shore trending East by South. We
had very much Rain all Night, so that we could not
carry much Sail; yet we had a very steddy Gale. At 8
this Morning the Weather clear'd up, and the Wind
decreas'd to a fine Top-gallant Gale, and settled at West
by South. We had more Rain these 3 Days past, than all
the Voyage in so short Time. We were now about 6
Leagues from the Land of *New-Guinea*, which appear'd
very high; and we saw 2 Head-lands, about 20 Leagues
asunder; the one to the East, and the other to the West,
which last is called the *Cape of Good Hope*. We found
Variation East 4 deg.

The 15th in the Morning between 12 and 2 a-Clock, it
blew a very brisk Gale at North-West, and look'd very
black in the South-West. At 2 it flew about at once to the
South-South-West, and rained very hard. The Wind
settled sometime at West-South-West, and we steered
East-North-East till 3 in the Morning: Then the Wind
and Rain abating, we steered East half North for fear of
coming near the Land. Presently after, it being a little
clear, the Man at the Bowsprit-end, call'd out, *Land on our
Starboard Bow*. We lookt out and saw it plain. I presently
sounded, and had but 10 Fathom soft Ground. The
Master, being somewhat scar'd, came running in haste

Table X.

New Guinea &c.

N.º 1.

C. Mabo

N.N.W. 12 L.   N.½ E. 6 L.

a

N.E. b. E. 7 L.   E. b. N. 9 L.

a

Thus shews Cape Mabo and ÿ Iʃlands to ÿ Weʃtward at theʃe Bearing N.N.
W. 12 L. alʃo ÿ loe Iʃl. to ÿ Eaʃtward of ÿ Cape at ÿ Bearing E. b. S.½ S. 7 L.
Theʃe are low Iʃlands.   E. b. S. ½ S. 7 L.

N.º 2.

S.W. b. S.   W. b. N.   W. N. W. 2 L.   N. b. E. 7 L.

N. N. E. ½ E.

a

When youw have Cape Mabo S. E. b. E. ÿ L. that shews ÿ Iʃlands to ÿ Northward
of the North Part of N. Guinea at theʃe Bearings & diʃtances.

N.E. b. E. ½ E.   E. N.   E. 10 L.
a   King will.ᵐ   Iʃland

N.º 3.

The Cape of Good Hope S. ½ E. 6 L.

S.S.E. 8 L.

a

Thus shews the Cape of Good Hope at theʃe bearings and diʃt. and ÿ land
to the E. and Weʃtward

a   S. b. W. ½ W. 9 L.

N.º 4.

S.E. ½ E.   Van Scoutens Iʃl.

a

Thus shews ÿ Iʃl. Providence and un Scoutens. at theʃe Bearings and Diʃt.

a   S. ½ E. 10 L.   The Iʃl. Providence S. ¼ W. 3 L.

N.º 5.

S.S.E. 10 L.

a

Thus shews S.ᵗ Mathias Iʃl. Diʃt. from the middle ÿ L.

a   S. S. W. ½ W. 7 L.

with this News, and said it was best to anchor: I told him no, but sound again; then we had 12 Fathom; the next Cast, 13 and a half; the 4th, 17 Fathom; and then no Ground with 50 Fathom Line. However we kept off the Island, and did not go so fast but that we could see any other Danger before we came nigh it. For here might have been more Islands not laid down in my Draughts besides This. For I search'd all the Draughts I had, if perchance I might find any Island in the one, which was not in the others; but I could find none near us. When it was Day, we were about 5 Leagues off the Land we saw; but, I believe, not above 5 Mile or at most 2 Leagues off it, when we first saw it in the Night.

This is a small Island, but pretty high; I named it *Providence*. About 5 Leagues to the Southward of this, there is another Island, which is called *William Scouten's Island*, and laid down in our Draughts: It is a high Island, and about 20 Leagues long.

It was by mere Providence that we miss'd the small Island. For had not the Wind come to West-South-West, and blown hard, so that we steered East-North-East; we had been upon it by our Course that we steered before, if we could not have seen it. This Morning we saw many great Trees and Logs swim by us; which it's probable came out of some great Rivers on the Main.

On the 16th we crossed the Line, and found Variation 6 deg. 26 min. East. The 18th by my Observation at Noon, we found that we had had a Current setting to the Southward, and probably that drew us in so nigh *Scouten's* Island. For this 24 Hours we steered East by North with a large Wind, yet made but an East by South half South Course; though the Variation was not above 7 deg. East.

The 21st we had a Current setting to the Northward,

o

which is against the true Trade Monsoon, it being now near the full Moon. I did expect it here, as in all other Places. We had Variation 8 deg. 45 min. East. The 22d we found but little Current; if any, it set to the Southward.

On the 23d in the Afternoon we saw 2 Snakes; and the next Morning another, passing by us, which was furiously assaulted by 2 Fishes, that had kept us Company 5 or 6 Days. They were shaped liked Mackarel, and were about that Bigness and Length, and of a yellow greenish Colour. The Snake swam away from them very fast, keeping his Head above Water; the Fish snapp'd at his Tail; but when he turn'd himself, that Fish would withdraw, and another would snap; so that by Turns they kept him employed; yet he still defended himself, and swam away a great Pace, till they were out of Sight.

The 25th betimes in the Morning, we saw an Island to the Southward of us, at about 15 Leagues distance. We steer'd away for it, supposing it to be that which the *Dutch* call *Wishart*'s Island; but finding it otherwise, I called it *Matthias*; it being that Saint's Day. This Island is about 9 or 10 Leagues long, mountainous and woody, with many Savannah's, and some Spots of Land which seem'd to be clear'd.

At 8 in the Evening we lay by, intending, if I could, to anchor under *Matthias* Isle. But the next Morning seeing another Island, about 7 or 8 Leagues to the Eastward of it, we steer'd away for it; at Noon we came up fair with its South-West-end, intending to run along by it, and anchor on the South-East-side: But the Tornadoes came in so thick and hard, that I could not venture in. This Island is pretty low and plain, and cloath'd with Wood; the Trees were very green, and appear'd to be large and tall, as thick as they could stand one by another. It is about 2 or 3 Leagues long, and at the South-West-point there is another small low woody Island, about a Mile round, and about a Mile from the other. Between them there runs a Riff of Rocks, which joyns them. (The biggest, I named *Squally Island.*)

Seeing we could not anchor here, I stood away to the Southward, to make the Main. But having many hard Squalls and Tornadoes, we were often forced to hand all our Sails and steer more Easterly to go before it. On the 26th at 4 a Clock it clear'd up to a hard Sky, and a brisk settled Gale; then we made as much Sail as we could. At 5 it clear'd up over the Land, and we saw, as we thought, Cape *Solomaswer* bearing South-South-East distance 10 Leagues. We had many great Logs and Trees swimming by us all this Afternoon, and much Grass; we steered in South-South-East till 6, then the Wind slackned, and we stood off till 7, having little Wind; then we lay by till 10, at which Time we made Sail, and steer'd away East all Night. The next Morning, as soon as it was light, we made all the Sail we could, and steer'd away East-South-East, as the Land lay; being fair in Sight of it, and not above 7 Leagues distance. We past by many small low woody Islands which lay between us and the Main, not laid down in our Draughts, We found Variation 9 deg. 50 min. East.

The 28th we had many violent Tornadoes, Wind, Rain, and some Spouts; and in the Tornadoes the Wind shifted. In the Night we had fair Weather, but more Lightning than we had seen at any Time this Voyage. This Morning we left a large high Island on our Larboard-side, called in the *Dutch* Draughts *Wishart*'s Isle, about 6 Leagues from the Main; and seeing many Smoaks upon the Main, I therefore steer'd towards it.

CHAP. IV

The main Land of New-Guinea. *Its Inhabitants.* Slinger's *Bay. Small Islands.* Garret Dennis *Isle described. Its Inhabitants. Their Proes.* Anthony Cave's *Island. Its Inhabitants. Trees full of Worms found in the Sea.* St. John's *Island. The main Land of* New-Guinea. *Its Inhabitants. The Coast described. Cape and Bay* St. George. *Cape* Orford. *Another Bay. The Inhabitants there. A large account of the Author's Attempts to Trade with them. He names the place Port* Mountague. *The Country thereabouts described, and its produce. A Burning Island described. A new passage found,* Nova Britannia. *Sir George* Rook's *Island.* Long *Island, and* Crown *Island, discovered and described. Sir R.* Rich's *Island. A burning Island. A strange Spout. A Conjecture concerning a new Passage Southward.* King William's *Island. Strange Whirlpools. Distance between Cape* Mabo, *and Cape* St. George, *computed.*

THE main Land, at this place, is high and mountainous, adorn'd with tall flourishing Trees; The Sides of the Hills had many large Plantations and Patches of clear'd Land; which, together with the Smoaks we saw, were certain Signs of its being well inhabited; and I was desirous to have some Commerce with the Inhabitants. Being nigh the Shore, we saw first one Proe; a little after, 2 or 3 more; and at last a great many Boats came from all the adjacent Bays. When they were 46 in Number, they approach'd so near us, that we could see each others Signs, and hear each other speak; though we could not understand them, nor they us. They made Signs for us to go in towards the Shore, pointing that way; it was squally Weather, which at first made me cautious of going too near; but the Weather beginning to look pretty well, I endeavoured to get into a Bay a-head of us, which we could have got into well enough at first; but while we lay by, we were driven so far to Leeward, that now it was more difficult to get in. The Natives lay in their Proes round us; to whom I shew'd Beads, Knives, Glasses, to

allure them to come nearer; but they would not come so
nigh, as to receive any thing from us. Therefore I threw
out some things to them, *viz.* a Knife fastned to a piece of
Board, and a Glass-bottle corked up with some Beads in
it, which they took up and seemed well pleased. They
often struck their left Breast with their right Hand, and as
often held up a black Truncheon over their Heads, which
we thought was a Token of Friendship; Wherefore we
did the like. And when we stood in towards their Shore,
they seem'd to rejoyce; but when we stood off, they
frown'd, yet kept us Company in their Proes, still pointing to the Shore. About 5 a-Clock, we got within the
Mouth of the Bay, and sounded several times, but had no
Ground, though within a mile of the Shore. The Bason
of this Bay was above 2 Miles within us, into which we
might have gone; but as I was not assured of Anchorage
there, so I thought it not Prudence to run in at this time;
it being near Night, and seeing a black Tornado rising
in the West, which I most fear'd: Besides, we had near
200 Men in Proes close by us. And the Bays on the Shore
were lined with Men from one end to the other, where
there could not be less than 3 or 400 more. What
Weapons they had, we know not, not yet their Design.
Therefore I had, at their first coming near us, got up all
our small Arms, and made several put on Cartouch
Boxes to prevent Treachery. At last I resolved to go out
again: Which when the Natives in their Proes perceived,
they began to fling Stones at us as fast as they could, being
provided with Engines for that purpose; (wherefore I
named this place *Slinger's* Bay:) But at the Firing of one
Gun they were all amaz'd, drew off and flung no more
Stones. They got together, as if consulting what to do; for
they did not make in towards the Shore, but lay still,
though some of them were killed or wounded; and many

more of them had paid for their Boldness, but that I was unwilling to cut off any of them; which if I had done, I could not hope afterwards to bring them to treat with me.

The next day we sailed close by an Island, where we saw many Smoaks, and Men in the Bays; out of which came 2 Canoas, taking much pains to overtake us, but they could not, though we went with an easy Sail; and I could not now stay for them. As I past by the South-East-Point, I sounded several times within a Mile of the Sandy Bays, but had no Ground: About 3 Leagues to the Northward of the South-East Point, we opened a large deep Bay, secur'd from West-North-West and South-West Winds. There were 2 other Islands that lay to the North-East of it, which secur'd the Bay from North-East Winds; One was but small, yet woody; the other was a League long, inhabited and full of Coco-Nut Trees. I endeavoured to get into this Bay; but there came such Flaws off from the high Land over it, that I could not; Besides, we had many hard Squalls, which deterr'd me from it; and Night coming on, I would not run any hazard, but bore away to the small inhabited Island, to see if we could get Anchoring on the East-side of it. When we came there, we found the Island so narrow, that there could be no Shelter; therefore I tack'd and stood toward the greater Island again: And being more than Mid-way between both, I lay by, designing to endeavour for Anchorage next Morning. Between 7 and 8 at Night, we spied a Canoa close by us; and seeing no more, suffered her to come aboard. She had 3 Men in her, who brought off 5 Coco-Nuts, for which I gave each of them a Knife and a String of Beads, to encourage them to come off again in the Morning: But before these went away, we saw 2 more Canoas coming; therefore we stood away to the Northward from them, and then lay by again till Day. We saw no more Boats this Night; neither design'd to suffer any to come aboard in the dark.

By nine a-Clock the next Morning, we were got within a League of the great Island, but were kept off by violent Gusts of Wind. These Squalls gave us warning of their Approach, by the Clouds which hung over the Mountains, and afterwards descended to the Foot of them; and then it is we expect them speedily.

On the 3d of *March*, being about 5 Leagues to Leeward of the great Island, we saw the Main Land a-head; and another great high Island to Leeward of us, distance about 7 Leagues; which we bore away for. It is called in the *Dutch* Draughts, *Garret Dennis* Isle. It is about 14 or 15 Leagues round; high and mountainous, and very woody: Some Trees appeared very large and tall; and the Bays by the Sea-side are well stored with Coco-nut-Trees; where we also saw some small Houses. The Sides of the Mountains are thick set with Plantations; and the Mould in the new clear'd Land, seem'd to be of a brown reddish Colour. This Island is of no regular Figure, but is full of Points shooting forth into the Sea; between which are many Sandy Bays, full of Coco-nut-Trees. The middle of the Isle lies in 3 deg. 10 min. South Latitude. It is very populous; The Natives are very black, strong, and well-limb'd People; having great round Heads, their Hair naturally curl'd and short, which they shave into several Forms, and dye it also of diverse Colours, *viz.* Red, White and Yellow. They have broad round Faces with great bottle Noses, yet agreeable enough, till they disfigure them by Painting, and by wearing great things through their Noses as big as a Man's Thumb and about four Inches long; these are run clear through both Nostrils, one end coming out by one Cheek-Bone, and the other end against the other; and their Noses so stretched, that only a small slip of them appears about the Ornament. They have also great Holes in their Ears, wherein they wear such stuff as in their Noses. They are very dextrous active Fellows in their Proes, which are very ingeniously built. They are narrow and long, with Outlagers on one side; the Head and Stern higher than the rest, and carved into many Devices, *viz.* some Fowl, Fish, or a Man's Head, painted or carv'd: And though it's but rudely done, yet the Resemblance appears plainly, and shews an ingenious Fancy. But with what Instruments they make their Proes or carved Work, I know not; for they seem to be utterly ignorant of Iron. They have very neat Paddles, with which they manage their Proes dextrously, and make great way through the Water. Their Weapons are chiefly Lances, Swords and Slings, and some Bows and Arrows: They have also wooden Fissgigs, for striking Fish. Those that came to assault us in *Slingers*-Bay on the Main, are in all Respects like these; and I believe these are alike treacherous. Their Speech is clear and distinct; the Words they used most, when near us, were *Vacousee Allamais*, and then they pointed to the Shore. Their Signs of Friendship, are either a great Truncheon, or Bough of a Tree full of Leaves, put on their Heads; often striking their Heads with their Hands.

The next Day, having a fresh Gale of Wind, we got under a high Island, about 4 or 5 Leagues round, very woody, and full of Plantations upon the Sides of the Hills; and in the Bays by the Water-side, are Abundance of Coco-nut-Trees. It lies in the Latitude of 3 deg. 25 min. South, and Meridian Distance from Cape *Mabo* 1316 m. On the South-East part of it are 3 or 4 other small woody Islands; one high and peek'd, the other low and flat; all bedeck'd with Coco-nut-Trees and other Wood. On the North there is another Island of an indifferent Heighth, and of a somewhat larger Circumference than the great high Island last mention'd. We past between this and the high Island. The high Island is called in the *Dutch* Draughts *Anthony Cave's Island*. As for the flat low Island, and the other small one, it is probable they were never seen by the *Dutch*; nor the Islands to the North of *Garret Dennis's Island*. As soon as we came near *Cave's Island*, some Canoas came about us, and made Signs for us to come ashore, as all the rest had done before; probably thinking we could run the Ship a-ground any where, as they did their Proes; for we saw neither Sail nor Anchor among any of them, though most *Eastern Indians* have both. These had Proes made of one Tree, well dug, with Outlagers on one side: They were but small, yet well shap'd. We endeavour'd to anchor, but found no Ground within a Mile of the Shore: We kept close along the North-side, still sounding till we came to the North-East-end, but found no Ground; the Canoas still accompanying us; and the Bays were covered with Men going along as we sail'd: Many of them strove to swim off to us, but we left them astern. Being at the North-East Point, we found a strong Current setting to the North-West; so that though we had steer'd to keep under the high Island, yet we were driven towards the flat one. At this time 3 of the Natives came aboard: I gave each of them a Knife, a Looking-Glass, and a String of Beads. I shew'd them Pumpkins and Coco-nut-shells, and made Signs to them to bring some aboard, and had presently 3 Coco-nuts out of one of the Canoas. I shewed them Nutmegs, and by their Signs I guess'd they had some on the Island. I also shew'd them some Gold-Dust, which they seem'd to know, and call'd out *Manneel, Manneel*, and pointed towards the

202 A VOYAGE TO NEW HOLLAND

Land. A while after these Men were gone, 2 or 3 Canoas
came from the flat Island, and by Signs invited us to their
Island; at which the others seem'd displeas'd, and us'd
very menacing Gestures and (I believe) Speeches to each
other. Night coming on, we stood off to Sea; and having
but little Wind all Night, were driven away to the
North-West. We saw many great Fires on the flat
Island. These last Men that came off to us, were all
black, as those we had seen before, with frizled Hair:
They were very tall, lusty, well-shap'd Men; They wear
great things in their Noses, and paint as the others, but
not much; They make the same Signs of Friendship, and
their Language seems to be one: But the others had Proes,
and these Canoas. On the Sides of some of these, we saw
the Figures of several Fish neatly cut; and these last were
not so shy as the others.

Steering away from *Cave's Island* South-South-East, we
found a strong Current against us, which set only in some
places in Streams; and in them we saw many Trees and
Logs of Wood, which drove by us. We had but little
Wood aboard; wherefore I hoisted out the Pinnace, and
sent her to take up some of this Drift-wood. In a little
time she came aboard with a great Tree in a tow, which
we could hardly hoist in with all our Tackles. We cut up
the Tree and split it for Fire-wood. It was much worm-
eaten, and had in it some live Worms above an Inch
long, and about the bigness of a Goose-quill, and having
their Heads crusted over with a thin Shell.

After this we passed by an Island, called by the *Dutch*
St. *John's Island*, leaving it to the North of us. It is about
9 or 10 Leagues round, and very well adorn'd with lofty
Trees. We saw many Plantations on the Sides of the Hills,
and Abundance of Coco-nut-Trees about them; as also
thick Groves on the Bays by the Sea-side. As we came near

Tab. XI. Squaly and other Islands on ye Coast of N Brittannia

N.1.
E.S.E. 3 L.

S.S.E 4 L.

S.S.E.E. 3L.   This is Squaly I. and sheweth thus at these Bearings

N.2.
S.E. 7 L.

S.b.w. 8 L.

S.b.w. ½ w. 6 L.

a   a

N.3.
S.S.E. 11 L.

a

Thus Sheweth Trecherons Hill and the Land to the E. and westward of it.
S.W.b.w.   Trecherons Hill
                                    w. ½ S. 7 L.
a   w. b. S.

N.4.
Swifshire I. N.w.b.w. 7 L.
                              N.E. b. N. 6 L.
                                                                    a

                              E. b. N. 5 L.
a

N.5.
w. b. N. 7 L.   N.W.b.w. 9 L.
                                                        N.W. 10 L.

E.b.N. 7 L.   E.b.S. 5 L.   E.S.E. 6 L.

N.6.
E. 6 L.

Thus Shuweth St. Iohns I. at these Bearings and Distances

a

a

it, 3 Canoas came off to us, but would not come aboard. They were such as we had seen about the other Islands: They spoke the same Language, and made the same Signs of Peace; and their Canoas were such, as at *Cave's Island*.

We stood along by St. *John's Island*, till we came almost to the South-East-Point; and then seeing no more Islands to the Eastward of us, nor any likelihood of anchoring under this, I steer'd away for the Main of *New-Guinea*; we being now (as I suppos'd) to the East of it, on this North-side. My Design of seeing these Islands as I past along, was to get Wood and Water, but could find no Anchor-Ground, and therefore could not do as I pur-pos'd. Besides, these Islands are all so populous, that I dar'd not send my Boat ashore, unless I could have anchor'd pretty nigh. Wherefore I rather chose to prose-cute my Design on the Main, the Season of the Year being now at hand; for I judg'd the Westerly Winds were nigh spent.

On the 8th of *March*, we saw some Smoaks on the Main, being distant from it 4 or 5 Leagues. 'Tis very high, woody Land, with some Spots of Savannah. About 10 in the Morning 6 or 7 Canoas came off to us: Most of them had no more than one Man in them; they were all black, with short curl'd Hair; having the same Orna-ments in their Noses, and their Heads so shav'd and painted, and speaking the same Words, as the Inhabi-tants of *Cave's* Island before-mentioned.

There was a Head-land to the Southward of us, be-yond which seeing no Land, I supposed that from thence the Land trends away more Westerly. This Head-land lies in the Latitude of 5 deg. 2 min. South, and Meridian distance from Cape *Mabo*, 1290 Miles. In the Night we lay by, for fear of over-shooting this Head-land. Between which and Cape St. *Maries*, the Land is high, Mountainous and Woody; having many Points of Land shooting out into the Sea, which make so many fine Bays. The Coast lies North-North-East and South-South-West.

The 9th in the Morning a huge black Man came off to us in a Canoa, but would not come aboard. He made the same signs of Friendship to us, as the rest we had met with; yet seem'd to differ in his Language, not using any of those Words which the others did. We saw neither Smoaks nor Plantations near this Head-land. We found here Variation 1 deg. East.

In the Afternoon, as we plied near the Shore, 3 Canoas came off to us; one had 4 Men in her, the others 2 apiece. That with the 4 Men, came pretty nigh us, and shew'd us a Coco-nut and Water in a Bamboo, making Signs that there was enough ashore where they lived; they pointed to the place where they would have us go, and so went away. We saw a small round pretty high Island, about a League to the North of this Head-land, within which there was a large deep Bay, whither the Canoas went; and we strove to get thither before Night, but could not; wherefore we stood off, and saw Land to the Westward of this Head-Land, bearing West by South half South, distance about 10 Leagues; and, as we thought, still more Land bearing South-West by South, distance 12 or 14 Leagues: But being clouded, it disappeared, and we thought we had been deceived. Before Night we opened the Head-Land fair, and I named it Cape St. *George*. The Land from hence trends away West-North-West about 10 Leagues, which is as far as we could see it; and the Land that we saw to the Westward of it in the Evening, which bore West by South half South, was another Point about 10 Leagues from

Cape St. *George*; between which there runs in a deep Bay for 20 Leagues or more. We saw some high Land in Spots like Islands, down in that Bay at a great distance; but whether they are Islands, or the Main closing there, we know not. The next Morning we saw other Land to the South-East of the Westermost Point, which till then was clouded; it was very high Land, and the same that we saw the day before, that disappear'd in a Cloud. This Cape St. *George* lies in the Latitude of 5 deg. 5 min. South; and Meridian distance from Cape *Mabo* 1290 Miles. The Island off this Cape, I called St. *George's* Isle; and the Bay between it and the West-Point, I named St. *George's* Bay. *Note*, No *Dutch* Draughts go so far as this Cape, by 10 Leagues. On the 10th in the Evening, we got within a League of the Westermost Land seen, which is pretty high and very woody, but no Appearance of Anchoring. I stood off again, designing (if possible) to ply to and fro in this Bay, till I found a Conveniency to Wood and Water. We saw no more Plantations, nor Coco-nut-Trees; yet in the Night we discerned a small Fire right against us. The next Morning we saw a Burning Mountain in the Country. It was round, high, and peaked at top (as most *Vulcano's* are,) and sent forth a great Quantity of Smoak. We took up a Log of drift Wood, and split it for Firing; in which we found some small Fish.

The Day after, we past by the South-West Cape of this Bay, leaving it to the North of us: When we were abreast of it, I called my Officers together, and named it Cape *Orford*, in Honour of my noble Patron; drinking his Lordship's Health. This Cape bears from Cape *St. George* South-West about 18 Leagues. Between them there is a Bay about 25 Leagues deep, having pretty high Land all round it, especially near the Capes, though they

themselves are not high. Cape *Orford* lies in the Latitude
of 5 deg. 24 min. South, by my Observation; and Meridian
distance from Cape *St. George*, 44 Miles West. The Land
trends from this Cape North-West by West into the Bay,
and on the other Side South-West *per Compass*, which is
South-West 9 deg. West, allowing the Variation which is
here 9 deg. East. The Land on each Side of the Cape, is
more Savannah than Wood-Land, and is highest on the
North-West-side. The Cape it self is a Bluff-point, of an
indifferent Heighth, with a flat Table Land at Top. When
we were to the South-West of the Cape, it appeared to be
a low Point shooting out; which you cannot see when a-
breast of it. This Morning we struck a Log of Drift-wood
with our Turtle-Irons, hoisted it in and split it for Fire-
wood. Afterwards we struck another, but could not get it
in. There were many Fish about it.

We steer'd along South-West as the Land lies, keeping
about 6 Leagues off the Shore; and being desirous to cut
Wood and fill Water, if I saw any Conveniency, I lay
by in the Night, because I would not miss any Place
proper for those Ends, for fear of wanting such Necessaries
as we could not live without. This Coast is high and
mountainous, and not so thick with Trees as that on the
other side of Cape *Orford*.

On the 14th, seeing a pretty deep Bay a-head, and
some Islands where I thought we might ride secure, we
ran in towards the Shore and saw some Smoaks. At 10
a-Clock we saw a Point, which shot out pretty well into
the Sea, with a Bay within it, which promised fair for
Water; and we stood in, with a moderate Gale. Being
got into the Bay within the Point, we saw many Coco-
nut-Trees, Plantations, and Houses. When I came within
4 or 5 Mile of the Shore, 6 small Boats came off to view us,
with about 40 Men in them all. Perceiving that they only

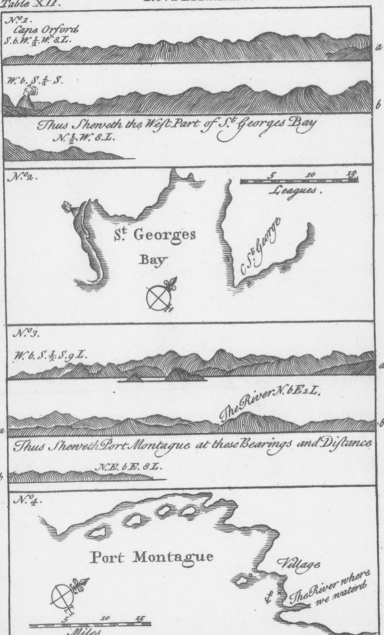

Table XII.

No. 1.
Cape Orford
S. b. W. ¼ W. 8 L.

a

W. b. S. ¼ S.

a

b

Thus Sheweth the West Part of St Georges Bay
N. ½ W. 8 L.

b

No. 2.

5   10   15
Leagues.

St Georges
Bay

C. St George

No. 3.

W. b. S. ¼ S. 9 L.

a

The River N. b E 1 L.

a

b

Thus Sheweth Port Montague at these Bearings and Distance
N. E. b E. 8 L.

b

No. 4.

Port Montague

Village

The River where
we water'd

5   10   15
Miles

J. Clark Sculpsit.

came to view us, and would not come aboard, I made
Signs and waved to them to go ashore; but they did not
or would not understand me; therefore I whistled a Shot
over their Heads out of my Fowling-piece, and then they
pull'd away for the Shore, as hard as they could. These
were no sooner ashore, but we saw 3 Boats, coming from
the Islands to Leeward of us, and they soon came within
call; for we lay becalm'd. One of the Boats had about 40
Men in her, and was a large well built Boat; the other 2
were but small. Not long after, I saw another Boat coming out of that Bay where I intended to go: She likewise
was a large Boat, with a high Head and Stern painted,
and full of Men; this I thought came off to fight us, as 'tis
probable they all did; therefore I fired another small Shot
over the great Boat that was nigh us, which made them
leave their Babling and take to their Paddles. We still
lay becalm'd; and therefore they rowing wide of us,
directed their Course toward the other great Boat that
was coming off: When they were pretty near each other,
I caus'd the Gunner to fire a Gun between them, which he
did very dextrously; it was loaden with round and
Partridge-shot; the last dropt in the Water somewhat
short of them, but the round Shot went between both
Boats, and grazed about 100 Yards beyond them; this so
affrighted them, that they rowed away for the Shore as
fast as they could, without coming near each other; and
the little Boats made the best of their Way after them:
And now having a gentle Breeze at South-South-East,
we bore into the Bay after them. When we came by the
Point, I saw a great Number of Men peeping from under
the Rocks: I ordered a Shot to be fired close by, to scare
them. The Shot graz'd between us and the Point; and
mounting again, flew over the Point, and graz'd a 2d
Time just by them. We were obliged to sail along close

by the Bays; and seeing Multitudes setting under the Trees, I ordered a 3d Gun to be fired among the Coco-nut-Trees, to scare them; for my Business being to Wood and Water, I thought it necessary to strike some Terrour into the Inhabitants, who were very numerous, and (by what I saw now, and had formerly experienc'd,) treacherous. After this I sent my Boat to sound; they had first 40, then 30, and at last 20 Fathom Water. We followed the Boat, and came to anchor about a quarter of a Mile from the Shore, in 26 Fathom Water, fine black Sand and Oaze. We rode right against the Mouth of a small River, where I hoped to find fresh Water. Some of the Natives standing on a small Point at the River's Mouth, I sent a small Shot over their Heads to fright them; which it did effectually. In the Afternoon I sent my Boat ashore to the Natives who stood upon the Point by the River's Mouth with a Present of Coco-nuts; when the Boat was come near the Shore, they came running into the Water, and put their Nuts into the Boat. Then I made a Signal for the Boat to come aboard, and sent both it and the Yawl into the River to look for fresh Water, ordering the Pinnace to lye near the River's Mouth, while the Yawl went up to search. In an Hour's time they return'd aboard with some Barrecoes full of fresh Water, which they had taken up about half a Mile up the River. After which, I sent them again with Casks; ordering one of them to fill Water, and the other to watch the Motion of the Natives, lest they should make any Opposition; but they did not, and so the Boats return'd a little before Sun-set with a Tun and half of Water; and the next Day by Noon brought aboard about 6 Tun of Water.

I sent ashore Commodities to purchase Hogs, &c. being informed that the Natives have plenty of them, as also of Yamms and other good Roots; But my Men returned without getting any thing that I sent them for; the Natives being unwilling to trade with us: Yet they admir'd our Hatchets and Axes; but would part with nothing but Coco-nuts; which they us'd to climb the Trees for; and so soon as they gave them our Men, they beckon'd to them to be gone; for they were much afraid of us.

The 18th, I sent both Boats again for Water, and before Noon they had filled all my Casks. In the Afternoon I sent them both to cut Wood; but seeing about 40 Natives standing on the Bay at a small Distance from our Men, I made a Signal for them to come aboard again; which they did, and brought me Word that the Men which we saw on the Bay were passing that way, but were afraid to come nigh them. At 4 a Clock I sent both the Boats again for more Wood, and they return'd in the Evening. Then I called my Officers to consult whether it were convenient to stay here longer, and endeavour a better Acquaintance with these People; or go to Sea. My Design of tarrying here longer, was, if possible, to get some Hogs, Goats, Yamms and other Roots; as also to get some Knowledge of the Country and its Product. My Officers unanimously gave their Opinions for staying longer here. So the next Day I sent both Boats ashore again, to fish and to cut more Wood. While they were ashore about 30 or 40 Men and Women past by them; they were a little afraid of our People at first; but upon their making signs of Friendship, they past by quietly; the Men finely bedeck'd with Feathers of divers Colours about their Heads, and Lances in their Hands; the Women had no Ornament about them, nor any Thing to cover their Nakedness, but a Bunch of small green Boughs, before and behind, stuck under a String which came round their Wastes. They carried large Baskets on their Heads, full of Yamms. And this I have

P

observ'd amongst all the wild Natives I have known, that they make their Women carry the Burdens, while the Men walk before, without any other Load than their Arms and Ornaments. At Noon our Men came aboard with the Wood they had cut, and had catch'd but 6 Fishes at 4 or 5 Hauls of the Sain, though we saw Abundance of Fish leaping in the Bay all the Day long.

In the afternoon I sent the Boats ashore for more Wood; and some of our Men went to the Natives Houses, and found they were now more shy than they us'd to be; had taken down all the Coco-nuts from the Trees, and driven away their Hogs. Our People made Signs to them to know what was become of their Hogs, &c. The Natives pointing to some Houses in the Bottom of the Bay, and imitating the Noise of those Creatures, seem'd to intimate that there were both Hogs and Goats of several Sizes, which they express'd by holding their Hands abroad at several Distances from the Ground.

At Night our Boats came aboard with Wood; and the next Morning I went my self with both Boats up the River to the Watering-place, carrying with me all such Trifles and Iron-work as I thought most proper to induce them to a Commerce with us; but I found them very shy and roguish. I saw but 2 Men and a Boy: One of the Men by some Signs was perswaded to come to the Boat's Side, where I was; to him I gave a Knife, a String of Beads, and a Glass-bottle; the Fellow call'd out, *Cocos, Cocos*, pointing to a Village hard by, and signified to us that he would go for some; but he never return'd to us. And thus they had frequently of late served our Men. I took 8 or 9 Men with me, and marched to their Houses, which I found very mean; and their Doors made fast with Withes.

I visited 3 of their Villages; and finding all the Houses thus abandon'd by the Inhabitants, who carried with them all their Hogs, &c. I brought out of their Houses some small Fishing-nets in Recompence for those Things they had receiv'd of us. As we were coming away, we saw 2 of the Natives; I shewed them the Things that we carried with us, and called to them, *Cocos, Cocos*, to let them know that I took these Things because they had not made good what they had promis'd by their Signs, and by their calling out *Cocos*. While I was thus employ'd, the Men in the Yawl filled 2 Hogsheads of Water, and all the Barrecoes. About 1 in the Afternoon I came aboard, and found all my Officers and Men very importunate to go to that Bay where the Hogs were said to be. I was loath to yield to it, fearing they would deal too roughly with the Natives. By 2 a-Clock in the Afternoon many black Clouds gather'd over the Land, which I thought would deter them from their Enterprize; but they sollicited me the more to let them go. At last I consented, sending those Commodities I had ashore with me in the Morning, and giving them a strict Charge to deal by fair means, and to act cautiously for their own Security. The Bay I sent them to was about 2 Miles from the Ship. Assoon as they were gone, I got all Things ready, that, if I saw Occasion, I might assist them with my great Guns. When they came to Land, the Natives in great Companies stood to resist them; shaking their Lances, and threatning them; and some were so daring, as to wade into the Sea, holding a Target in one Hand and a Lance in the other. Our Men held up to them such Commodities as I had sent, and made Signs of Friendship; but to no Purpose; for the Natives waved them off. Seeing therefore they could not be prevailed upon to a friendly Commerce, my Men, being resolved to have some Provision among them, fired some Muskets to scare them away; which had the desired Effect upon all but 2 or 3, who stood still in a

menacing Posture, till the boldest dropt his Target and
ran away; they suppos'd he was shot in the Arm: He and
some others felt the Smart of our Bullets, but none were
kill'd; our Design being rather to fright than to kill them.
Our Men landed, and found Abundance of tame Hogs
running among the Houses. They shot down 9, which
they brought away, besides many that ran away wounded.
They had but little Time; for in less than an Hour after
they went from the Ship, it began to rain: Wherefore
they got what they could into the Boats; for I had
charg'd them to come away if it rain'd. By that Time the
Boat was aboard, and the Hogs taken in, it clear'd up;
and my Men desir'd to make another Trip thither before
Night; this was about 5 in the Evening; and I consented,
giving them Order to repair on Board before Night. In
the Close of the Evening they returned accordingly,
with 8 Hogs more, and a little live Pig; and by this Time
the other Hogs were jerk'd and salted. These that came
last, we only drest and corn'd till Morning; and then
sent both Boats ashore for more Refreshments, either of
Hogs or Roots: But in the Night the Natives had convey'd away their Provisions of all Sorts. Many of them
were now about the Houses, and none offer'd to resist our
Boats landing, but on the contrary were so amicable,
that one Man brought 10 or 12 Coco-nuts, left them on the
Shore after he had shew'd them to our Men, and went
out of Sight. Our People finding nothing but Nets and
Images, brought some of them away; which 2 of my
Men brought aboard in a small Canoa; and presently
after, my Boats came off. I order'd the Boatswain to take
care of the Nets, till we came at some place where they
might be disposed of for some Refreshment for the Use of
all the Company: The Images I took into my own
Custody.

Fishes taken on the
Coast of New
Guinea.

This Fish his fins & Taill is ~~~~ Blew. w.th Blew spots all over y.e Body.

In the Afternoon I sent the Canoa to the Place from whence she had been brought; and in her, 2 Axes, 2 Hatchets (one of them helv'd,) 6 Knives, 6 Looking-glasses, a large of Bunch of Beads, and 4 Glass-bottles. Our Men drew the Canoa ashore, placed the Things to the best Advantage in her, and came off in the Pinnace which I sent to guard them. And now being well stock'd with Wood, and all my Water-casks full, I resolv'd to sail the next Morning. All the Time of our Stay here, we had very fair Weather; only sometimes in the Afternoon we had a Shower of Rain, which lasted not above an Hour at most: Also some Thunder and Lightning, with very little Wind. We had Sea and Land-breezes; the former between the South-South-East, and the latter from North-East to North-West.

This Place I named Port *Mountague*, in Honour of my noble Patron. It lies in the Latitude of 6 deg. 10 min. South, and Meridian distance from Cape *St. George*, 151 Miles West. The Country hereabouts is mountainous and woody, full of rich Valleys and pleasant fresh Water-brooks. The Mould in the Valleys is deep and yellowish; that on the Sides of the Hills of a very brown Colour, and not very deep, but rocky underneath; yet excellent planting Land. The Trees in general are neither very streight, thick, nor tall; yet appear green and pleasant enough: Some of them bore Flowers, some Berries, and others big Fruits; but all unknown to any of us. Coco-nut-Trees thrive very well here; as well on the Bays by the Sea-side, as more remote among the Plantations. The Nuts are of an indifferent Size, the Milk and Kernel very thick and pleasant. Here is Ginger, Yamms, and other very good Roots for the Pot, that our Men saw and tasted. What other Fruits or Roots the Country affords, I know not. Here are Hogs and Dogs; other

Land-Animals we saw none. The Fowls we saw and knew, were Pidgeons, Parrots, Cockadores and Crows like those in *England*; a Sort of Birds about the Bigness of a Black-Bird, and smaller Birds many. The Sea and Rivers have Plenty of Fish; we saw Abundance, though we catch'd but few, and these were Cavallies, Yellow-tails and Whip-rays.

We departed from hence on the 22d of *March*, and on the 24th in the Evening we saw some high Land bearing North-West half West; to the West of which we could see no Land, though there appeared something like Land bearing West a little Southerly; but not being sure of it, I steered West-North-West all Night, and kept going on with an easy Sail, intending to coast along the Shore at a distance. At 10 a Clock I saw a great Fire bearing North-West by West, blazing up in a Pillar, sometimes very high for 3 or 4 Minutes, then falling quite down for an equal Space of Time; sometimes hardly visible, till it blazed up again. I had laid me down having been in-disposed this 3 Days: But upon a Sight of this, my chief Mate called me; I got up and view'd it for about half an Hour, and knew it to be a burning Hill by its Intervals: I charg'd them to look well out, having bright Moon-light. In the Morning I found that the Fire we had seen the Night before, was a burning Island; and steer'd for it. We saw many other Islands, one large high Island, and another smaller, but pretty high. I stood near the *Vulcano*, and many small low Islands with some Shoals.

March the 25th 1700, in the Evening we came within 3 Leagues of this Burning-hill, being at the same Time 2 Leagues from the Main. I found a good Channel to pass between them, and kept nearer the Main than the Island. At 7 in the Evening I sounded, and had 52 Fathom fine Sand and Oaze. I stood to the Northward to get clear of this Streight, having but little Wind and fair Weather. The Island all Night vomited Fire and Smoak very amazingly; and at every Belch we heard a dreadful Noise like Thunder, and saw a Flame of Fire after it, the most terrifying that ever I saw. The Intervals between its Belches, were about half a Minute; some more, others less: Neither were these Pulses or Eruptions alike; for some were but faint Convulsions, in Comparison of the more vigorous; yet even the weakest vented a great deal of Fire; but the largest made a roaring Noise, and sent up a large Flame 20 or 30 Yards high; and then might be seen a great Stream of Fire running down to the Foot of the Island, even to the Shore. From the Furrows made by this descending Fire, we could in the Day Time see great Smoaks arise, which probably were made by the sulphureous Matter thrown out of the Funnel at the Top, which tumbling down to the Bottom, and there lying in a Heap, burn'd till either consumed or extinguished; and as long as it burn'd and kept its Heat, so long the Smoak ascended from it; which we perceived to increase or decrease, according to the Quantity of Matter discharged from the Funnel. But the next Night, being shot to the Westward of the Burning-Island, and the Funnel of it lying on the South-side, we could not discern the Fire there, as we did the Smoak in the Day when we were to the Southward of it. This Vulcano lies in the Latitude of 5 deg. 33 min. South, and Meridian distance from Cape St. *George*, 332 Miles West.

The Eastermost Part of *New-Guinea* lies 40 Miles to the Westward of this Tract of Land; and by Hydrographers they are made joyning together: But here I found an Opening and Passage between, with many Islands; the largest of which lye on the North-side of this Passage or Streight. The Channel is very good, between the Islands and the Land to the Eastward. The East-part of *New-Guinea*, is high and mountainous, ending on the North-East with a large Promontory, which I nam'd *King William*'s Cape, in Honour of his present Majesty. We saw some Smoaks on it; and leaving it on our Larboard-side, steer'd away near the East Land; which ends with two remarkable Capes or Heads, distant from each other about 6 or 7 Leagues. Within each Head were two very remarkable Mountains, ascending very gradually from the Sea-side; which afforded a very pleasant and agreeable Prospect. The Mountains and lower Land were pleasantly mixt with Wood-Land and Savannahs. The Trees appeared very green and flourishing; and the Savannahs seem'd to be very smooth and even; no Meadow in *England* appears more green in the Spring, than these. We saw Smoaks, but did not strive to anchor here; but rather chose to get under one of the Islands, (where I thought I should find few or no Inhabitants,) that I might repair my Pinnace, which was so crazy that I could not venture ashore any where with her. As we stood over to the Islands, we look'd out very well to the North, but could see no Land that way; by which I was well assur'd that we were got through, and that this East-Land does not join to *New-Guinea*; therefore I named it *Nova-Britannia*. The North-West Cape, I called Cape *Glocester*, and the South-West-point Cape *Anne*; and the North-West Mountain, which is very remarkable, I call'd Mount *Glocester*.

This Island which I called *Nova-Britannia*, has about 4 deg. of Latitude: The Body of it lying in 4 deg. and the Northermost part in 2 deg. 30 min. and the Southermost in 6 deg. 30 min. South. It has about 5 deg. 18 min. Longitude from East to West. It is generally high, moun-tainous Land, mixt with large Valleys; which, as well

Table XIII Dampiers Passage and Islands on y.e Coast of N. Guinea

N.º 1.

S.S.W ½ W. 9 L.

a.

W. 12 L.

a

Thus shews y.e S.W. Land when your in y.e S. Part of y.e Entrance of Cap.t Damp. Paſ.

N.w.b.w ½ w. 8 L.

N.w.b.N. 9 L.

N.N. w ½ w. 10 L.

W. b.N ½ N. 5 L.

N. ½ w. 7 L.

N.E.b.E. 10 L.

N.º 2.

E. b. N. 5 L.

a

a

S. ½ E. 5 L.

S.w. b. w ½ w. 3 L.

W. b.S. 5 L.

S.w. b. S. 6 L.

W. 2 L.

N.º 3.

S.w. b w. 3 L.

W. b.S ½ S. 5 L.

S.S.W ½ W. 6 L.

W. ½ S. 2 L.

N.º 4.

N.N.W. 4 L.

W. b.S. 11 L.

W

N. 5.

S.E ½ E 6 L.

S. b. w. 6 L:

S.w. b. w. 3 L.

W. 2 ½ L.

as the Mountains, appeared very fertile; and in most
Places that we saw, the Trees are very large, tall and
thick. It is also very well inhabited with strong well-
limb'd *Negroes*, whom we found very daring and bold
at several Places. As to the Product of it, I know no
more than what I have said in my Account of *Port
Mountague:* But it is very probable this Island may
afford as many rich Commodities as any in the World;
and the Natives may be easily brought to Commerce,
though I could not pretend to it under my present
Circumstances.

Being near the Island to the Northward of the *Vulcano*,
I sent my Boat to sound, thinking to anchor here; but
she return'd and brought me Word that they had no
Ground, till they met with a Riff of Coral Rocks about a
Mile from the Shore. Then I bore away to the North-side
of the Island, where we found no anchoring neither. We
saw several People, and some Coco-nut-Trees, but could
not send ashore for want of my Pinnace, which was out of
order. In the Evening I stood off to Sea, to be at such a
distance, that I might not be driven by any Current upon
the Shoals of this Island, if it should prove calm. We had
but little Wind, especially the Beginning of the Night; but
in the Morning I found my self so far to the West of the
Island, that the Wind being at East-South-East, I
could not fetch it; wherefore I kept on to the Southward,
and stemm'd with the Body of a high Island about 11 or
12 Leagues long, lying to the Southward of that which I
before designed for. I named this Island Sir *George Rook's*
Island.

We also saw some other Islands to the Westward;
which may be better seen in my Draught of these
Lands, than here described. But seeing a very small
Island lying to the North-West of the long Island which

was before us, and not far from it; I steer'd away for that; hoping to find anchoring there: And having but little Wind, I sent my Boat before to sound; which, when we were about 2 Miles distance from the Shore, came on Board and brought me Word that there was good anchoring in 30 or 40 Fathom Water, a Mile from the Isle, and within a Riff of the Rocks which lay in a half Moon, reaching from the North-part of the Island to the South-East: so at Noon we got in and anchored in 36 Fathom, a Mile from the Isle.

In the Afternoon I sent my Boat ashore to the Island, to see what Convenience there was to haul our Vessel ashore in order to be mended, and whether we could catch any Fish. My Men in the Boat rowed about the Island, but could not land by Reason of the Rocks and a great Surge running in upon the Shore. We found Variation here, 8 deg. 25 min. West.

I design'd to have stay'd among these Islands till I had got my Pinnace refitted; but having no more than one Man who had skill to work upon her, I saw she would be a long Time in repairing; (which was one great Reason why I could not prosecute my Discoveries further:) And the Easterly Winds being set in, I found I should scarce be able to hold my Ground.

The 31st in the Forenoon we shot in between 2 Islands, lying about 4 Leagues asunder; with Intention to pass between them. The Southermost is a long Island, with a high Hill at each End; this I named *Long Island*. The Northermost is a round high Island towering up with several Heads or Tops, something resembling a Crown; this I named *Crown-Isle*, from its Form. Both these Islands appear'd very pleasant, having Spots of green Savannahs mixt among the Wood-land: The Trees appeared very green and flourishing, and some of them looked white and full of Blossoms. We past close by *Crown-Isle*; saw many Coco-nut-Trees on the Bays and the Sides of the Hills; and one Boat was coming off from the Shore, but return'd again. We saw no Smoaks on either of the Islands, neither did we see any Plantations; and it is probable they are not very well peopled. We saw many Shoals near *Crown-Island*, and Riffs of Rocks running off from the Points, a Mile or more into the Sea. My Boat was once over-board, with Design to have sent her ashore; but having little Wind, and seeing some Shoals, I hoisted her in again, and stood off out of Danger.

In the Afternoon, seeing an Island bearing North-West by West, we steer'd away North-West by North, to be to the Northward of it. The next Morning, being about Mid-way from the Islands we left Yesterday, and having this to the Westward of us; the Land of the Main of *New Guinea* within us to the Southward, appear'd very high. When we came within 4 or 5 Leagues of this Island to the West of us, 4 Boats came off to view us; one came within call, but return'd with the other 3 without speaking to us: So we kept on for the Island; which I named Sir *R. Rich*'s Island. It was pretty high, woody, and mixt with Savannah's like those formerly mentioned. Being to the North of it, we saw an Opening between it and another Island 2 Leagues to the West of it, which before appear'd all in One. The Main seemed to be high Land, trending to the Westward.

On *Tuesday* the 2d of *April*, about 8 in the Morning, we discovered a high peeked Island to the Westward, which seem'd to smoak at its Top. The next Day we past by the North-side of the Burning Island, and saw a Smoak again at its Top; but the Vent lying on the South-side of the Peek, we could not observe it distinctly, nor see the Fire. We afterwards opened 3 more Islands, and some

Land to the Southward, which we could not well tell whether it were Islands or Part of the Main. These Islands are all high, full of fair Trees and Spots of green Savannahs; as well the Burning Isle as the rest; but the Burning Isle was more round and peek'd at Top, very fine Land near the Sea, and for two Thirds up it. We also saw another Isle sending forth a great Smoak at once; but it soon vanished, and we saw it no more. We saw also among these Islands 3 small Vessels with Sails, which the People on *Nova Britannia* seem wholly ignorant of.

The 11th at Noon, having a very good Observation, I found my self to the Northward of my Reckoning; and thence concluded that we had a Current setting North-West, or rather more Westerly, as the Land lies. From that Time to the next Morning, we had fair clear Weather, and a fine moderate Gale from South-East to East by North: But at Day-break, the Clouds began to fly, and it lightned very much in the East, South-East, and North-East. At Sun-rising, the Sky look'd very red in the East near the Horizon; and there were many black Clouds both to the South and North of it. About a Quarter of an Hour after the Sun was up, there was a Squall to the Windward of us; when on a sudden one of our Men on the Fore-castle called out that he saw something astern, but could not tell what: I look'd out for it, and immediately saw a Spout beginning to work within a Quarter of a Mile of us, exactly in the Wind. We presently put right before it. It came very swiftly, whirling the Water up in a Pillar about 6 or 7 Yards high. As yet I could not see any pendulous Cloud, from whence it might come; and was in Hopes it would soon lose its Force. In 4 or 5 Minutes Time, it came within a Cable's Length of us, and past away to Leeward; and then I saw a long pale Stream, coming down to the whirling Water. This

Fishes taken on the Coast of New Guinea

*This Fish fins & tail are blew on y̆ edges & red in the
middle with blew spots all over y̆ Body, but y̆ Belly white.*

A Pike Fish Conger on y̆ Coast of New Guinea

*This Fish is a pale red with blew spots on y̆ body the
long Tail blew in y̆ midle & white on y̆ side.*

Stream was about the Bigness of a Rainbow: The upper
End seem'd vastly high, not descending from any dark
Cloud, and therefore the most strange to me; I never
having seen the like before. It past about a Mile to
Leeward of us, and then broke. This was but a small
Spout, not strong nor lasting; yet I perceived much Wind
in it, as it past by us. The Current still continued at
North-West a little Westerly, which I allow'd to run a
Mile *per* Hour.

By an Observation the 13th at Noon, I found my self
25 min. to the Northward of my Reckoning; whether
occasion'd by bad Steerage, a bad Account, or a
Current, I could not determine; but was apt to judge it
might be a Complication of all; for I could not think it
was wholly the Current, the Land here lying East by
South, and West by North, or a little more Northerly
and Southerly. We had kept so nigh as to see it, and at
farthest had not been above 20 Leagues from it, but sometimes much nearer; and it is not probable that any Current should set directly off from a Land. A Tide indeed
may; but then the Flood has the same Force to strike in
upon the Shore, as the Ebb to strike off from it: But a
Current must have set nearly along Shore, either Easterly
or Westerly; and if any thing Northerly or Southerly, it
could be but very little in Comparison of its East or West
Course, on a Coast lying as this doth; which yet we did
not perceive. If therefore we were deceiv'd by a Current,
it is very probable that the Land is here disjoyn'd, and that
there is a Passage through to the Southward, and that the
Land from *King William's* Cape to this Place is an Island,
separated from *New-Guinea* by some Streight, as *Nova-
Britannia* is by that which we came through. But this
being at best but a probable Conjecture, I shall insist no
farther upon it.

The 14th we passed by *Scouten's* Island and *Providence* Island, and found still a very strong Current setting to the North-West. On the 17th we saw a high Mountain on the Main, that sent forth great Quantities of Smoak from its Top: This *Vulcano* we did not see in our Voyage out. In the Afternoon we discovered *King William's* Island, and crowded all the Sail we could, to get near it before Night; thinking to lye to the Eastward of it till Day, for fear of some Shoals that lye at the West-end of it. Before Night we got within 2 Leagues of it, and having a fine Gale of Wind and a light Moon, I resolv'd to pass through in the Night; which I hop'd to do before 12 a-Clock, if the Gale continued; but when we came within 2 Miles of it, it fell calm; yet afterwards by the Help of the Current, a small Gale, and our Boat, we got through before Day. In the Night we had a very fragrant Smell from the Island. By Morning-light we were got 2 Leagues to the Westward of it; and then were becalm'd all the Morning; and met such whirling Tides, that when we came into them, the Ship turn'd quite round; and though sometimes we had a small Gale of Wind, yet she could not feel the Helm when she came into these Whirlpools: Neither could we get from amongst them, till a brisk Gale sprung up; yet we drove not much any way, but whirl'd round like a Top. And those Whirlpools were not constant to one Place, but drove about strangely; and sometimes we saw among them large Riplings of the Water, like great Over-falls, making a fearful Noise. I sent my Boat to sound, but found no Ground.

The 18th, Cape *Mabo* bore S. distance 9 Leagues. By which Account it lies in the Latitude of 50 min. South, and Meridian distance from Cape S. *George* 1243 Miles. S. *John's* Isle lies 48 Miles to the East of Cape St. *George*; which being added to the Distance between Cape

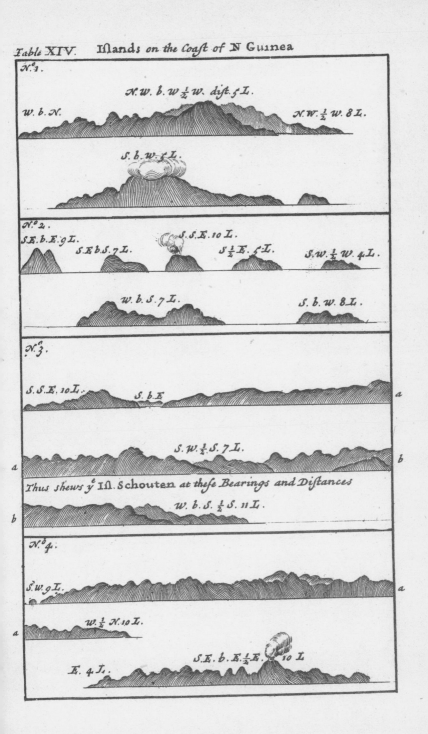

Table XIV. *Iſlands on the Coaſt of* N Guinea

Nº 1.

N.W. b. W ½ W. diſt. 5 L.

W. b. N.

N.W. ½ W. 8 L.

S. b. W. 5 L.

Nº 2.

S.E. b. E. 9 L.

S.S.E. 10 L.

S.E. b. S. 7 L.

S ½ E. 5 L.

S.W. ½ W. 4 L.

W. b. S. 7 L.

S. b. W. 8 L.

Nº 3.

S.S.E. 10 L.

S. b. E

a

a

S. W. ½ S. 7 L.

b

Thus ſhews ye *Iſl.* Schouten *at theſe Bearings and Diſtances*

W. b. S. ½ S. 11 L.

b

Nº 4.

S. W. 9 L.

a

W. ½ N. 10 L.

a

S.E. b. E ½ E. 10 L.

E. 4 L.

St. *George* and Cape *Mabo*, makes 1291 Meridional Parts; which was the furthest that I was to the East. In my outward bound Voyage I made Meridian distance between Cape *Mabo* and Cape St. *George*, 1290 Miles; and now in my Return, but 1243; which is 47 short of my distance going out. This Difference may probably be occasion'd by the strong Western Current which we found in our Return, which I allowed for after I perceiv'd it; and though we did not discern any Current when we went to the Eastward, except when near the Islands; yet it is probable we had one against us, though we did not take Notice of it because of the strong Westerly Winds. King *William's* Island lies in the Latitude of 21 Min. South, and may be seen distinctly off of Cape *Mabo*.

In the Evening we past by Cape *Mabo*; and afterwards steer'd away South-East, half East, keeping along the Shore, which here trends South-easterly. The next Morning seeing a large Opening in the Land, with an Island near the South-side; I stood in, thinking to anchor there. When we were shot in within 2 Leagues of the Island, the Wind came to the West, which blows right into the Opening. I stood to the North Shore; intending, when I came pretty nigh to send my Boat into the Opening, and sound, before I would adventure in. We found several deep Bays, but no Soundings within 2 Miles of the Shore; therefore I stood off again. Then seeing a Ripling under our Lee, I sent my Boat to sound on it; which return'd in half an Hour, and brought me Word that the Ripling we saw was only a Tide, and that they had no Ground there.

CHAP. V

The A's return from the Coast of New-Guinea. *A deep Channel. Strange Tides. The Island* Ceram *described. Strange Fowls. The Islands* Bonao, Bouro, Misacombi, Pentare, Laubana, *and* Potoro. *The Passage between* Pentare *and* Laubana. *The Island* Timor. Babao *Bay. The Island* Rotte. *More Islands than are commonly laid down in the Draughts. Great Currents. Whales. Coast of* New-Holland. *The* Tryal-Rocks. *The Coast of* Java. Princes *Isle. Streights of* Sunda. *Thwart-the-way Island. Indian Proes, and their Traffick. Passage through the Streight. Arrival at* Batavia.

THE Wind seeming to incline to East, as might be expected according to the Season of the Year; I rather chose to shape my Course as these Winds would best permit, than strive to return the same way we came; which, for many Leagues, must have been against this Monsoon: Though indeed on the other hand, the Dangers in that way, we already knew; but what might be in this, by which we now proposed to return, we could not tell.

We were now in a Channel about 8 or 9 Leagues wide, having a Range of Islands on the North-side, and another on the South-side, and very deep Water between, so that we had no Ground. The 22d of *April* in the Morning, I sent my Boat ashore to an Island on the North-side, and stood that way with the Ship. They found no Ground till within a Cable's length of the Shore, and then had Coral Rocks; so that they could not catch any Fish, though they saw a great many. They brought aboard a small Canoa, which they found a-drift. They met with no Game ashore, save only one party-colour'd Parrakite. The Land is of an indifferent Height; very Rocky, yet cloathed with tall Trees, whose bare Roots run along upon the Rocks. Our People saw a Pond of Salt Water, but found no fresh. Near this Island we met a pretty strong Tide, but found neither Tide nor Current off at some distance.

On the 24th, being about 2 Leagues from an Island to the Southward of us, we came over a Shoal, on which we had but 5 Fathom and a half. We did not descrie it, till we saw the Ground under us. In less than half an Hour before, the Boat had been sounding in discoloured Water, but had no Ground. We mann'd the Boat presently, and tow'd the Ship about; and then sounding, had 12, 15 and 17 Fathom, and then no Ground with our Hand-lead. The Shoal was rocky; but in 12 and 15 Fathom we had oazy Ground.

We found here very strange Tides, that ran in Streams, making a great Sea; and roaring so loud, that we could hear them before they came within a Mile of us. The Sea round about them seem'd all broken, and tossed the Ship so that she would not answer her Helm. These Riplings commonly lasted 10 or 12 minutes, and then the Sea became as still and smooth as a Mill-pond. We sounded often when in the midst of them, and afterwards in the smooth Water; but found no Ground, neither could we perceive that they drove us any way.

We had in one Night several of these Tides, that came most of them from the West; and the Wind being from that Quarter, we commonly heard them a long time before they came; and sometimes lowered our Topsails, thinking it was a Gust of Wind. They were of great length from North to South, but their breadth not exceeding 200 Yards, and they drove a great pace: For though we had little Wind to move us, yet these would soon pass away, and leave the Water very smooth; and just before we encountred them, we met a great Swell, but it did not break.

Q

The 26th we saw the Island *Ceram*; and still met some Riplings, but much fainter than those we had the 2 preceeding Days. We sail'd along the Island *Ceram* to the Westward, edging in withal, to see if peradventure we might find a Harbour to anchor in, where we might water, trim the Ship, and refresh our Men.

In the Morning we saw a Sail to the North of us, steering in for the West-end of *Ceram*, as we likewise were. In the Evening, being near the Shore on the North-side of the Island, I stood off to Sea with an easy Sail; intending to stand in for the Shore in the Morning, and try to find Anchoring, to fill Water, and get a little Fish for refreshment. Accordingly in the Morning early, I stood in with the North-West-point of *Ceram*; leaving a small Island, called *Bonao*, to the West. The Sail we saw the Day before, was now come pretty nigh us, steering in also (as we did) between *Ceram* and *Bonao*. I shortned Sail a little for him; and when he got a-breast of us, not above 2 Miles off, I sent my Boat aboard. It was a *Dutch* Sloop, come from *Terranate*, and bound for *Amboyna*: My Men whom I sent in the Boat, bought 5 Bags of new Rice, each containing about 130 pounds, for 6 *Spanish* Dollars. The Sloop had many rare Parrots aboard for Sale, which did not want price. A *Malayan* Merchant aboard, told our Men, that about 6 Months ago he was at *Bencola*, and at that time the Governour either dyed or was kill'd, and that the Commander of an *English* Ship then in that Road succeeded to that Government.

In the Afternoon, having a Breeze at North and North-North-East, I sent my Boat to sound, and standing after her with the Ship, anchored in 30 Fathom Water oazy Sand, half a Mile from the Shore, right against a small River of fresh Water. The next Morning I sent both the Boats ashore to Fish; they return'd about 10 a-Clock,

This Bird was taken on the Coast of New Guinea

A Stately Land Fowl found on the Coast of New Guinea

A Strange Land Fowl found on the Island Ceram. described

with a few Mullets and 3 or 4 Cavallies, and some Pan-Fish. We found Variation here, 2 deg. 15 min. East.

When the Sea was smooth by the Land-Winds, we sent our Boats ashore for Water; who, in a few Turns, filled all our Casks.

The Land here is low, swampy and woody; the Mould is a dark Grey, friable Earth. Two Rivers came out within a Bow-shot of each other, just opposite to the place where we rode: One comes right down out of the Country; and the other from the South, running along by the Shore, not Musquet-shot from the Sea-side. The Northermost River is biggest, and out of it we filled our Water; our Boats went in and out at any time of Tide. In some places the Land is overflown with fresh Water, at full Sea. The Land hereabouts is full of Trees unknown to us, but none of them very large or high; the Woods yield many wild Fruits and Berries, such as I never saw elsewhere. We met with no Land-Animals. The Fowls we found, were Pidgeons, Parrots, Cockadores, and a great number of small Birds unknown to me. One of the Master's Mates killed 2 Fowls as big as Crows; of a black Colour, excepting that the Tails were all white. Their Necks were pretty long, one of which was of a Saffron-colour, the other Black. They had very large Bills, much like a Rams-horn; their Legs were strong and Short, and their claws like a Pidgeon's; their Wings of an ordinary length: Yet they make a great Noise when they fly, which they do very heavily. They feed on Berries, and perch on the highest Trees. Their Flesh is sweet; I saw some of the same Species at *New-Guinea,* but no where else.

May the 3d, at 6 in the Morning we weighed, intending to pass between *Bonao* and *Ceram*; but presently after we got under Sail, we saw a pretty large Proe coming about the North-West-point of *Ceram*. Wherefore I stood to the North to speak with her, putting aboard our Ensign. She seeing us coming that way, went into a small Creek, and skulked behind a Point a while: At last discovering her again, I sent my Boat to speak with her; but the Proe row'd away, and would not come nigh it. After this, finding I could not pass between *Bonao* and *Ceram*, as I purposed; I steer'd away to the North of it.

This *Bonao* is a small Island, lying about 4 Leagues from the North-West Point of *Ceram*. I was inform'd by the *Dutch* Sloop before-mentioned, that notwithstanding its smallness, it hath one fine River, and that the *Dutch* are there settled. Whether there be any Natives on it, or not, I know not, nor what its Produce is. They further said, that the *Ceramers* were their mortal Enemies; yet that they were settled on the Westermost Point of *Ceram* in spite of the Natives.

The next Day, as we approach'd the Island *Bouro*, there came off from it a very fragrant Scent, much like that from *King William*'s Island; and we found so strong a Current setting to the Westward, that we could scarce stem it. We plied to get to the Southward, intending to pass between *Bouro* and *Keelang*.

In the Evening, being near the West-end of *Bouro*, we saw a Brigantine to the North-West of us, on the North-side of *Bouro*, standing to the Eastward. I would not stand East or West for fear of coming nigh the Land which was on each side of us, *viz. Bouro* on the West, and *Keelang* on the East. The next Morning we found our selves in Mid-channel between both Islands; and having the Wind at South-West we steer'd South-South-East, which is right through between both. At 11 a-Clock it fell calm, and so continued till Noon; by that time the Brigantine, which we saw a-Stern the Night before, was

Table XV.   Gilolo and other Islands between it and Bouro

No. 1. Thus Sheweth ye S.E. Part of Gilolo at
these Bearings and at ye same time ye Est.
Mellel and ye small Isl. to ye N. ward of it.

N.¼ W. 8 L.   {Gilolo}   N.b.E. 9 L.   E.b.N.¼ N. 6 L.   E.½ S. 8 L.   a

a   S. 11 L.   S.b.w. 5 L.   b

b   S.S.E. 2½ L. ye Isl. that lay to ———— ye N. ward of Mellel
                                                S.w.b.S. 6 L.

b
Thus Sheweth ye Isl. Mellel and the Small Isl. that ly to the Northward of it.

No. 2.

N.N.W. ½ W. 7 L.   S.W. Part of Gilolo   N.N.E. ½ E. 8 L.

All this Land makes Thus at these Bearings ye first being ye S.w. Part of Gilolo, and
the Land that bears S.E. is Part of Mellel. and ye W.½ S. Bearing is a smal high Isl. by
it selfe. this was taken at once from ye parting line.

E.N.E.¼ N. 9 L.   S.E. 10 L.   W.½ S. 8 L.

No. 3.

N.E. 5 Miles   River S.E. 2 Miles
                                                                                        a
N.E. b. N. 2 Miles the small Isl.

S.w. b. W. 4. Miles

a   b
Thus shews ye N.W. Part of Ceram and ye Bay where wee watered and the Isl.
Bona at these Bearings, the River S.W. 2 Miles at ye same time.
W.S.w. ½ L.   W.b.S.½ S. 3 L.   Isl. Bona   W. 4 L.
b

No. 4.

N.w. Point of Ceram   E.½ N. 9 L.   The Island Bonao
                                                                                        a

S.E.b.S. 4 L.
a   b
Thus Sheweth the N.w. Part of Ceram the Isl. Bona and the Land and
Isl. that leys to the Southward of Bona & Bouro.
b   c
c.   S.w. b. S. 9 L.

got 2 or 3 Leagues a-head of us. It is probable she met a strong Land-wind in the Evening, which continued all Night; she keeping nearer the Shore, than I could safely do. She might likewise have a Tide or Current setting Easterly, where she was; though we had a Tide setting Northwardly against us, we being in Mid-channel.

About 8 at Night, the Brigantine which we saw in the Day, came close along by us on our Weather-side: Our Guns were all ready before Night, Matches lighted, and small Arms on the Quarter-Deck ready loaden. She standing one way, and we another; we soon got further asunder. But I kept good watch all the Night, and in the Morning saw her a-Stern of us, standing as we did. At 10 a-Clock, having little Wind, I sent the Yawle aboard of her. She was a Chinese Vessel, laden with Rice, Arrack, Tea, Porcellane, and other Commodities, bound for *Amboyna.* The Commander said that his Boat was gone ashore for Water, and ask'd our Men if they saw her; for she had been wanting 2 or 3 Days, and they knew not what was become of her. They had their Wives, and Children aboard, and probably came to settle at some new *Dutch* Factory. The Commander also inform'd us, that the *Dutch* had lately settled at *Ampulo, Menippe, Bonao,* and on a Point of *Ceram.* The next Day we past out to the Southward between *Keelang* and *Bouro.* After this, we had for several Days a Current setting Southerly, and a great tumbling Sea, occasion'd more by the strong Current than by Winds, as was apparent by the jumping of its Waves against each other; and by Observation I found 25 Miles more Southing then our Course gave us.

On the 14th we discovered the Island *Misacomby,* and the next Day sail'd along to the West on the North-side of the Island. In some Charts it is called *Omba*; it is a mountainous Island, spotted with Woods and Savan-

nahs; about 20 Leagues long, and 5 or 6 broad. We saw
no signs of Inhabitants on it. We fell in nearest to the
West-end of it; and therefore I chose to pass on to the
Westward, intending to get through to the Southward
between this and the next Isle to the West of it, or between any other 2 Islands to the West, where I should
meet with the clearest Passage; because the Winds were
now at North-East and East-North-East, and the Isle
lies nearly East and West; so that if the Winds continued,
I might be a long time in getting to the East-end of it,
which yet I knew to be the best Passage. In the Night,
being at the West-end, and seeing no clear Passage, I
stood off with an easie Sail, and in the Morning had a
fine Land-wind, which would have carried us 5 or 6
Leagues to the East, if we had made the best of it; but we
kept on only with a gentle Gale, for fear of a Westerly
Current. In the Morning, finding we had not met with
any Current as we expected; assoon as it was Light, we
made Sail to the Westward again.

After Noon, being near the end of the Isle *Pentare*,
which lies West from *Misacomby*, we saw many Houses and
Plantations in the Country, and many Coco-nut-Trees
growing by the Sea-side. We also saw several Boats
sailing cross a Bay or Channel at the West-end of
Misacomby, between it and *Pentare*. We had but little
Wind, and that at North, which blows right in, with a
Swell rowling in withal; wherefore I was afraid to venture
in, though probably there might be good Anchoring, and
a Commerce with the Natives. I continued steering to
the West, because the Night before, at Sun-setting, I saw
a small round high Island to the West of *Pentare*, where I
expected a good Passage.

We could not that Day reach the West-end of *Pentare*,
but saw a deep Bay to the West of us, where I thought

Table XVI Bouro and other Islands between it and Ambo

No. 1.

This Isl. makes Thus at these Bearings when ý Isl. Bona shews at ý other side

S. W. ½ S. 11 L.   S. W. b. W. 14 L.

Isl. Bouro

No. 2.

S. W. ½ S. 5 L.   W. b. S. 5 L.   W. ½ S. 12 L.

Ambolow

Thus Shews the Isl. Ambolow and Bouro at these Bearings

a   I. Bouro   b

b   N. N. W. 7 L.

No. 3.

E. S. E. ½ S. 10 L.   Ambo   S. E. 9 L.   a

a   S. S. E. 7 L.   S. ½ E. 8 L.

At these Bearings Sheweth ý Isl. Ambo and ý Islands as you see to ý South Westward of it.

S. S. W. ½ W. 9 L.   S. W. 11 L.   S. W. ½ W. 12 L.

No. 4.

W. ½ N. 11 L.   The Passage w.ch wee came through

Thus Sheweth ý Islands Laubana and Panterra at these Bearings w.ch wee came between at ý Bearings N. W. b. N also ý Islands between that and Ambo as you see.

Part of Ambo.

might be a Passage through, between *Pentare* and *Laubana*. But as yet the Lands were shut one within an other, that we could not see any Passage. Therefore I ordered to sail 7 Leagues more Westerly, and lye by till next Day. In the Morning we look'd out for an Opening, but could see none; yet by the distance and bearing of a high round Island called *Potoro*, we were got to the West of the Opening, but not far from it. Wherefore I tack'd and stood to the East; and the rather, because I had reason to suppose this to be the Passage we came through in the *Cygnet* mentioned in my Voyage round the World; but I was not yet sure of it, because we had rainy Weather, so that we could not now see the Land so well as we did then. We then accidentally saw the Opening, at our first falling in with the Islands; which now was a Work of some time and difficulty to discover. However before 10 a Clock we saw the Opening plain; and I was the more confirm'd in my Knowledge of this Passage, by a Spit of Sand and 2 Islands at the North-East part of its Entrance. The Wind was at South-South-West, and we plied to get through before Night; for we found a good Tide helping us to the South. About 7 or 8 Leagues to the West of us we saw a high round piked Mountain, from whose Top a Smoak seem'd to ascend as from a *Vulcano*. There were 3 other very high piked Mountains, 2 on the East, and 1 on the West of that which smoaked.

In our plying to get through between *Pentare* and *Laubana*, we had (as I said) a good Tide or Current setting us to the Southward. And it is to be observed, that near the Shores in these Parts we commonly find a Tide setting Northwardly or Southwardly, as the Land lyes; but the Northwardly Tide sets not above 3 Hours in 12, having little strength; and sometimes it only checks the contrary Current, which runs with great Violence, especially in narrow Passes, such as this, between 2 Islands. It was 12 at Night before we got clear of 2 other small Islands, that lay on the South-side of the Passage; and there we had a very violent Tide setting us through against a brisk Gale of Wind. Notwithstanding which, I kept the Pinnace out, for fear we should be becalm'd. For this is the same place, through which I passed in the Year 1687, mentioned in my Voyage round the World, (*pag.* 309.) Only then we came out between the Western small Island and *Laubana*, and now we came through between the two small Islands. We sounded frequently, but had no Ground. I said there, that we came through between *Omba* and *Pentare:* For we did not then see the Opening between those 2 Islands; which made me take the West-side of *Pentare* for the West-end of *Omba*, and *Laubana* for *Pentare*. But now we saw the Opening between *Omba* and *Pentare*; which was so narrow that I would not venture through: Besides, I had now discovered my Mistake, and hop'd to meet with the other Passage again, as indeed we did, and found it to be bold from Side to Side, which in the former Voyage I did not know. After we were through, we made the best of our way to *Timor*; and on *May* the 18th in the Morning, we saw it plain, and made the high Land over *Laphao* the *Portugueze* Factory, as also the high Peak over our first Watering-place, and a small round Island about mid-way between them.

We coasted along the Island *Timor*, intending to touch at *Babao*, to get a little Water and Refreshments. I would not go into the Bay where we first water'd, because of the Currents which there whirl about very strangely, especi-ally at Spring-tides, which were now setting in; besides, the South-East Winds come down in Flaws from the Mountains, so that it would have been very dangerous for us. Wherefore we crowded all the Sail we could, to get to *Babao* before Night, or at least to get Sight of the sandy Island at the Entrance of the Bay; but could not. So we plied all Night; and the next Morning entered the Bay.

There being good Ground all over this Bay, we anchored at 2 a Clock in 30 Fathom Water, soft oazy Ground. And the Morning after I sent my Boat ashore with the Sain to fish. At Noon she return'd and brought enough for all the Ship's Company. They saw an *Indian* Boat at a round rocky Island about a Mile from them.

On the 22d, I sent my Boat ashore again to fish: At Noon she return'd with a few Fish, which serv'd me and my Officers. They catch'd one Whiteing, the first I had seen in these Seas. Our People went over to the rocky Island, and there found several Jarrs of Turtle, and some hanging up a drying, and some Cloaths; their Boat was about a Mile off, striking Turtle. Our Men left all as they found. In the Afternoon a very large Shark came under our Stern; I never had seen any near so big before. I put a Piece of Meat on a Hook for him, but he went a-Stern and return'd no more. About Mid-night, the Wind being pretty moderate, I weigh'd and stood into the Bottom of the Bay, and ran over nearer the South Shore, where I thought to lye and Water, and at convenient Times get Fish for our Refreshment. The next Morning I sent my Pinnace with 2 Hogsheads and 10 Barrecoes for Water; they return'd at Noon with the Casks full of Water, very thick and muddy, but sweet and good. We found Variation, 15 min. West.

This Afternoon, finding that the Breezes were set in here, and that it blew so hard that I could neither fish nor fill Water without much Difficulty and Hazard of the Boat; I resolved to be gone, having good Quantity of

Water aboard. Accordingly at half an Hour after 2 in the Morning we weighed with the Wind at East by South, and stood to Sea. We coasted along by the Island *Rotte*, which is high Land, spotted with Woods and Savannahs. The Trees appear'd small and shrubby, and the Savannahs dry and rusty. All the North-side has sandy Bays by the Sea. We saw no Houses nor Plantations.

The next Day we crowded all the Sail we could to get to the West of all the Isles before Night, but could not; for at 6 in the Evening we saw Land bearing South-West by West. For here are more Islands than are laid down in any Draughts that I have seen. Wherefore I was oblig'd to make a more Westerly Course than I intended, till I judg'd we might be clear of the Land. And when we were so, I could easily perceive by the Ship's Motion. For till then, being under the Lee of the Shore, we had smooth Water; but now we had a troubled Sea which made us dance lustily. This turbulent Sea, was occasion'd in Part by the Current; which setting out slanting against the Wind, was by it raised into short cockling Seas. I did indeed expect a South-West Current here, but not so very strong as we found it.

On the 26th we continued to have a very strong Current setting Southwardly; but on what Point exactly, I know not. Our whole Distance by Log was but 82 Miles, and our Difference of Latitude since Yesterday-noon by Observation 100 Miles, which is 18 Miles more than the whole Distance; and our Course, allowing no Lee-way at all, was South 17 Deg. West, which gives but 76 Miles Difference of Latitude, 24 less than we found by Observation. I did expect (as has been said) we might meet a great Current setting to the South Yesterday, because there is a constant Current setting out from among those

Islands we pass'd through between *Timor* and the Isles
to the West of it, and, 'tis probable, in all the other
Openings between the Islands, even from the East-end
of *Java* to the End of all that Range that runs from
thence, both to the East and West of *Timor*; but being
got so far out to Sea as we were, though there may be a
very great Current, yet it does not seem probable to me
that it should be of so great Strength as we now found:
For both Currents and Tides lose their Force in the
open Sea, where they have room to spread; and it is
only in narrow Places, or near Head-lands, that their
Force is chiefly felt. Besides in my Opinion, it should
here rather set to the West than South; being open to the
narrow Sea, that divides *New-Holland* from the Range of
Islands before-mentioned.

The 27th, we found that in the last 24 Hours we had
gone 9 Miles less South than the Log gave: So that 'tis
probable we were then out of the Southern Current,
which we felt so much before. We saw many Tropick-
Birds about us. And found Variation 1 deg. 25 min. West.

On *June* the 1st, we saw several Whales, the first we
had at this Time seen on the Coast: But when we were
here before, we saw many; at which Time we were
nearer the Shore than now. The Variation now, was
5 deg. 38 min. West.

I design'd to have made *New-Holland* in about the
Latitude of 20 deg. and steer'd Courses by Day to make
it, but in the Night could not be so bold; especially since
we had sounding. This Afternoon I steer'd in South-
West, till 6 a-Clock; then it blowing fresh, and Night
coming on, I steer'd West-South-West, till we had 40
Fathom; and then stood West, which Course carries
along Shore. In the Morning again from 6 to 12 I steer'd
West-South-West, to have made the Land, but, not

seeing it, I judged we were to the West of it. Here is very good Soundings on this Coast. When we past this way to the Eastward, we had, near this Latitude of 19 deg. 50 min. 38 Fathom, about 18 Leagues from the Land: But, this Time, we saw not the Land. The next Morning I saw a great many Scuttle-Fish-bones, which was a Sign that we were not far from the Land. Also a great many Weeds continually floating by us.

We found the Variation increase considerably as we went Westward. For on the 3d, it was 6 deg. 10 min. West; on the 4th, 6 deg. 20 min. and on the 6th, 7 deg. 20 min. That Evening we saw some Fowls like *Men of War Birds* flying North-East, as I was told; for I did not see them, having been indisposed these 3 or 4 Days.

On the 11th we found the Variation 8 deg. 1 min. West; on the 12th, 6 deg. 0 min. I kept on my Course to the Westward till the 15th, and then altered it. My Design was to seek for the *Tryal Rocks*; but having been sick 5 or 6 Days, without any fresh Provision or other good Nourishment aboard, and seeing no Likelihood of my Recovery, I rather chose to go to some Port in Time, than to beat here any longer; my People being very negligent, when I was not upon Deck my self: I found the Winds variable, so that I might go any way, East, West, North, or South; wherefore, its probable I might have found the said Rocks, had not Sickness prevented me; which Discovery (when ever made) will be of great use to Merchants trading to these Parts.

From hence nothing material happened, till we came upon the Coast of *Java*. On the 23d we saw *Princes-Isle* plain, and the Mouth of the Streights of *Sunda*. By my Computation, the Distance between *Timor* and *Princes-Isle*, is 14 deg. 22 min. The next Day in the Afternoon, being abreast of *Crockadore* Island, I steer'd away East-

North-East for an Island that lies near Mid-way between *Sumatra* and *Java*, but nearest the *Java* Shore; which is by *English* Men called *Thwart-the-way*. We had but small Winds till about 3 a-Clock, when it freshned, and I was in good Hopes to pass through before Day: But at 9 a Clock the Wind fell, and we got but little. I was then abreast of *Thwart-the-way*, which is a pretty high long Island; but before 11, the Wind turned, and presently afterward it fell calm. I was then about 2 Leagues from the said Island; and, having a strong Current against us, before Day we were driven astern 4 or 5 Leagues. In the Morning we had the Wind at North-North-West; it look'd black and the Wind unsettled: So that I could not expect to get through. I therefore stood toward the *Java* Shore, and at 10 anchored in 24 Fathom Water, black oazy Ground, 3 Leagues from the Shore. I sounded in the Night when it was calm, and had 54 Fathom, coarse Sand and Coral.

In the Afternoon before, we had seen many Proes; but none came off to us; and in the Night we saw many Fires ashore. This Day a large Proe came aboard of us, and lay by our Side an Hour. There were only 4 Men in her, all *Javians*, who spoke the *Malayan* Language. They ask'd if we were *English*; I answered, we were; and presently one of them came aboard, and presented me with a small Hen, some Eggs and Coco-nuts; for which I gave some Beads and a small Looking-Glass, and some Glass-Bottles. They also gave me some Sugar-canes, which I distributed to such of my Men as were scorbutick. They told me there were 3 *English* Ships at *Batavia*.

The 28th at 2 in the Afternoon we anchored in 26 Fathom Water; presently it fell calm and began to rain very violently, and so continued from 3 till 9 in the Evening. At 1 in the Morning we weigh'd with a fine

Land-wind at South-South-East; but presently the Wind coming about at East, we anchored; for we commonly found the Current setting West. If at any Time it turn'd, it was so weak, that it did us little good; and I did not think it safe to venture through without a pretty brisk leading Gale; for the Passage is but narrow, and I knew not what Dangers might be in the way, nor how the Tide sets in the Narrow, having not been this way these 28 Years, and all my People wholly Strangers: We had the Opening fair before us.

While we lay here, 4 *Malayan* Proes came from the Shore, laden with Coco-nuts, Plantains, Bonanoes, Fowls, Ducks, Tobacco, Sugar, &c. These were very welcome, and we purchased much Refreshment of them. At 10 a-Clock I dismiss'd all the Boats, and weigh'd with the Wind at North-West. At half an Hour past 6 in the Evening, we anchored in 32 Fathom Water in a coarse Sort of Oaze. We were now past the Island *Thwart-the-way*, but had still one of the small Islands to pass. The Tide begun to run strong to the West; which obliged me to anchor while I had Soundings, for Fear of being driven back again or on some unknown Sand. I lay still all Night. At 5 a Clock the next Morning, the Tide began to slacken: At 6, I weig'd with the Wind at South-East by East, a handsom Breeze. We just weather'd the *Button*; and sounding several Times, had still between 30 and 40 Fathom. When we were abreast of the *Button*, and about 2 Leagues from the Westermost point of *Java*, we had 34 Fathom, small Peppery Sand. You may either come between this Island and *Java*, or, if the Wind is Northerly, run out between the Island *Thwart-the-way* and this last small Island.

The Wind for the most Part being at East and East by South, I was obliged to run over towards the *Sumatra*

Shore, sounding as I went, and had from 34 to 23 Fathom. In the Evening I sounded pretty quick, being got near the *Sumatra* Shore; and, finding a Current setting to the West, between 8 and 9 a-Clock we anchored in 34 Fathom. The Tide set to the West from 7 in the Evening to 7 this Morning; and then, having a small Gale at West-South-West, I weigh'd and stood over to the *Java* Shore.

In the Evening having the Wind between East-North-East and South-East by East, we could not keep off the *Java* Shore. Wherefore I anchored in 27 Fathom Water, about a League and a half off Shore. At the same Time we saw a Ship at anchor near the Shore, about 2 Mile to Leeward of us. We found the Tide setting to the Westward, and presently after we anchored it fell calm. We lay still all Night, and saw many Fires ashore. At 5 the next Morning, being *July* the 1st, we weigh'd and stood to the North for a Sea-breeze: At 10 the Wind coming out, I tack'd and had a fine brisk Gale. The Ship we saw at anchor, weigh'd also and stood after us. While we past by *Pulo Baby*, I kept sounding, and had no less than 14 Fathom. The other Ship coming after us with all the Sail she could make, I shortned Sail on Purpose that she might overtake us, but she did not. A little after 5, I anchored in 13 Fathom good oazy Ground. About 7 in the Evening, the Ship that followed us, past by close under our Stern; she was a *Dutch* Fly-boat; they told us they came directly from *Holland*, and had been in their Passage six Months. It was now dark, and the *Dutch* Ship anchored within a Mile of us. I order'd to look out sharp in the Morning; that so soon as the *Dutch* Man began to move, we might be ready to follow him; for I intended to make him my Pilot. In the Morning at half an hour after 5 we weigh'd, the *Dutch* Man being under Sail before;

and we stood directly after him. At 8, having but little Wind, I sent my Boat aboard of him, to see what News he had brought from *Europe*. Soon after, we spied a Ship coming from the East, plying on a Wind to speak with us, and shewing *English* Colours. I made a Signal for my Boat, and presently bore away towards her; and being pretty nigh, the Commander and Super-cargoe came aboard, supposing we had been the *Tuscany* Galley, which was expected then at *Batavia*. This was a Country Ship, belonging to Fort St. *George*, having come out from *Batavia* the Day before, and bound to *Bencola*. The Commander told me that the *Fleet-frigat* was at Anchor in *Batavia* Road, but would not stay there long: He told me also, that his Majesty's Ships commanded by Captain *Warren* were still in *India*, but he had been a great while from the Coast and had not seen them. He gave me a Draught of these Streights, from the *Button* and *Cap* to *Batavia*, and shew'd me the best way in thither. At 11 a Clock, it being calm, I anchored in 14 Fathom good oazy Ground.

At 2 a Clock we weigh'd again; the *Dutch* Ship being under Sail before, standing close to *Mansheters* Island; but finding he could not weather it, he tack'd and stood off a little while, and then tack'd again. In the mean Time I stood pretty nigh the said Island, sounding, but could not weather it. Then I tack'd and stood off, and the *Dutch* stood in towards the Island; and weathered it. I being desirous to have room enough, stood off longer, and then went about, having the *Dutch* Ship 4 Points under my Lee. I kept after him; but as I came nearer the Island, I found a Tide setting to the West, so that I could not weather it. Wherefore at 6 in the Evening I anchored in 7 Fathom oazy Ground, about a Mile from the Island: The *Dutch* Ship went about 2 Miles further, and anchored also; and we both lay still all Night. At 5 the next Morning we weigh'd again, and the *Dutch* Ship stood away between the Island *Cambusses* and the Main; but I could not follow, because we had a Land-wind. Wherefore I went without the *Cambusses*, and by Noon we saw the Ships that lay at the careening Island near *Batavia*. After the Land-wind was spent, which we had at South-East and South-South-East; the Sea-breeze came up at East. Then we went about; and the Wind coming afterward at East-North-East, we had a large Wind to run us into *Batavia* Road: And at 4 in the Afternoon, we anchored in 6 Fathom soft Oaze.

CHAP. VI

The A. continues in Batavia-Road, *to refit, and to get Provisions.* English *Ships then in the Road. Departure from* Batavia. *Touch at the* Cape of Good Hope. *And at* St. Helena. *Arrival at the Island of* Ascension. *A Leak Sprung. Which being impossible to be stopped; the Ship is lost, but the Men saved. They find Water upon the Island. And are brought back to* England.

WE found in *Batavia* Road a great many Ships at anchor, most *Dutch*, and but one *English* Ship named the *Fleet-frigat*, commanded by one *Merry*. We rode a little without them all. Near the Shore lay a stout China Junk, and a great many small Vessels, *viz.* Brigantines, Sloops and *Malayan* Proes in abundance. Assoon as I anchored, I sent my Boat aboard the *Fleet-frigat*, with orders to make them strike their Pendant, which was done soon after the Boat went aboard. Then my Clerk, whom I sent in the Boat, went for the Shore, as I had directed him; to see if the Government would answer my Salute: But it was now near Night, and he had only time to speak with the *Ship-bander*, who told him that the Government would have answered my Salute with the same number of Guns, if I had fired as soon as I anchored; but that now it was too late. In the Evening my Boat came aboard, and the next Morning I my self went ashore, visited the *Dutch* General, and desir'd the Priviledge of buying such Provision and Stores, as I now wanted; which he granted me.

I lay here till the 17th of *October* following, all which time we had very fair Weather, some Tornadoes excepted. In the mean time I supplied the Carpenter with such Stores as were necessary for refitting the Ship; which prov'd more leaky after he had caulk'd Her, then she was before: So that I was obliged to carreen her, for which purpose I hired Vessels to take in our Guns, Ballast, Provision and Stores.

The *English* Ships that arriv'd here from *England*, were first the *Liampo*, commanded by Captain *Monk*, bound for *China*; next, the *Panther*, commanded by Captain *Robinson*; then the *Mancel*-Frigat, commanded by Captain *Clerk*. All these brought good Tidings from *England*. Most of them had been unfortunate in their Officers; especially Captain *Robinson*, who said that some of them had been conspiring to ruin him and his Voyage. There came in also several *English* Country Vessels; first a Sloop from *Ben-jarr*, commanded by one *Russel*, bound to *Bengale*; next, the *Monsoon*, belonging to *Bengale*: She had been at *Malacca* at the same time that his Majesty Ship the *Harwich* was there: Afterwards came in also another small Ship from *Bengale*.

While we stay'd here, all the forenamed *English* Ships sailed hence; the 2 *Bengale* Ships excepted. Many *Dutch* Ships also came in here, and departed again before us. We had several Reports concerning our Men of War in *India*, and much talk concerning Rovers who had committed several Spoils upon the Coast, and in the Streights of *Malacca*. I did not hear of any Ships sent out to quash them. At my first coming in, I was told that 2 Ships had been sent from *Amboyna* in quest of me; which was lately confirm'd by one of the Skippers, whom I by accident met with here. He told me they had 3 Protests against me; that they came to *Pulo-Sabuda* on the Coast of *New-Guinnea* 28 Days after my departure thence, and went as far as *Scouten's* Island, and hearing no further News of me, return'd. Something likewise to this purpose Mr. *Merry*, Commander of the *Fleet-frigat*, told me at my first arrival here; and that the General at *Batavia* had a

Copy of my Commission and Instructions; but I look'd upon it as a very improbable thing.

While we lay here, the *Dutch* held several Consultations about sending some Ships for *Europe* sooner than ordinary: At last the 16th of *October* was agreed upon for the Day of Sailing, which is 2 Months sooner than usual. They lay ready 2 or 3 Days before, and went out on the 10th. Their Names were, the *Ostresteen,* bound to *Zea-land*; the *Vanheusen,* for *Enchiehoust*; and the 3 *Crowns,* for *Amsterdam,* commanded by *Skipper Jacob Uncright,* who was Commadore over all the rest. I had by this time finished my Business here, *viz.* fitted the Ship, recruited my self with Provision, filled all my Water; and the time of the Year to be going for *Europe* being now at hand, I prepar'd to be gone also.

Accordingly on the 17th of *October,* at half an Hour after 6 in the Morning, I weigh'd Anchor from *Batavia,* having a good Land-wind at South, and fair Weather: And by the 19th at Noon, came up with the 3 *Dutch* Ships before-mentioned. The 29th of *November* in the Morning we saw a small Hawk flying about the Ship till she was quite tired. Then she rested on the Mizen-Top-Sail-Yard, where we catch'd her. It is probable she was blown off from *Madagascar* by the violent Northerly Winds; that being the nighest Land to us, though distance near 150 Leagues.

The 30th of *December,* we arrived at the *Cape of Good Hope*; and departed again on the 11th of *January,* 1701. About the end of the Month, we saw abundance of Weeds or Blubber swim by us, for I cannot determine which. It was all of one Shape and Colour. As they floated on the Water, they seem'd to be of the breadth of the Palm of a Man's Hand, spread out round into many Branches about the Bigness of a Man's Finger.

They had in the middle a little Knob, no bigger than the Top of a Mans Thumb. They were of a Smoak-colour; and the Branches, by their pliantness in the Water, seem'd to be more simple than Gellies, I have not seen the like before.

The 2d of *February*, we anchored in St. *Helena* Road, and set sail again from thence on the 13th.

On the 21st we made the Island of *Ascension*, and stood in towards it. The 22d between 8 and 9 a-Clock, we sprung a Leak, which increased so that the Chain-pump could not keep the Ship free. Whereupon I set the Hand-pump to work also, and by 10 a-Clock suck'd her: Then wore the Ship, and stood to the Southward, to try if that would ease her; and then the Chain-pump just kept her free. At 5 the next Morning we made Sail and stood in for the Bay; and at 9 anchored in 10 and a half Fathom, sandy Ground. The South-point bore South-South-West distance 2 Miles, and the North-point of the Bay, North-East half North, distance 2 Miles. As soon as we anchored, I ordered the Gunner to clear his Powder-room, that we might there search for the Leak, and endeavour to stop it within board if possible; for we could not heel the Ship so low, it being within 4 Streaks of the Keel; neither was there any convenient place to haul her ashore. I ordered the Boatswain to assist the Gunner; and by 10 a-Clock the Powder-room was clear. The Carpenter's Mate, Gunner, and Boatswain went down; and soon after I followed them my self, and ask'd them whether they could come at the Leak: They said they believed they might, by cutting the Cieling; I told the Carpenter's Mate (who was the only Person in the Ship that understood any Thing of Carpenters-work,) that if he thought he could come at the Leak by cutting the Cieling without weakening the Ship, he might do it for he had stopp'd one Leak so before; which though not so big as this, yet having seen them both, I thought he might as well do this as the other. Wherefore I left him to do his best. The Ceiling being cut, they could not come at the Leak; for it was against one of the *Foot-hook-Timbers*, which the Carpenter's Mate said he must first cut, before it could be stopp'd. I went down again to see it, and found the Water to come in very violently. I told them I never had known any such thing as cutting Timbers to stop Leaks; but if they who ought to be best Judges in such Cases, thought they could do any good, I bid them use their utmost Care and Diligence, promising the Carpenter's Mate that I would always be a Friend to him if he could and would stop it: He said, by 4 a-Clock in the Afternoon he would make all well, it being then about 11 in the Forenoon. In the Afternoon my Men were all employ'd, pumping with both Pumps; except such as assisted the Carpenter's Mate. About one in the Afternoon I went down again, and the Carpenter's Mate was cutting the After-part of the Timber over the Leak. Some said it was best to cut the Timber away at once; I bid them hold their Tongue, and let the Carpenter's Mate alone; for he knew best, and I hop'd he would do his utmost to stop the Leak. I desir'd him to get every thing ready for stopping the violence of the Water, before he cut any further; for fear it should overpower us at once. I had already ordered the Carpenter to bring all the Oakam he had, and the Boatswain to bring all the waste Cloaths, to stuff in upon Occasion; and had for the same purpose sent down my own Bedcloaths. The Carpenter's Mate said he should want short Stantions, to be placed so that the upper-end should touch the Deck, and the under-part rest on what was laid over the Leak; and presently took a Length for them. I ask'd the Master-Carpenter what he thought best to be done: He replied till the Leak was all open, he could not tell. Then he went away to make a Stantion, but it was too long: I ordered him to make many of several Lengths, that we might not want of any Size. So, once more desiring the Carpenter's Mate to use his utmost Endeavours, I went up, leaving the Boatswain and some others there. About 5 a Clock the Boatswain came to me, and told me the Leak was increased, and that it was impossible to keep the Ship above Water; when on the contrary I expected to have had the News of the Leak's being stopt. I presently went down, and found the Timber cut away, but nothing in Readiness to stop the Force of the Water from coming in. I ask'd them why they would cut the Timber, before they had got all Things in Readiness: The Carpenter's Mate answered, they could do nothing till the Timber was cut, that he might take the Dimensions of the Place; and that there was a Chaulk which he had lined out, preparing by the Carpenter's Boy. I ordered them in the mean Time to stop in Oakam, and some Pieces of Beef; which accordingly was done, but all to little Purpose: For now the Water gush'd in with such Violence, notwithstanding all our Endeavours to check it, that it flew in over the Cieling; and for want of Passage out of the Room overflow'd it above 2 Foot deep. I ordered the Bulkhead to be cut open, to give Passage to the Water that it might drain out of the Room; and withal ordered to clear away abaft the Bulk-head, that we might bail: So now we had both Pumps going, and as many bailing as could; and by this Means the Water began to decrease; which gave me some Hope of saving the Ship. I ask'd the Carpenter's Mate, what he thought of it; He said, *Fear not*; *for by* 10 *a Clock at Night I'll engage to stop the Leak.* I

went from him with a heavy Heart; but putting a good
Countenance upon the Matter, encouraged my Men,
who pump'd and bail'd very briskly; and, when I saw
Occasion, I gave them some Drams to comfort them.
About 11 a Clock at Night, the Boatswain came to me,
and told me, that the Leak still encreased; and that the
Plank was so rotten, it broke away like Dirt; and that
now it was impossible to save the Ship; for they could
not come at the Leak, because the Water in the Room
was got above it. The rest of the Night we spent in
Pumping and Bailing. I worked my self to encourage
my Men, who were very diligent; but the Water still
encreas'd, and we now thought of nothing but saving
our Lives. Wherefore I hoisted out the Boat, that, if the
Ship should sink, yet we might be saved: And in the
Morning we weighed our Anchor, and warp'd in nearer
the Shore; yet did but little good.

In the Afternoon, with the Help of a Sea-breeze, I ran
into 7 Fathom, and anchored; then carried a small
Anchor ashore, and warp'd in till I came into 3 Fathom
and a half. Where having fastned her, I made a Raft to
carry the Men's Chests and Bedding ashore; and, before
8 at Night, most of them, were ashore. In the Morning I
ordered the Sails to be unbent, to make Tents; and then
my self and Officers went ashore. I had sent ashore a
Puncheon, and a 36 Gallon Cask of Water, with one
Bag of Rice for our common use: But great Part of it
was stolen away, before I came ashore; and many of my
Books and Papers lost.

On the 26th following, we, to our great Comfort,
found a Spring of fresh Water, about 8 Miles from our
Tents, beyond a very high Mountain, which we must
pass over: So that now we were, by God's Providence,
in a Condition of subsisting some Time; having Plenty

of very good Turtle by our Tents, and Water for the fetching. The next Day I went up to see the Watering-place, accompanied with most of my Officers. We lay by the way all Night, and next Morning early got thither; where we found a very fine Spring on the South-East-side of the high Mountain, about half a Mile from its Top: But the continual Fogs make it so cold here, that it is very unwholsome living by the Water. Near this Place, are Abundance of Goats and Land-crabs. About 2 Mile South-East from the Spring, we found 3 or 4 shrubby Trees, upon one of which was cut an Anchor and Cable, and the Year 1642. About half a Furlong from these, we found a convenient Place for sheltering Men in any Weather. Hither many of our Men resorted; the hollow Rocks affording convenient Lodging; the Goats, Land-crabs, *Men of War Birds*, and Boobies, good Food; and the Air was here exceeding wholsome.

About a Week after our coming ashore, our Men that liv'd at this new Habitation, saw 2 Ships making towards the Island. Before Night they brought me the News; and I ordered them to turn about a Score of Turtle, to be in Readiness for their Ships if they should touch here: But before Morning they were out of Sight, and the Turtle were releas'd again. Here we continued without seeing any other Ship till the second of *April*; when we saw 11 Sail to Windward of the Island: But they likewise past by. The Day after appear'd 4 Sail, which came to anchor in this Bay. They were his Majesty's Ships the *Anglesey*, *Hastings* and *Lizard*; and the *Canterbury East-India* Ship. I went on board the *Anglesey* with about 35 of my Men; and the rest were dispos'd of into the other 2 Men of War.

We sail'd from *Ascension*, the 8th; and continued aboard till the 8th of *May:* At which Time the Men of

War having miss'd St. *Jago*, where they design'd to Water, bore away for *Barbadoes*: But I being desirous to get to *England* as soon as possible, took my Passage in the Ship *Canterbury*, accompanied with my Master, Purser, Gunner, and 3 of my superiour Officers.

NOTES

Page 8, l. 20. *Don Pedro de Ponto:* When the Spaniards first took over the Canary Islands from Portugal in 1480, colonization was not far advanced, and many new settlers were needed. English adventurers took up lands in the islands, among them one Bridges, brother of a Lord Mayor of London. It is possible that he was the ancestor of the Teneriffe governor, whose name was more commonly rendered as de Ponte.

Page 21, ll. 4-5. In Dampier's time the Newfoundland fishery played a large part in English maritime economy. From 5000 to 10,000 seamen were said to be employed in it, and they were available for impressment into the Navy in time of war. The fishery demanded great quantities of salt, which was obtained from France and Portugal and from certain tropical localities where shallow lagoons of sea-water were exposed to the heat of the sun. Besides the salt-pans at Mayo, described by Dampier, there were others on the Venezuela coast and at St. Kitts in the Leeward Islands.

Page 33, ll. 26-7. The friendship between England and Portugal, now so long-standing as to be traditional, already existed when Dampier wrote. It had been continuous since the revolt of Portugal against Spanish overlordship in 1640. Portuguese independence had received the backing of Charles I, Cromwell, and Charles II, and in return for diplomatic and military aid the English had received trading privileges in the Portuguese colonies. Charles II's marriage with Catherine of Braganza marks a well-known stage in the alliance.

Page 65, l. 13. *Rift*: reefed.

Page 68, l. 21. The half-minute glasses were used in estimating the speed of the ship through the water. The log, a piece of wood, attached to the knotted log-line, was thrown overboard and allowed to drift astern. At the moment when a given mark on the line passed overboard the half-minute glass was turned. The number of knots in the line which had run out when the half-minute was up was equal to the speed of the ship in sea-miles per hour. Hence the usual expression of speed in knots. The calculation of longitude depended largely upon the correct estimation of the ship's speed, and thus the accuracy of the half-minute glass was important. The method is now obsolete, the modern rotating patent-log being a quite different instrument which records mechanically the total distance run. The *stray-line* mentioned in the text was the amount run out before the glass was first turned and the timing begun.

Page 70. *A Table of Variations:* It will be observed that Dampier did not express longitudes from the meridian of Greenwich, but from various points visited on his voyage. On the other hand John Welbe, the author of the project of 1715, printed after the Introduction, reckoned his longitudes (inaccurately) from Greenwich. The Royal Observatory at Greenwich was founded in 1676, and the "Capt. Hally" mentioned by Dampier on this page was Edmund Halley, the Astronomer-Royal.

Page 75, l. 8. *The New East-India Company:* In 1698, the original East India Company, dating from 1600, having fallen out of favour with William III's government, a new East India Company was established by Act of Parliament. The two companies traded in rivalry until 1702, when they agreed to unite. The amalgamation was completed in 1708-9, the joint body taking the title of the United East India Company, and enduring until 1858.

Page 81, l. 3. *Abrohles, an Appellative Name for Shoals:* The Portuguese *abrolhos* adopted by the Dutch and English, and meaning "Open your eyes" or "Look out!"

Page 100, l. 23. *just like the Hottentot's Houses:* the possible significance of these objects in the record of exploration is referred to in the Introduction.

Page 104, l. 6. *Nun-buoy:* a buoy attached to the anchor to mark its position and facilitate raising it if foul of a rock.

Page 121, l. 10. *Advantages of the Torrid Zone:* a reminder that at that time the greatest commercial profits were expected from possessions in tropical climates, producing exotic goods not obtainable nearer home. In addition to vegetable products, it was also a common belief that gold was more likely to be found in hot climates.

Page 124, ll. 5-11. The suspicion that Australia might be an archipelago intersected by sea-channels was not finally dispelled for another hundred years.

Page 126. It is evident from Dampier's remarks that his principal object in coasting Western Australia was to obtain water, and that he did not expect to make fruitful discoveries there.

Page 139, l. 12. There was no treaty or principle of international law by which the Dutch claimed a monopoly of navigating the eastern seas, although they did claim to monopolize the trade of some (not all) of their land-territories, as did other colonial powers. In any case, Dampier's was not a trading expedition.

Page 147, l. 7. *Island Ende:* now commonly named Flores.

Page 147, l. 11. *Captain More:* a title, not a personal name: the Portuguese *capitão-mor*, equivalent of captain-major or military governor-in-chief.

Page 150, l. 16. *A Long-Boat in a frame:* probably a contemporary printer's error for "in frame," that is, in pieces, convenient for stowage, and to be assembled when required.

Page 151, ll. 11-13. The burning or charring and subsequent paying with lime were for the purpose of killing worm and preventing its entry. Fishermen in some English districts still char or scorch the planking of their boats as a precaution against worm.

Page 177, l. 13. By passing the Straits of Omba, Dampier entered the Banda Sea and was in the region of the Spice Islands.

Page 196, l. 1. *The main Land:* Not the main land of New Guinea, as Dampier afterwards explains, but that of his new discovery of New Britain.

Page 199, l. 14. *Garret Dennis:* Gerard de Nys.

Page 203, l. 9. *the main of New-Guinea:* on examining it Dampier found it to be separated from New Guinea by his Dampier Passage.

Page 205, l. 13. *St. George's Bay:* this was actually the mouth of a strait, not recognized as such by Dampier. It cuts off from his New Britain the eastern portion subsequently named New Ireland by Captain Philip Carteret, the discoverer of the separation.

Page 216, l. 24. *I named it Nova Britannia:* Dampier apparently did not name his newly discovered strait, which is now Dampier Strait.

Page 226, l. 26. *Bencola:* Bencoolen, a factory of the East India Company, near the southern end of Sumatra.

Page 237, l. 29. *English Ships at Batavia:* the number of English traders in the Far East encountered or casually mentioned by Dampier, not only here, but in his account of his previous voyage,

should serve to modify the common belief that the Dutch mono-
polized the business of the Asiatic Archipelago and its surrounding
coasts.

Page 238, l. 8. *these 28 years:* a reference to Dampier's early voyage
to the Far East, when nineteen years of age.

Page 240, l. 9. *a Country Ship:* after the Restoration of Charles II in
1660, which was also the occasion of a reorganization of the East
India Company, that body did not itself engage in the port-to-port
trade in the East, but contented itself with the monopoly of shipping
cargoes to England. Its factories were therefore fed by local shipping,
chiefly owned by Asiatic merchants, and known as the country
ships. By Dampier's time Englishmen were taking part in the local
Asiatic trades and becoming owners of the country ships, as is in-
dicated by his allusion on this page.

INDEX

OF PERSONS, PLACES AND SHIPS, etc.

ABROHLO Shoals or Abrohles, 63, 81, 91
Achin, 49
Admiralty, Condition of ships supplied by, xxix *et seq.*
Africa, xi, 36, 52, 60; Africa, South, xii, xxxvi
African Coast, West, xvi
Allegrance, Island of, 2
All Saints, the bay of, 32
Amabie, native kingdom in Timor, 171
Ambergreece, 96
Amboyna, xx, 110, 226, 229, 243
America, x, xiii, xiv, xviii, xxiii, li, 60, 69, 122, 165, 166
Ampulo, 229
Amsterdam, 244
Anamabao, Island of (Anabao), xxxix, 132, 133, 134, 135, 156, 171
Anamabeans, 139
H.M.S. *Anglesey*, 249
Angola, 36, 37, 42
Anne, Cape of, 216
Anne, Queen, lv
Antarctic Ocean, xxii, xxvii
Antelope of London, merchantman, 75, 76
Antipodes, xi, xii
Abreu, Antonio d', xii
Aristotle, 113
Arnhem Land, xx, xxiv
Ascension, Island of, lxv, lxx, lxxii, xlv, lvi, 245, 249
Asiatic Archipelago, xiv
Australia, xii, xiii, xiv, xv, xvi, xviii, xxiii, xxvii, xxviii, li
Australia, Eastern, xxix, liii
Austrialia del Espiritu Santo, xviii

Australia, Northern, xxix, xxxviii
Australia, Western, xix, xx, xxi, xxxviii
Australian Exploration before Dampier's time, x *et seq.*
Axes, 84, 209, 213
Azimuth Compass, lxix

BABAO, port in Copang Bay, xl, xliv, 140, 146, 149, 150, 151, 158, 159, 176, 177, 183, 185, 232, 233
Bahia, Port of, xxxiv, xxxv, xlvi, 32, 33, 36, 39, 49, 52, 53, 55, 56, 58, 59; Exports from, 37
Bahia, commodities brought to, by European ships, 37
Bahia de Todos los Santos, 30, 32, 34, 56; description of, 35 *et seq.*
Balboa, Spaniards under, xii
Bande-Isles, 179
Banditti, 57
Bantam, xviii
Barbacue, 135, 143, 181, 182
Barbados (Barbadoes), xlv, xlvi, 21, 250
Barefoot, Captain, 10, 26
Batavia, xxii, xxiii, lii, 162, 164, 173, 237, 240, 241, 243, 244
Batavia-Roads, xliv, lxxi, 240, 241, 242
Baya, 108
Beachy Head, Battle of, xxxi
Beads (string of), 37, 184, 196, 197, 198, 201, 210, 212, 237
Bencola, Island of, 226, 240
Bengal, Bay of, 75
Bengale, 243
Ben-jarr, 243
Bird-Isle, 179, 180

Blake, Admiral, 3, 4
Bonao, Island of, 226, 227, 228, 229
Borneo, xiii
Bougainville, xv, lvi
Bouro, Island of, 228, 229
Brasilian trade, 39, 40
Brazil, xxxiii, xlviii, 16, 21, 23, 24, 27, 30, 31, 32, 36, 52, 56, 59, 60, 65, 68, 75, 80, 82, 99, 108, 123, 144, 167
Burning Isle (see Volcano), 178, 179, 214, 215, 219, 220
Button, Island of, 238, 240
Byron, lvi
Byzantine libraries, xi

CAIMANES Island, 56
Calicut, xii
California, xxi
Cambusses, Island of, 241
Campbell, John, lvi
Campeachy, bay of, 47, 51, 52
Canary Islands, xxxii, 7, 9
Canterbury East India Ship, lxxii, xlv, 249, 250
Cap, Island of, 240
Cape Verde Islands, xxxiii, 9, 11, 20, 21, 22, 27
Carlos II, xxvi
Carpentaria, Gulf of, xviii, xx, xxiii, xxiv
Carteret, lvi
Cave Island, Anthony, xlii, 201, 202, 203
Cave Island, Anthony, description of Natives, 201, 202
Celebes, xiii, 188
Central America, Spaniards Colony of, xxi
Ceram, Island of, xliv, 179, 226, 227, 228, 229
Ceramers (Natives of Ceram), 228
Charles II, lii
Charles V, xiii
Chaulk, 247
Chile, xxi, xxiii, xxiv

China, lii, 78, 243
Chinese Trade to Laphao, 162
Church, John, lv
Ciccale harbour, 164
Clerk, Captain, 243
Cock, Mr., English Merchant at Bahia, 37, 62
Cockle Island, 188
Concordia, Dutch Post in Timor, xxxix, xl, 133, 135, 156, 157, 158, 168, 174
Concordia, the Governor of, 133 et seq., 151 et seq.
Cook, James, xv, xxvii, xxviii, xlii, xliii, lvi
Cooke, Edward, x
Copang Bay or Cupang, 139, 140, 150, 156, 171
Copang, Native Kingdom in Timor, 135, 171, 173
Copper, 165
Coral Rocks, 63, 81, 89, 158, 185, 217, 224
Cotton-Hammock, 40, 41
Council of Trade and Plantations, xxvi
Crockadore Island, 236
Cross Island, 150
Crown Isle, 218, 219
Cupangayans (see Copang), 172, 173, 174
Cygnet, 231

DAMPIER Archipelago, xxxvii
Dampier's Passage, xliii
Darien, Isthmus of, xxvi
Dee, John, xxviii
Defoe, lvi
Deptford, xxx, xxxi, xxxii
Diemen, Anthony van, xxi, xxiii, xxiv
Dieppe Maps, showing Australia, xiv, xv, xvii, xxiv, xxxviii
"Discourse of the Winds, etc., in the Torrid Zone," by W. Dampier, 30
Downs, the, xxx, xxxii, 1
Drake, Sir Francis, xxvii, li, lii

Du Halde's History of China, lv
Duke Privateer, liv
Dungeness, 1
Dutchess Privateer, liv

EAST India Companies, li, 137
East India Waggoner, or Pilot-Book, 67, 68
East Indian Trade, xxviii
East Indies, xvii, xviii, xxi, xxiv, xxviii, li, 15, 24, 44, 46, 47, 76, 78, 99, 105, 189
Eastern Archipelago (Indian), xii, lii
Enchiehoust, 244
Ende, Island of, 141, 147, 148, 175
Endeavour, xlii
Equator, Crossing of, 28, 29, 193

FAYAL, one of the Western Islands, 10
Fetter, Island of, xli, 177
Finisterre, Cape of, 2
Fisher, George, Dampier's 1st Lieutenant, xxxi, xxxii, xxxiii, xxxiv, xxxv, xlvi, xlvii, xlviii, xlix, l
Fissgigg (used for fishing), 181, 186, 200
Flamborough-head at Timor, 141, 159
Fleet-frigat (English ship), 240, 242, 243
Fogo, Island of, 26
Forteventura, Island of, 8
Foot-hook Timbers, 246
Frape-boat for taking Salt, 13, 14, 15
French Jesuits in China, Publications of, lv
Funnel, William, ix, liv

GAMA, Vasco da, xii
Gamba, 36
Garcia, Andres, xxxii, xxxiii
Garret Dennis Island, xlii, 199, 201

Garret Dennis Isle, description of natives, 199, 200
Gennesareth, Lake of, 67
Gibraltar, xlvii
Gilolo, Island of (Northern-most of Moluccas), xxix, xliv
Glasses (looking glass or glass bottle), 37, 184, 198, 201, 210, 213, 237
Glocester, Cape of, 216
Glocester, Mountain, 216
Goa, 162, 163, 172, 173, 175
Goa, the Viceroy of, 58, 163, 171, 172, 175
Gold, 39, 105, 145, 162, 165, 170, 172, 201, (manneel—native word 201.)
Gomera, Island of, 8
Good Hope, Cape of, xiii, xix, xxi, xxix, xxxviii, xlv, li, lxxi, 58, 65, 67, 79, 84, 100, 122, 192, 244
Good Hope, storm whilst near the Cape, 77 *et seq.*
Good Hope, the rounding of the Cape, 67 *et seq.*
Grand Canary Island, 7, 8
Gray, Sir Albert, ix
Great Australian Bight, xxiv
Great Barrier Reef (coste dangereuse), xv
Guinea, Coast of (Africa), 36, 42, 49, 105
Guinea-Trade (Africa), 39

HAGUE, Cape de, 1, 2
Hakluyt, Richard, xxviii
Hally, Captain, or Halley, xxxvi, 2, 70
Hammond, Captain, 58, 75
Harris, John, lv
Harwich, H.M.S., 243
Hastings, H.M.S., 249
Hatchets, 184, 209
Hawkins, John, xxxii
Hedges Mr., 75
Henriquez, Antonio (*see* Captain More), 163, 172

Henry VIII, xiv
Horn, Cape, xxviii, xxix
Hottentots, xxxviii
Hottentots' houses, 100
Hughes, Jacob, Master of *Roebuck*, xlvi

INDIA, xii, li, lii, 240, 243
Indian Ocean, xiii, xix, xxvi, xliv, li
Iron, 135, 162, 172, 182, 200
Ivory, 39

JAMAICA, 17, 56, 185
Janszoon, Willem, xviii, xix
Java, Island of, xiii, xix, xx, xliv, lxxi, 78, 235, 236, 237, 238, 239
Javians, 237
Jolly Prize, xxx

KEELANG, Island of, 228, 229
King William, Cape of, 216, 221
King William's Island, xli, xliv, 190, 191, 222, 223, 228
Knapton, James, ix, lvii
Knives, 184, 196, 197, 198, 201, 210, 213
Kosiway Island, 180

LAGOA, town of, 16
Laguna, the town of, 4, 5, 6, 7, 8
Lancastrio, Don John de, 36
Lancerota, one of the Canary Islands, 2
Lances, wooden, used by New Hollanders, 101, 102, 103
Laphao Bay or Liphao, 145, 146, 148, 153, 160, 163, 164, 172, 177, 232; Portuguese Settlement, xl, xli, 175
Laphao, inhabitants of, 161 *et seq.*
Larentucka on Island of Ende (Lorantuca), 147, 148, 175
Laubana, Island of, 141, 231, 232
Laughton, Sir J. K., xlix

Liampo (English ship), 243
Lisbon, xxxv, 58
Littleton, Sir Edward, 75
Lizard, H.M.S., 249
Lizard, the, 2
Lok, Michael, xxviii
Londonderry, xxxi
Long Island, 218
Lortribie, native kingdom in Timor, 171
Louis XIV, lii
Luca-parros Islands, 178

MABO, Cape, of New Guinea, xli, xliv, 187, 191, 192, 200, 203, 205, 222, 223
Macao (Chinese Trade), from, 162, 172
Madagascar, xxix, 244
Magellan, Ferdinand, xii
Magellan, Straits of, xvii, 52, 122
Maio or Mayo, Isle of, xxxiii, 9, 10, 11, 12, 15, 21, 22, 25
Malacca, xii, 243
Malacca, Straits of, xii, 243
Malayans, 159, 186
Mancel-Frigat (English Ship), 243
Manila, xix
Mansheters, Island of, 240
Marcgrave, 113
Maria Van Diemen, Cape, xxii
Matthias Island, 194
Mauritius, xxii
Mayo, Governor of, 18
Mendosa, Alexis, 148, 163, 171
Mendana, Alvaro de, xvii, xviii, xxiii
Menippe, Island of, 229
Mercator, Gerard, xvi
Merry, Captain, 242, 243
Mindanao, Island of, 186
Mindanayans, 185
Misicomba, Island of, or Misicomby (*see* Omba Island)
Monk, Captain, 243
Monsoon (English Ship), 243
Montague, Port, xlii, 213, 217

More, Captain (Antonio Henriquez at Timor), 147, 163, 172, 175
Mother of Pearl, 170
Money, types of in I Mayo, 20
Mutiny, reference to, 31, 32, 59, 138, 139, 147

NAMQUIMAL, Native kingdom in Timor, 171
Narborough, Sir John, lii
Negro's, Inhabitants of I. Mayo, 19
Negroes, used as slaves in Bahia, 40, 41, 42
New-Britain, Island of, liii, lxxi (Nova-Britannia)
New East India Company, 75
Newfoundland, 11, 21
New Guinea, xiii, xvii, xviii, xxi, xxiii, xxvii, xxviii, xxix, xli, xlii, xliii, lxxi, 82, 94, 123, 125, 177, 180, 183, 185, 186, 187, 190, 191, 192, 203, 215, 216, 219, 221, 227, 243
New Guinea, description of main land, 198
New Guinea, Inhabitants, 196, 197, 198
New Guinea Coast, Islands of, 129, 180
New Hebrides, xvii, xviii
New Holland, x, xx, xxii, xxiv, xxxix, lxx, lxii, 27, 65, 75, 76, 79, 82, 90, 91, 94, 95, 96, 104, 105, 109, 121, 123, 124, 126, 235
New Holland, description of the Coast, 105
New Hollanders, 100 et seq., 122
Newport of London, a merchant man, 10
"New Voyage Round the World," by W. Dampier, xxvi, lii, 10, 11, 103, 124, 188, 231, 232
New Zealand, xxii, li, liii
North West Passage, li

Norwood, John, Boatswain of the Roebuck, xlvi
Nova Britannia (New Britain), xliv, liii
Nova Britannia, Island of (New Britain), 216, 220, 221

OAKHAM, 246, 247
Omba, Island of, xli, 141, 177, 178, 229, 230, 232
Oratavia, 2, 3, 6
Orford, Cape of, xlii, 205, 206
Ortelius, Abraham, xvi
Ostresteen, Dutch ship, 244
PALMA, 7, 8
Panama, Isthmus of, xii
Panther (English Ship), 243
Paterson, William, Scottish explorer, xxvi
Pentare, Island of (see Pintare), 230, 231, 232
Pearls, 8
Petiver's, Mr., Centuria (see Dammara), 110
Pernambuc, or Pernambuco, Port of, xxxiv, 30, 31, 56
Peru, xvii, xviii, xxi, xxvii, li
Philip II, xxxii
Philippine Islands, xii, xiii, xviii
Pidgeon Island, 190
Pinose, Town of, 16
Pintare, Island of (see Pentare), 141
Piso, 113
Plate, River, 52
Plymouth, 1
Pobumbie, Native kingdom in Timor, 171
Ponto, Don Pedro de, xxxii, 8
Porcelane, 162, 172, 229
Porta Nova, 161, 163, 172
Porto Bello, liv
Portugal, 23, 173
Portuguese discovery in the fifteenth century, xii
Potoro, Island of, 231
Prado, Diego de, xviii, xix
Praya, Port in Island of St. Iago, 21, 23

Princes-Isle, 236
Providence Island, 193, 222
Ptolemy of Alexandria, xi
Pulo Baby, Island of, 239
Pulo-Sabuda (Sabuti), Island of,
　lxxi, 184 *et seq.*, 189, 243
Pulo-Sabuda, natives of, 185,
　186; Trade with, 184
Puncheon, 248

QUEENSLAND, xviii
Quiros, Fernandez de, xvii, xviii

RAY'S, Mr., supplement, 108,
　110
Ria Janeria, 30, 56
Rich's Island, Sir R., 219
Robinson, Captain, 243
Roe-buck, H.M.S., xxx, xxxi,
　xxxii, xxxiii, xxxvi, xl, xlii,
　xliv, xlv, xlvi, xlix, lviii, lxv, 1
Roebuck Bay, xxxvii
Roebuck, H.M.S., Dampier's un-
　published account of the loss
　of, lvii *et seq.*
Roe-buck, H.M.S., careening, 150
　et seq., 243; leak and wreck,
　245 *et seq.*
Rogers, Captain Woodes, ix, liv
Rooke, Sir George, xxxi, xlvii,
　xlix
Rook's Island, Sir George, 217
Rosemary Island, 96, 104, 105,
　123
Rosemary Islands, 124
Rotee, Island of, or Rotte, 131,
　132, 234
Royal Sovereign, H.M.S., xlvii
Rumphius, Mr., 110
Russel, Captain, 243
Rotz of Dieppe, Jean, xiv

ST. ANTONIO, harbour in
　Port Bahia, 34
St. Augustine, Cape, 30, 31
St. George's Bay, xlii, 205
St. George, Cape of, xlii, 204,
　205, 206, 213, 215, 222, 223

St. George, Fort, 240
St. George's Isle, 205 *et seq.*
St. George's Island, description
　of natives, 206, 207, 209, 210,
　211, 212
St. Helena, xlv, 245
St. Iago, xxxiii, 20, 21, 28, 30,
　37, 39, 61, 138, 250; roads, 26
St. Iago Town, 21, 22, 23
St. John's Island, xlii, 202, 203,
　222
St. John's, town of, 16
St. Maries, Cape of, 204
St. Pauls Port, 57
St. Peter, 67
Salt, 12, 13, 15, 20-22
Salt-Pond (Salina), 11, 12
Salt-Tortuga, Island of, 12
Salvadore, Cape, 63, 64, 67
Santa Cruz, xvii, xxxii, 2, 3, 4, 7,
　8, 9, 10
Santa Cruz, Governor of, 8, 9
Saracen scholars, xi
Saragossa, Treaty of, xiii
Scouten's Island (William), 193,
　222, 243
Sesial(1), Portuguese port, "Por-
　to del Roy de Portugal," xl,
　146, 148, 149
Shark's Bay, xxxvii, 84, 86, 87,
　92, 94, 98, 124, 126
Shovell, Sir Cloudesley, xlvii
Silver, 152, 170
Slinger's Bay, 197, 200
Solomaswer, Cape of, 195
Solomon Islands, xvii, xxiii
Solor, Island of, 147, 175
South Pole, xxix
South Seas, Admiralty's desire
　for accurate discovery in, xxvii
South Sea Company, liv
Spanish Succession, War of, x
Spice Islands (or Moluccas),
　xii, xiii, xvi
Spithead, 1
Spout, a Strange, 220, 221
Squally Island, 195
Sumatra, 49, 78, 237, 238, 239

Sundy, Streights of (or Sunda), 76, 78, 236
Surinam, 108
Swift, lvi

TASMAN, Abel, xxi, xxii, xxiii, xxiv, xxvii, xxix, xxxvii, xxxviii, liii
Tasmania, formerly Van Diemen's Land, xxii, xxiii
Tasman's Draught of the Coast, 94
Teneriffe, Island of, xxxii, 2, 7, 8, 10
Teneriffe, Pike of, 6, 10
Terra Australis (Incognita), xi, xvii, xxxviii, xli, xlii, li, 121, 122, 123
Terranate, 226
Thomas, Earl of Pembroke, lxv
Thwart-the-way, Island of, 273, 238
Tierra de Fuego, xvii, xxvii, 122
Timor and Anabao, Indian Inhabitants of, 130, 131, 134, 135, 136, 169, 170, 171
Timor, Island of, xxxviii, xxxix, xli, xliv, lxx, lxxi, 16, 78, 107, 126, 127, 128, 129, 132, 133, 134, 135, 140, 144, 150, 155, 156, 158, 160, 164, 175, 177, 179, 185, 189, 232, 235, 236
Timor, description of the coast, 129 et seq.
Timor, Dutch Fort at, lxx, 128, 133, 134, 136, 137, 138, 139, 162, 169, 171, 173
Timor, the Dutch Governour of, 136 et seq.
Timor, outside trading, 172, 173
Timor, the Portuguese Governour of, 144 et seq.
Timor, Portuguese Settlement at the Island of, lxxi, 128, 144
Three Crowns, Dutch Ship, 244
Torres, Luis Vaez de, xviii, xix, xxvii, xxviii

Torres Strait, ix, xxiii, xxiv, xli
Tristian d'Aconha, Island of, 67
Tryal Rocks, xliv, 236
Turtle Isles, 178, 179
Tuscany Galley, The, 240

UNCRIGHT, Skipper Jacob, 244
Urdaneta, Andres de, xiii
Utrecht, Treaty of, liv

Vanheusen, Dutch Ship, 244
Variations, a table, of 70 et seq.
Varthema, Ludovici di, xii
Visscher, Frans, xxi
"Voyages and Discoveries" by W. Dampier, lii
"Voyage to New Holland," by W. Dampier, liii
Vulcano (on a burning island), 178, 205, 214, 215, 217, 222, 231

WAFER, Lionel (Buccaneer), xxvi
Waiela, Island of, 180
Wallis, lvi
Walpole, lv
Warren, Captain, 240
Water, the search for on the 1st reaching of Australia, 82 et seq.
West Indies, li, 7, 12, 14, 24, 44, 46, 47, 50, 52, 56, 85, 99, 166, 168, 189
White Island, 182
William III, x
Willughby's, Mr., History of Fishes, 113
Willughby's Ichthyol, 113
Wishart Island, 194, 195
Wood, Professor G. A., xvii
Woodward, Dr., lxx
Wytfliet, Cornille, xvii, xviii

ZEALAND, 244

INDEX

OF BIRDS, FISH, FRUIT, FLOWERS, etc.

AGNUS Castus (Carrepat), 49
Albicore-fish, 63
Alcea Novæ Hollandiæ, 109
Alligators, 19, 53, 86, 140, 143, 169
Amelanchier Lob (*see* Tab. 3, Fig. 3), 109, 110
Amphisbæna, or 2-headed snake (Cobra de dos Cabesas), 53
Apples, 7
Apple-tree, 45, 47, 165
Apricocks, 7
Arack or Arrack, 145, 229
Arbor Hortensis Javanorum (*see* Dammara), 110
Armadillo, 53
Arisah's (Fruit), 47
Asses, 7, 18, 20, 21, 25

BAMBOO, used for carrying water, 104
Bardana major (*see* Crista), 108
Barrama's, 55
Barly, 7
Bass, 169, 185
Bats, 185, 189
Beans, 7
Bees, 169
Bees-wax, 162, 172
Beeves, 168
Bill-Birds, 50, 51
Black-Birds, 168, 214
Blubber, off the Cape of Good Hope, 244, 245
Bonano's or Bonanoes, 46, 167, 238
Boneta's, 18, 28, 80, 86
Boobies, or Booby's, 50, 63, 98, 106, 127, 169, 185, 249
Breams (fish), 97, 169

Buffalo, 135, 140, 143, 145, 146, 147, 150, 151, 153, 159, 168, 170
Bullocks, 25
Bulls, 18
Burgoo (porridge), 104
Butter, 75

CABBAGES, 7, 75, 157
Cabbage trees, 49
Cackatoos, 143
Cachora's de agua (water-dogs), 53, 55
Calabash (tree), 47, 143, 165, 166
Calalaloo (herb), 168
Callavances (kind of French bean), 17, 50
Canary-wine, 6, 7
Cashews, 46, 47
Cana-fistula-trees, 165, 166
Cassava, 50
Cattle, black, 53, 157
Cavallies, 55, 169, 214, 227
Centumpees (animal), 168
Cherries, 7
Cinnamon-trees, 46
Citrons, 7, 23, 167
Coches, 7
Cockadores (fowl), 214, 227
Cockatoes, 168
Cockles, 87, 169, 188, 189, 190
Cockle-Merchants (fish), or oyster-crackers, 169
Cocks (wild and tame), 8, 168, 169
Cockrecoes, 50
Coco-nuts, 46, 131, 135, 145, 161, 167, 184, 198, 201, 204, 208, 209, 210, 212, 213, 237, 238

Coco-nut trees, 44, 157, 166, 198, 199, 200, 201, 202, 205, 206, 208, 213, 217, 219, 230

Coco-plumbs (Munsheroo's), 46

Cocos (native word for coco-nut), 210, 211

Cod-fruit, 105

Coire, 172

Colutea Novæ Hollandiæ, 111

Comesserie tree, 43

Conchs (shell-fish), 107

Conies, 7

Conger-eels, 55, 169

Conyza Novæ Hollandiæ, 111

Coquinda's, 55

Cotton, 43

Cotton-apple, 45

Cotton-flower from Baya, 108

Cotton-trees, 44, 45, 165

Cotyledon aquatica (see Mohoh), 111

Cows, 7, 18

Coyre-cables, 44

Crabs, land-, 249

Crab-catchers, 25, 50, 52, 85, 96, 169, 185

Craw-fish, 169

Crista Pavonis Brasiliana Bardanae, 108

Crocodiles, 19, 86

Crows, 106, 168, 185, 214, 227

Crows, chattering-, 50

Crufia's, type of land-fowl, 18

Cucumbers, 50

Cuchora's or dog-fish, 55

Curresoes (see Mackeraws), 50, 51

Currecoo's, 50, 52

Curlews [Great], 17, 25, 50, 85, 106

Custard-apples, 23, 24, 46

DAMMARA ax Nova Hollandia 110

Deer 7, 8, 25

Delphin Belgis (fish), 113

Dogs, 17. 41, 213

Dog-fish (see Cuchora's), 97, 169

Dolphins, 18, 64, 90, 113, 131, 186, 191

Doves, 50

Ducks, 8, 25, 50, 52, 85, 169, 238

Ducks Muscovy, 50, 52

Dunghill-Fowls, 8, 22, 52, 181

EAGLES, 85, 168

Eggs, 237

Erica (see Dammara), 110

Erica Marina (see Fucus), 109

Equisetum Novæ Hollandiæ, 111

FABA Aegyptia (see Mohoh), 111

Filix Brasiliana Osmundæ, 108

Fig-Tree, 166

Fishing-hawks, 169

Flamingo's, 17, 18, 50

Flesh-flies, 103, 104

Flying-Fish, 10

Foxes, 53

Frogs, 53

Fry, Small, 79

Fustick, a Dye-Wood, 37, 50

Fucus, 109

Fucus ex Nova Guinea, 111, 112

Fucus ex Nova Guinea Fluviatilis Pisanæ, 112

GALDENS, 25, 50, 52, 85

Gannets, 82

Garden-Herbs Various, 50

Gar-fish, 18, 55, 79, 86, 169

Geese, 169

Ginger, 213

Goats, xii, 7, 18, 25, 53, 145, 146, 153, 168, 175, 209, 210, 249

Goldens (bird), 169, 185

Gorasses (fish), 55

Gormorants, 85, 96

Grain, like Beans on Isle Rosemary, 96

Grandpisces, 169

Grapes, Wild, 46

Groopers (fish), 55
Guano's or Gunanoes, 19, 53, 85, 86, 168
Guaparva (fish), 113
Guaperva maxima Candata (fish), 113
Guaracapema (fish), 113
Guarapucu (fish), 113
Guava's or Guavoes, 7, 23, 46, 167
Guinea-Hens, or Gallena Pintata, 17, 20, 25, 138
Guitteba tree, 43
Gulls, 85, 96
Gurabuca (fish), 113

HAWKS, 25, 106, 168, 244
Hawksbill (see Sea-Turtle), 56
Helichrysum (see Scabious), 109
Hens, 8, 168, 169, 237
Hens, Clocking,–50, 51, 52
Herons, 25, 169
Herring, 55
Hippopotomus, 87
Hogs, 7, 25, 53, 147, 153, 159, 168, 170, 175, 208, 209, 210, 211, 212, 213
Hog-plumbs, 46
Horses, 7, 25, 53, 168: Lancerot, 7, 8

INDICO, 43
Indian Corn, 168, 170
Ingwa's, 48

JACA, 157, 167, 184
Jacks, 145
Jasminum Brasilianum, 108
Jenetees, 50, 51
Jennipah's (Jennipapah's, 46, 47

KIDS, 145
Kites, 106

LAND-FOWLS near Shark's Bay, 85
Lapwings (bird), 80

Larks, 106, 127
Lemons, 7, 23, 157, 167
Leopards, 53
Libby Tree, 184
Limes, 5, 7, 23, 46, 167
Limpits, 86, 96, 107
Lizards, 53, 106, 168
Locust-Trees, 165
Loggerhead (see Sea-Turtle), 56

MACKRIL or Mackarels, 8, 169, 181, 194
Maho tree, 143, 165
Maccaw's, 50
Mackeraws (see Chattering-crows), 50
Maiz, 7, 22, 25, 43
Malmesy wine, 6, 8
Malvaceous (see Alcea), 109
Mamoons (see Papahs), 46
Manchineel-apples, 46
Mangoe, 46, 145, 167
Mangroves, 43, 44, 89, 106, 130, 131, 132, 155, 156, 165
Mangrovy land on Timor, 129, 130
Men of War birds, 50, 63, 127, 169, 185, 236, 249
Mendibees, 49
Melons (water and musk), 23, 50, 157, 167, 168
Mericasah's fruit, 47, 48
Mohoh Insulæ Timor, 111
Momoo (see cotton-flower), 108
Monkeys, 25, 37, 53, 168
Monk-fish, 98
Miniota's, sort of land-fowl, 18
Mules, 7, 25
Mullets, 18, 55, 169, 185, 227
Mungaroo's, 48
Muscles, 86, 107
Muscovada sugar, 38
Musteran-de-ova's, 48, 49
Mutton, 75

NODDY birds, 50, 99, 106
Nutmegs, 184, 201

OAKS, 43
Oatmeal, 75, 104, 126
Old-Wives (fish), 97, 107, 185
Olio de Boy, 55
Onions, 7
Oranges, 5, 7, 23, 46, 61, 157, 167, 184
Orange, China, 46
Ostridges, 50
Otee, 48
Oysters, 86, 87, 96, 107, 159, 169

PAPAH-TREE, 24
Papah's, kind of fruit, 7, 23, 24, 25, 46
Palm, 161, 165, 166, 167
Palm-berries (Dendees), 49
Palmeto-leaves, 151, 161, 186
Palmeto-trees (see Palmeto-leaves), 190
Pan-fish, 227
Papaes (fruit), 184
Parracots (fish), 107, 169
Parrakites, 25, 37, 50, 168, 224
Parrots, 25, 37, 50, 96, 143, 168, 186, 214, 227
Parsnips. 75
Partridges, 8
Peaches, 7
Peas, 7
Pears, 7
Pease, 148
Pecary or Pica (see hogs), 53
Pelicans, 50, 85, 106
Pentango's, 47, 48
Periwinkles, 86, 96, 107
Petrels (foul-weather birds), 65, 66, 67
Petumbo's, 48
Phæcena (see Porpuss), 113
Physick-nuts (Pineon), 49
Pidgeons, 8, 25, 50, 51, 143, 181, 185, 189, 190, 214, 227
Pig (see hogs), 212
Pike-fish, 182
Pine-apples, 50, 157, 167, 184
Pintado-Birds (or Painted Bird), 65, 66, 79

Pines, trees like, 129, 166, 167
Pippin, 46
Plantains, 46, 167, 184, 238
Plumbs, 7
Pomecitrons, 46, 157
Pomegranates, 7, 23, 46, 157, 167
Porposes, 18, 29, 56, 79
Porpusses, and Bottle-nose Porpuss, 113
Potato's, 7, 50, 184
Pulse scrub of New Holland, 105
Pumkins, 7, 50, 75, 168, 201
Pumplemusses, 46
Pumplenose (fruit-tree), 157
Pursly, 168

QUINCES, 23
Quince-Tree, 24

RABBITS, 53
Rabek's, type of land-fowl, 18
Raccoons (Rackoon), 85, 88, 105
Rapuntium Novæ Hollandiæ, 108
Rasperages (fish), 169
Rattle-Snake, 53
Ray, kind of fish (Sea-Devil), 86, 169
Rice, 148, 162, 168, 172, 173, 226, 229, 248
Ricinoides Novæ Hollandiæ, 109
Ringing-Birds, 168, 169
Rock-fish, 107, 169, 185
Rosemary Shrubs, 96, 111
Rum, 39, 61

SAGO Cakes, 184
St. Iago, Animals in, 25
Sallads, 157
Sampier, 168
Sanamunda (see Dammara), 110
Sandall-Wood, 162, 166, 172
Sapiera tree, 43
Sargazo (see Fucus), 109
Sassafras, 50
Savannahs of Bahia, 43

25

Savannah of New Holland, 100, 106
Savannah of Timor, 165
Scabiosa Novæ Hollandiæ, 109
Scorpions, 168
Scrubs, Fruits, etc., found on New Holland, Coast 105
Scuttle-bones (or Shells or Fish), 79, 80, 90, 169, 236
Sea-Fowls, 65 et seq., 82, 169
Sea-Mews, 82
Sea-pies (Sea-fowl), 106
Sea-snakes, 93, 127
Seal, 80
Serpents, 53
Serrew, 55
Sevil-Orange 24, 46
Sharks, 28, 64, 86, 87, 88, 96, 107, 178, 191, 233
Shark's Bay, Condition of foliage to be found there, 84
Shear-waters (Fowl), 64, 80
Sheep, 7, 53, 168, 175
Shell-fish various, 55, 56, 96, 107
Shrimps, 169
Silver-fish, 18
Silk-Cotton, 15, 16
Skates, 86, 90
Skipjacks, 80
Snakes, various (see Serpents), 53, 54, 86, 98, 106, 168, 194
Snake-Root, 50
Snappers, 18, 97
Snooks (fish), 55, 169
Solanum spinosum Novæ Hollandiæ, 109
Speckled-Wood, 50
Sour-Sops, 46
Sting-rays (fish), 169
Stock-Fish, 75
Sugar, 23, 37, 38, 39, 61, 238
Sugar, Brazil, 38
Sugar-canes, 43, 60, 237

TAMARINS (Tree), or Tamarind, 161, 166
Tarpoon's, 55
Tea, 162, 172, 229

Teal, 50, 52
Ten-pounders (fish), 169
Thornbacks, 86, 90
Thrift (see Scabious), 109
Timor, the fruits of, 167, 168
Toads, 53
Tobacco, 37, 39, 43, 238
Toddy-trees, 157, 161
Tortoise, 159
Trees, description of near Shark's Bay, 84, 85
Tresabo, top of Coco-nut tree, 44
Tropick-birds, 235
Tunny, 113
Turnips, 7, 24, 25
Turtle, xii, 88, 90, 135, 233, 249
Turtle-Doves, 25, 51, 106
Turtle (Green), 19, 56, 87, 96, 106, 140, 169
Turtle, Sea, 19, 56
Tygers, 53

VERDONA, or Green-Wine, 6, 7
Vermiatico tree, 43

WATER-SERPENTS, 90
Water-Fowls, near Shark's Bay, 85
Water-Snake, 90, 96, 125
Water-Spaniel, 66
West-India Cotton Scrub, 45
Whale(s), 18, 39, 40, 55, 64, 65, 76, 79, 80, 90, 91, 98, 106, 126, 131, 235
Wheat, 7
Whip-rays (fish), 169, 185, 214
Whiteing, 233
Widgeons, 50, 52
Wilks (shell-fish), 107
Wolves, 106
Worms, 158, 202

YAMS, 50, 208, 209, 213
Yellow-tails (fish), 214
Yemma's, 50

411/10